MW01491744

THE COMPLETE GUIDE TO SPRING TRAINING 2025 / FLORIDA

KEVIN REICHARD

August
Publications

August Publications
215 10th Av. S., Unit 621
Minneapolis, MN 55415
augustpublications.com

ISBN 978-1-938532-86-3 (Print)

ISBN 978-1-938532-87-0 (eBook)

10 9 8 7 6 5 4 3

Designer (cover): Natalie Nowytski

CONTENTS

ACKNOWLEDGEMENTS

We can pinpoint the exact moment normalcy returned to the Florida spring-training experience: Feb. 24, 2024.

On that date the Tampa Bay Rays hosted the Atlanta Braves in the reopening of Charlotte Sports Park, a year after the Rays spent spring training at Tropicana Field and Orlando. In Port Charlotte, the ballpark and training facilities sustained serious water damage following Hurricane Ian in September 2022—serious enough that spring training was shifted to the Trop and Disney's ESPN Wide World of Sports. It was just the latest setback in a long line of challenges beginning with the COVID-19 shutdown in 2020.

But normalcy reigned at Charlotte Sports Park. The beer flowed smoothly, the autographs were abundant, and fans were content. It was a refreshingly normal spring-training opener.

It was a good day for spring-training fans. We find spring-training attendees to be among the most unique in all of baseball because of their unbridled optimism for everything related to America's Pastime. This book is dedicated to those hearty souls who plan their vacations around a trip to spring training, saving up for a week of travel throughout Florida.

No matter what obstacle is placed in their path, spring-training fans arrive in Florida with tubes of sunscreen and big smiles. And in these times, they're rewarded with a return to normalcy. This book is for you.

Thanks go to the readers of *Spring Training Online*, the Internet gathering spot for the true spring-training fans detailed above.

—Kevin Reichard
July 2024

WARM BREEZES, COLD BEER, SUNNY SKIES

People ask me what I do in the winter when there's no baseball. I'll tell you what I do. I stare out the window and wait for spring.—Rogers Hornsby

No news is usually the best news. For teams and fans, spring training 2024 was free of drama: No schedule delays, no canceled games, no natural disasters impacting game schedules. The only news was generated on the field—not in the stands.

In 2024, the things we love about spring training—the player access, the fun food offerings, the intimacy of games in smaller ballparks—returned. Some of the game changes we saw after the COVID shutdown continued, such as paperless ticketing and contactless concessions. These changes to spring training were accelerated by but ultimately made inevitable thanks to the evolution of ballpark technology.

This is great news. Because, as we all know, there's no better time of year than spring training in Florida. From that first flight into Tampa or Palm Beach to that first view of TigerTown and JetBlue Park to that first pitch on the initial day of workouts, a day during Grapefruit League season is truly a day to remember.

Spring training is America's annual transformation from darkness to light, from cold to warm, when millions of baseball fans—both hardcore and casual—descend upon warmer climes to shed their winter blues. It's especially true for those of us in cold-weather climes like Minneapolis-St. Paul, Detroit, and Toronto. Baseball's spring training is not a luxury but a necessity, our reward for living in climates filled with overcast skies, snow, ice, and rain.

Beer and brats in hand, we arrive at Florida spring-training games every February and March to soak up some sun and catch some baseball. We wait months for that first whiff of freshly mown grass at the ballpark, that first foul ball, that first inevitable sunburn. Who cares whether the starting pitcher is some kid likely to begin the season as a Double-A Erie Seawolf? As long as the drinks are cold and the dogs are hot, all is right with the world.

We begin planning our winter getaways months in advance, juggling airline schedules and hotel openings to ensure the maximum number of games. We show up to morning workouts just to stand by the fences and be part of the action. We slather ourselves with sunscreen while waiting in line to enter Hammond Stadium or Roger Dean Chevrolet Stadium. And we take spring-training performances a lot more seriously than do many players and managers.

This book is both for the hardcore baseball fan scouting out their favorite team in depth, and the casual fans heading to spring training more in search of the perfect suntan than this year's spring phenom. In fact, the casual fan is more likely to get something out of this book than the hardcore fan. While the hardcores just want to know the shortest route between their hotel and the ballpark, the casual fan knows that the richness of spring training is augmented with visits to local restaurants, shopping areas, historic ballpark sites, and area attractions.

Spring training in Florida is a relaxed, sprawling affair. Most teams train in the Tampa, Fort Myers, and Palm Beach areas. You tend to focus on a team or two in a specific area and then schedule other activities around an afternoon exhibition game. It's a very laid-back environment: A spring-training game in Florida's Lakeland or Bradenton tends to be a subdued affair, rich with tradition.

INSIDER'S TIP

If you're one of those people who goes to spring training both in Florida and Arizona, you may want to check out the Arizona edition of *The Complete Guide to Spring Training*. It's available via the August Publications website, *amazon.com*, *bn.com* and the Apple Bookstore.

We've arranged this book by area: Gulf Coast (where the Boston Red Sox, Minnesota Twins, and Tampa Bay Rays train), Sarasota County (where the Atlanta Braves and Baltimore Orioles train), greater Tampa Bay (where the Detroit Tigers, New York Yankees, Philadelphia Phillies, Pittsburgh Pirates, and Toronto Blue Jays train), and Florida's east coast (where the Houston Astros, Miami Marlins, New York Mets, St. Louis Cardinals, and Washington Nationals train). Plan your time well and you can see a lot of baseball in a short amount of time.

What can we expect in 2025? Expect players to report around Feb. 12 or so, with exhibition and Grapefruit League games beginning Feb. 21-22 and the regular season launching March 27 (March 18 if you count the Dodgers/Cubs games scheduled for Tokyo). (Yes, we updated the eBook version with tentative schedules. It's a free download if you buy the eBook from August Publications or Amazon.) For up-to-the-minute information, check out *springtrainingonline.com*.

When it comes to restaurants and attractions, things can change quickly. The listings here were current as of July 2024. In past editions, there were plenty of situations where a restaurant or bar we listed went out of business by the time this book was released. And despite to a return to normalcy, today's economic climate is far from normal, so we're seeing some restaurants and shops go out of business—but, on the flip side, we're seeing plenty of new businesses open as well. When in doubt, check this book's website, *springtrainingonline.com*, for up-to-the-minute information.

And don't forget there's a normal amount of change between each spring-training season as well, with baseball teams implementing changes from season to season. Quite often there are small changes to spring-training venues in terms of food, drink, and parking, with the upgrades announced right before spring training begins. We do our best to track these changes, but given the deadlines of book publishing, we obviously can't include them all in this book. The best place to keep track of the changes in spring training is in our twice-weekly Spring Training Online newsletter. You can sign up for a free subscription at *springtrainingonline.com*.

A SHORT HISTORY OF SPRING TRAINING

Sanford Municipal Athletic Field, where Jackie Robinson first trained as a
Montreal Royal. *Courtesy Florida Historical Society.*

Spring training has been around almost as long as professional
baseball. Boss Tweed—yes, *that* Boss Tweed—arranged for his New
York Mutuals, an amateur team made up mostly of volunteer
firemen with the Mutual Hook and Ladder Company Number 1, to
train in New Orleans in 1869. Yes, the Mutuals were ostensibly
amateur, but like everything with the notorious Boss Tweed, there

are multiple layers to this tale. Many of the players were likely paid under the table—a good investment given how baseball's popularity was due partially to its appeal to gamblers. Winning for a team owner worked on several levels.

The best evidence for openly pro teams heading to spring training points to the Cincinnati Red Stockings and the Chicago White Stockings holding organized baseball camps in New Orleans in 1870. By 1886, spring training had spread throughout professional baseball, with at least four professional teams holding a formal training camp, and *The Sporting News* hailing the development in its inaugural March 17, 1886, issue:

> The preparatory work now being done by two or three prominent clubs in the country marks one of the most sensible departures from the old rut in base-ball that has ever been made. It has always been a matter of wonder to professional and amateur athletes that men having thousands of dollars invested in a business of which so much depends on the physical condition of their men, should pay so little attention to the matter of training these people for the arduous work that was expected of them during the six months covering the championship season. Take these same men and let them put the money that they have invested in base-ball in horseflesh. Would they dare send their horses out on a trotting or running circuit in the spring without training them....
>
> Man is the superior animal and really needs more care and attention than the horse. Yet for years ball players have been sent out in the spring with muscles soft and flabby, carrying from ten to twenty pounds of extra flesh, and told to "play ball." Well, they have played ball, but the games have been "yaller," and many a man has come in from a first game with a shoulder, a leg or an arm that has impaired his effectiveness for an entire season....

That first season saw the Chicago White Stockings go to Hot Springs, Arkansas, for spring training, while the Philadelphia Phillies headed for Charleston, South Carolina, for some games against local talent. The White Stockings were owned and managed by Al Spalding (the same Spalding who founded the sporting-goods firm that exists to this day), who told *The Sporting News* of his plans to literally "boil" the members of his team in Hot Springs for two weeks:

> "It's a great scheme," said Mr. Spalding yesterday, leaning back in his chair and stroking his forehead. "I wonder whatever made me think of it. All the boys are enthusiastic about it and all want to go. I have written to a professor down there, and he is making arrangements to build a vat in which he can boil the whole nine at once....I boil out all the alcoholic microbes which may have impregnated the systems of these men during the winter while they have been away from me and Anson....If that don't work I'll send 'em all over to Paris and have 'em inoculated by Pasteur."

By 1890 *Frank Leslie's Illustrated Newspaper* was reporting on Henry M. Flagler's effort to capitalize on spring training by building a ballpark, complete with scenic grandstand, press box, and two private boxes, to host spring training in downtown St. Augustine, Florida. An early investor in Standard Oil, Flagler turned his attention to Florida and tourism in 1885, bringing railroads and flashy hotels to Florida's Treasure Coast, eventually extending the line down to Key West. He certainly had associations with baseball: he brought semi-pro baseball to St. Augustine and famously built diamonds at his leading properties across Florida (including The Breakers and the Royal Poinciana in Palm Beach), hiring African-American players to play exhibitions in the spring. It was a good business move for a hotelier and railroad owner: fans would pay to travel to spring training on Flagler's trains and stay at his hotels.

Flagler was not the only entrepreneur to combine baseball and tourism: Henry Plant combined his "Plant system" of railroad lines from Connecticut to Florida with the Tampa Bay Hotel and a slew of ballplayers and exhibition games. At nearby Plant Field, Babe Ruth reportedly hit one of the longest home runs of his career. The Tampa Bay Hotel is now part of the University of Tampa campus, and Plant Field is now the site of the college's football stadium. (We discuss the Plant baseball legacy further in the Tampa-St. Petersburg chapter.)

By the turn of the century, spring training was firmly established as a baseball ritual, with most American and National League teams heading out of town so players could train (or, in many cases, dry out) and managers could evaluate. In those days, spring training was a considerably looser affair: players would gather in a Florida, California, Texas, Arkansas, or Louisiana city, work out for several days, play in a few exhibitions, sweat out the winter booze, perhaps sample some of the local delights (many teams held spring training in Hot Springs, with the city's notable gambling establishments as an inducement to report), and then make their way back to their homes while barnstorming daily against local teams. Ever wonder why every small-town ballpark on a rail line features a ballpark where Babe Ruth once played? The teams would take the trains back to their hometowns and stop frequently for ballgames—and a quick payday—against the local heroes.

Even so, spring training was rarely a strenuous activity in the past. Take the Cleveland Indians of the 1920s, who trained in Lakeland at a ballpark still standing, Henley Field. Most teams worked out only once a day, either for an hour or two; the rest of the time the players were free to play golf and carouse—which many of them did. In the 1924 *Reach Guide*, Jack Ryder reported that Indians manager Tris Speaker was a firm believer in a single, brief but intense daily workout.

Other teams of that era were a bit more dedicated. The Brooklyn Dodgers were known for their three-hour workouts, while Pat Moran, manager of the Cincinnati Reds, held 10 a.m. and 2 p.m. workouts. Ryder seemed to approve of the Reds' schedule:

It is the observation of this writer that the policy of Manager Moran is the best of those outlined. Ball players are young men, many of them merely boys, full of pepper and anxious to work. They all enjoy the spring training after the long lay-off of the winter. They do not ask to coddled or favored with light labor. In fact, the more work they can get, provided it is not up to the point of exhaustion, the better they like it. Furthermore, the policy of two sessions a day of practice leaves the boys less time to themselves and keeps them together more, which is always a good thing for a team. They have less temptation to get into bad habits or bad company and the younger recruits are more apt to follow the good example set by the veterans on the team. It must not be understood that Manager Moran is a hard driver or forces his players too far, quite the reverse. If he sees that any one of the athletes is lazy or inclined to shirk, he is after him at once with a sharp stick, but there are not many such cases. In most instances, the Reds leader has to curb the ambition of his men instead of urging them on. This he constantly does, not allowing any man to get an inch beyond the limit of his strength.

Small Florida communities were suddenly known across the nation because of the shine provided by major-league baseball. St. Petersburg. Plant City. Orlando. Lakeland. Vero Beach. Fort Lauderdale. Sarasota. Bradenton. Tampa. Fans are dismayed these days when MLB teams look for new training facilities, but the practice is not new: since the turn of the century, cities have sought to promote themselves to tourists after building spring-training facilities and guaranteeing revenues to teams. Look at the cities where the Philadelphia Athletics trained between 1903 and 1914: Jacksonville, Spartanburg (South Carolina), Shreveport, Montgomery (Alabama), Dallas, New Orleans, Atlanta, San Antonio, and back to Jacksonville. No more than two years spent in a single city, and whoever made the best offer to a team in January usually landed the spring training in March. That pattern prevailed until World War II.

Case in point: tiny Bogalusa, Louisiana, which hosted the St. Louis Browns (the predecessor to the Baltimore Orioles) for spring training in 1921. The city lured the Brownies with the construction of a new grandstand and inexpensive accommodations at the Pine Tree Inn. The *Bogalusa Enterprise and American* of March 10, 1921 reported how pleased the Brownies were with the facilities:

"When we ask for something at the hotel," said one of the best known players in the American League, "we are not told that 'it will be looked into,' but within a shorter time than one would expect in the best hotel in America, we are served. I never saw people so hospitable in all my life, they simply go out of their way in Bogalusa to make it enjoyable for us and I know there is not a member of the team who will not leave

Bogalusa with regret when we finish our training, and I also know that if it was left to the members of the team as to where we would train next spring, that it would be Bogalusa by 100 percent."

Manager Coleman of the Terre Haute, Ind., team of the Central League, and former manager of the Mobile club, said that the club house built here for the Browns was by far better than any club house on the American League circuit and that it passed Detroit, which had the best in the league. "The grounds," said Mr. Coleman, "are great and by next year they can be made as good as any in the country."

All of this, apparently, was not enough: the Brownies never returned to Bogalusa for spring training, heading in 1922 for Mobile, Alabama.

Each team has a unique spring-training history, and we present some of the highlights in each team chapter. We also point out former spring-training sites worth a visit. There was one period that bears further discussion, however: spring training during the war years. We all associate spring training with warmer climes, but there was a time when major-league teams trained close to home. Travel restrictions during World War II kept teams north of the Ohio River and east of the Mississippi River; the St. Louis Browns and Cardinals were exempted and trained in the greater St. Louis area.

As a result, teams trained in such exotic locales as Evansville and French Lick, where both the Chicago Cubs and Chicago White Sox trained in 1943 and 1944. The East Coast teams didn't stray too far from home, either: The Brooklyn Dodgers trained at the West Point fieldhouse between drills, and the Boston Braves trained at Choate School in Wallingford, Connecticut.

When the war ended, normalcy resumed—and that included baseball, which returned to springs spent mostly in Florida and Arizona. As travel and demographics changed, so did spring training. Rather than writing off spring training as a necessary expense, baseball teams saw spring training evolve into a profit center: instead of being limited to boozy journalists and clubby insiders, spring training opened to everyone with enough money for admission.

REMEMBERING JACKIE ROBINSON IN SPRING TRAINING

While spring training past and present has been focused on the process of establishing rosters and whipping players into game shape, there was a period when spring training was central in America's consciousness for a different reason: when Jackie Robinson integrated Major League Baseball.

Robinson's feat in baseball racial integration is celebrated annually by Major League Baseball, marking his debut in 1947 with the Brooklyn Dodgers. But that wasn't exactly his first stint in a Dodgers uniform, and it could be argued that Robinson began the process of integrating MLB by donning a Montreal Royals uniform during spring training 1946. It was then that racial integration in Major League Baseball burst on the national stage, and all the drama surrounding Robinson in the spring of 1946 paved the way for his Dodgers tenure in 1947. The Grapefruit League and Florida played a central role in this drama as well—some for good, some for bad.

Some of the facilities where Robinson made history are still standing and in use. If you're in Florida for an extended spring-training trip or live in Florida, we'd recommend a day trip to take in some of these sites. We'll cover the high points of spring training 1946 for Robinson and the Dodgers, aligning them to venues you can visit today.

The first thing to know when you consider spring training 1946 from the Dodgers' point of view: in the 1946 season Brooklyn fielded 21 farm teams, ranging from the Montreal Royals and St. Paul Saints at the Triple-A level to the Fort Worth Cats in the Texas League, the Nashua Dodgers in the New England League, the Trois-Rivieres Royals in the Canadian-American League, and the Daytona Beach Islanders of the Florida State League, then a Class-D league. Besides serving as home of the Islanders, City Island Ballpark was also the spring-training home of the Brooklyn Dodgers MLB squad for a single year before the team shifted spring training to Cuba in 1947. But it was not the only site used by the Dodgers organization, with the team's 700-plus players spread out in eastern Florida camps.

Jackie Robinson, a UCLA football and baseball star, was playing for the Kansas City Monarchs of the Negro American League in August 1945 when he was approached by Dodgers President/General Manager Branch Rickey about playing for the Dodgers. Rickey had been scouting the Negro Leagues under the guise of forming a new Negro Leagues team, the Brooklyn Brown Dodgers, but was instead searching for someone up to integrating MLB for the first time in the 20th century—someone with the cool and the guts to walk away from a fight, according to Rickey. Today, this integration could be seen as an inevitable development of history, but at a time when Jim Crow laws ruled the South and America's major institutions remained segregated, Rickey's desire to integrate Major League Baseball was far from an assured success. There were plenty of voices calling for the integration of America's Pastime—progressive politicians, the African-American press, Communists—but in an era where Blacks were still being lynched in the South, integration was a brave move.

Technically, Robinson signed a 1946 contract in August 1945 with the International League's Montreal Royals, which was announced to the press in October 1945. Minor League Baseball integration would precede Major League integration by a year, with the belief that Robinson's debut would not generate too much controversy in the cosmopolitan and international Montreal—a belief borne out by a relatively uneventful 1946 season. He was not the only Black player Rickey signed, with pitcher Johnny Wright joining Robinson in camp in Sanford, a small community located north of Orlando.

The choice of Daytona as the home of the Dodgers' spring training in 1946 was not an accident: Rickey sought a community that was comparatively racially progressive by the standards of the day. Though in the Deep South, Daytona was known for being relatively integrated and home to Bethune-Cookman College, one of the leading Black institutions of higher learning in the country, led by Mary McLeod Bethune. Yes, we know *relatively* is carrying a lot of weight here, but situations must be viewed through the lens of the time.

The Montreal Royals camp was located at Sanford Municipal Athletic Field, near downtown Sanford and next to the current Sanford Memorial Stadium (which we discuss in our Orlando chapter). While the major leaguers were training at Daytona's City Island Ballpark, the minor leaguers were scattered across eastern Florida. Kelly Field, located in the Black part of Daytona, was pressed into service as a training site, and after soliciting advice from Dodgers broadcaster Red Barber, who recommended his Florida hometown as a training site, Rickey selected Sanford for Royals and Saints workouts. Kelly Field was a familiar site for pro baseball players, with Hall of Famers like Satchel Paige and Larry Doby having played games there. Kelly Field also once hosted games for Bethune-Cookman University and served as a center of social life in the predominately Black neighborhood.

Sanford was also home to the Dodgers' pre-camp meetings. Players would gather at the Mayfair Hotel, where "Rickey University" would convene in the ballroom, with Rickey and coaches going over the finer points of the Dodgers' approach to baseball. It was at Sanford Municipal Athletic Field during spring training 1946 where Rickey unveiled his latest innovation, the electric pitching machine.

Training camp did not start smoothly for Robinson: on the second day he was warned that Sanford residents did not want him there, leading Rickey and the Dodgers to move the Royals training camp to Daytona Beach. Robinson's presence there did not generate the same sort of reaction it did among some quarters in Sanford— and, indeed, it's hard to say whether loudmouths who promised violence in Sanford really spoke for any sizable portion of the populace. But as long as the Dodgers and Robinson promised to recognize the city's segregation laws, local officials promised peace. And those segregation laws extended to City Island Ballpark, remnants you can still see at the modern Jackie Robinson Ballpark: the shaded first-base grandstand seating is the former whites-only section, while the unshaded grandstand down the third-base line was the Black seating area.

On March 17, 1946, Robinson made his Montreal Royals debut at City Island Ballpark against the Dodgers, before a crowd of over 4,000. Rickey, a devout Methodist, was not on hand for the Sunday game, but he didn't miss much past the history of Robinson integrating pro baseball: the Dodgers won, while Robinson went hitless and scored a run. There were no incidents in the stands or on the field, and Robinson won praise from Brooklyn manager Leo Durocher, who said he "looked like a real ballplayer out there."

Things did not go so smoothly when Robinson and the Royals played on the road. A game against the Jersey City Giants at Jacksonville's Durkee Field was cancelled by the head of the city's Parks and Public Property department, dubiously arguing that a city ordinance prohibited competitions between whites and Blacks. In DeLand, a game between the Royals and the Double-A Indianapolis Indians was cancelled by city officials under some questionable circumstances: they said the electric lines underneath the field used by the lighting system needed to be dug up and tested. After that, a second scheduled game in Jacksonville was cancelled after Durkee Field was locked up and the Jersey City Giants headed to Gainesville. Finally, in one last act of Deep South prejudice, Robinson and Wright were ordered from the Sanford Municipal Athletic Field dugout by a local police officer when in town to scrimmage the St. Paul Saints. Robinson was in the lineup and had batted in the top of the second inning, but he was later removed after the officer threatened to arrest the pair if they remained in the dugout, arguing that local segregation laws prohibited Blacks from playing on the same field as whites.

So, at the end of the day, Jackie Robinson's monumental feat of integrating spring training comprised several games at City Island Ballpark and less than two innings played at Sanford Municipal Athletic Field. The next year the Dodgers shifted training to Cuba, where in the past Black ballplayers like Josh Gibson and Satchel Paige were welcomed and the team had the use of the new Gran Stadium, which still stands and served as home to landmark MLB games in recent years. But the cost of operating spring training in Cuba, far from other MLB and MiLB teams in Florida, was too much for the Dodgers to bear, so for spring training 1948 the team set its sights on a permanent base in Vero Beach. The Dodgers were attracted to the area by Bud Holman, a local entrepreneur and director of Eastern Air Lines. He persuaded Buzzie Bavasi (then the farm director of the Brooklyn Dodgers) to consolidate spring training for the Dodgers and their farm teams. The city of Vero Beach wasn't sure this was a good idea—as a matter of fact, the city refused to put in a swimming pool that Holman requested—so technically the Dodgers contracted with Holman, who in turn leased the land from the city.

The Dodgers were so pleased with spring training in Vero Beach that by 1952 the Dodgers signed a 21-year lease with the city for a true Dodgertown at a former Naval air base. As part of the lease, the Dodgers agreed that the entire major-league club and 50 percent of the Dodgers' farm teams would train in Vero Beach. The players were put up in former Naval barracks.

The Dodgers then furthered their commitment a few months later by investing $100,000 in a new ballpark, named Holman Stadium, with 1,500 steel seats brought from Ebbets Field in Brooklyn and New York City's Polo Grounds. Holman Stadium has an impressive lineage: it was designed by Norman Bel Geddes (designer of the Futurama building at the 1964 New York World's Fair and the creative genius behind one of the three proposed domed stadiums for the Dodgers that, alas, was never built) and engineered by Captain Emil Praeger, whose firm (Praeger-Kavanagh-Waterbury) also engineered Dodger Stadium in Los Angeles and Shea Stadium in New York City.

You may have time to hit some of the Jackie Robinson landmarks during your spring-training travels. The old City Island Ballpark in Daytona Beach is now Jackie Robinson Ballpark, complete with exhibits telling the story of Robinson's exploits. The ballpark doesn't host spring training—interestingly, the last MLB team to train there was the Montreal Expos—but it is home to the Single-A Daytona Tortugas. During February and March, fittingly, the ballpark is also home to the Bethune-Cookman University baseball team.)You can see a schedule at the Bethune-Cookman University website: *bcuathletics.com*.) Baseball is still played at Vero Beach's Dodgertown, now run by Major League Baseball. There's plenty of baseball there between youth and college tournaments, and strolling through Dodgertown and taking a gander at Holman Stadium is well worth a visit: it still feels like the spring home of the Dodgers in many ways. In Sanford, a short drive from Orlando, Sanford Municipal Athletic Field has been replaced by Sanford Memorial Stadium. We discuss Sanford Memorial Stadium in more depth in our Orlando chapter; suffice it to say it's a classic 1951 ballpark hosting all manner of high-school and youth baseball each spring. Jacksonville's Durkee Field is now J. P. Small Memorial Stadium, and it still stands, complete with a history exhibit about Robinson and the venue's history as a Negro Leagues home. And Kelly Field has been restored by the local minor-league Daytona Tortugas, with the field ready for play and a permanent display installed honoring the field's history installed by SABR. It's located at George Engram

A SHORT HISTORY OF SPRING TRAINING

Boulevard and Keech Street, behind the Midtown Cultural & Educational Center.

And there's one more landmark you may want to drive by if you're in Sanford. As noted, Robinson didn't spend too much time in Sanford before threats of violence forced him and Johnny Wright to Daytona Beach. During Robinson's time there, he roomed at 612 Sanford Avenue, hosted by David and Viola Brock after they were vetted personally by Rickey. That house is still there. It was deemed a "mansion" by Rickey in 1946, and the four-bedroom home still has plenty of curb appeal. It was a stop, albeit a short one, on Robinson's journey to the majors.

Sanford Municipal Athletic Field. *Courtesy Florida Historical Society.*

SPRING TRAINING: AN AMERICAN TRADITION

We live in an increasingly crowded sports marketplace, but one thing remains constant: the appeal of low-tech, low-stress spring training, a time considered by many to be the best time in the baseball season. While the grandstands aren't wooden anymore and you never see pitchers running wind sprints in the outfield during a

SPRING TRAINING: AN AMERICAN TRADITION

game, spring training is still a celebration of everything that is right with baseball.

Spring training has remained a cornerstone activity for baseball fans hardcore and casual, though it has certainly changed over the years. In the not-too-distant past, spring training could be attended on a whim, with plenty of good seats available at the gate and fewer than a thousand fans in the stands. Those days are long gone and, in this age of fans seeking great experiences of all sorts, spring training has exploded in popularity over the last 20 years.

How popular is spring training? Attendance has been down the last few years, as you might expect. Overall, 7,345 fans per game were on hand for spring-training games in Arizona, Florida, and Las Vegas, up from 7,026 fans per game played on a limited schedule in 2022. Yes, more on approaching normalcy: In 2019, the last "normal" spring training, 7,623 fans per game attended spring training in Arizona, Florida, and Las Vegas.

The *Wall Street Journal* estimated that spring training generates some $1.3 billion in spending in a normal season. Locally, the Florida Sports Foundation estimates that in a normal year the Grapefruit League generates a $687.1 million economic impact, with 52 percent of fans arriving from out of state, while the Baltimore Orioles estimate the team has generated $584.5 million in economic impact for the state of Florida since 2015. Big numbers tend to be a little abstract, to be sure, but the economic impact is there.

THE PLANNING PROCESS

Though the beginning of spring training marks the official beginning of the baseball season, teams prepare for training camp months in advance. Planning starts before the end of the prior season, when team equipment managers start organizing supplies in advance of spring training, and team officials begin finalizing spring-training schedules.

Truck Day is now regarded by many as the unofficial launch to spring training. In late January and early February, each team ships its equipment from its home ballpark to its spring-training site. Most MLB teams have turned this rather mundane shipment into a full-fledged event, flooding social media with photos of trucks being loaded, leaving the ballpark, and arriving at the spring-training facility. Several teams have sold naming rights to the event; JetBlue, for example, is the sponsor of the Boston Red Sox Truck Day.

We're talking some serious baggage here. In 2024, the Philadelphia Phillies shipped the following to Clearwater via three 28-foot equipment trailers:

- 10,000 cups
- 2,400 baseballs
- 2,000 short-and-long sleeved shirts
- 1,200 bats
- 900 pairs of socks
- 600 pairs of pants
- 600 batting practice hats
- 350 pairs of shorts
- 300 batting gloves
- 250 batting practice tops
- 200 fleeces
- 200 light jackets
- 140 batting helmets
- 125 leather and elastic belts
- 75 pairs of assorted spike and turf shoes
- 40 heavy jackets
- 20 coolers
- several bikes

The Houston Astros sent a slightly more eclectic set of merchandise to Florida:

- 30 pounds of resin
- 150 batting helmets
- 150 belts
- 200 cases of sunflower seeds
- 250 jerseys
- 300 caps
- 300 cartons of bubble gum
- 1,000 pair of baseball pants
- 2,000 pounds of laundry detergent
- 8,400 baseballs (700 dozen)
- 1 case of Silly String (for use by mascot Orbit)

- 1 4-wheeler (for use by mascot Orbit)

Spring training now requires a certain level of planning from fans as well. Timeshares and hotels must be reserved, relatives must be warned, vacations must be requested, and school schedules must be consulted. We understand. It can be difficult at times to plan for spring training. In this chapter, we'll go through the steps needed to prepare for your spring travels.

At all times, you can catch schedules both permanent and tentative at *springtrainingonline.com*.

INSIDER'S TIP
We do a Spring Training Online newsletter, and we send out issues when schedules are updated. It's free, and you can sign up at *springtrainingonline.com*.

PLANNING YOUR TRIP

There are three ways to approach a visit to spring training: for games, for workouts, or for both. We love doing both—workouts in the morning, a game in the afternoon—but there are plenty of folks who focus on games as their spring-training experience.

For many, spring training begins when it does for players: on reporting day, this year in the middle of February (think Valentine's Day). Decades ago, that first reporting day was a big deal. Players were reentering the baseball world from their offseason jobs, and they were subject to a physical, a weigh-in, and a general evaluation by team officials. With players mostly out of touch between October and February, there were always some surprises on reporting day, mostly of the unpleasant kind, when a player should show up fat and out of shape.

For today's baseball player, the game is a full-time job. Virtually every player trains in the offseason or plays winter ball, and organizations keep close tabs on most players, especially the well-paid prospects and superstars. There are very few surprises come that first reporting date, as many players have already been hanging out around training facilities for several weeks, months, or the entire offseason.

Many fans like to show up for those first practices, as hordes of players run through drills. Many practice areas are set up for fan comfort, with shaded seating and even concessions. There are some big rewards to showing up for workouts: players tend to be accessible at those initial workouts and more willing to sign autographs after practice. We cover every team's practice schedule individually; there's no uniform MLB schedule to practices, and every team sets its own start time and location. (We update them on *springtrainingonline.com*.) The actual workout period is quite short, running the 10 days or so from reporting dates to the first game, when the schedule changes.

INSIDER'S TIP

Practices are organized, and while MLB teams have added many creature comforts to workout facilities, they don't feel compelled to share their organizational plan with you. You're welcome to observe from a respectful distance—either in the stands in the main ballpark or somewhere next to a practice field—and teams are very explicit about where you're allowed to watch. Some teams rope off access to specific areas of the training complex at certain times. At the end of the day, the attitude from many MLB teams is that workouts are for players, not for fans.

Another thing regarding practice schedules: teams have general times for workouts, but the specifics will vary from day to day. Some teams will post morning practice updates on their Instagram accounts, but the practice is hardly uniform in the baseball world.

When games begin around February 21-22, workouts are curtailed. Most teams will gather in the morning for workouts, but the real focus is the afternoon game. You can show up early and see who you can catch at the morning workout. (Indeed, that's one of the big advantages of a modern spring facility like CACTI Park of the Palm Beaches: they are designed to bring fans close to practice areas before you ever hit the ballpark.) Conversely, if a team is on the road, the regulars not scheduled for the trip will often work out in the morning during a regularly scheduled workout time.

In fact, this emphasis on games versus long workouts designed to sweat the booze from out-of-shape players is perhaps the biggest shift in the modern age of spring training. Most players come to spring training in shape, so the need for intense physical workouts is mitigated. Most teams have their basic rosters mostly set weeks before spring training, but some roster spots are won and lost during spring training. Take, for example, Aaron Judge. When the New York Yankees were close to breaking camp in 2017, the front office had not decided whether to keep Judge on the roster or send him to Triple-A Scranton/Wilkes-Barre. In the end, the Yankees went with Judge in right field in somewhat of a last-minute decision, and the rest was history. Now, Judge's case is a little unusual in that most teams have an idea of their Opening Day lineup well before camp breaks. Indeed, for most teams, the last week of spring training is to determine the last two pitchers in the bullpen, the fifth outfielder should a team carry five, the backup catcher, etc.

So why go to practices? Eagerness to begin the season. Enthusiasm for the upcoming campaign. Desire to snare an autograph. Baseball in the sun.

Though you'll find plenty of fans milling around camp after players report, the real action starts when games begin at the end of February. This, for most fans, is the real beginning of spring training. And although the starting lineups during those first few weeks of games will bear little resemblance to the Opening Day lineup, enough stars will be present to make those games worthwhile. In general, you'll need a long lineup card to keep track of all the players shuttling on and off the field for those games. Technically, any team playing on the road is required by Major League Baseball to feature four regulars from the previous season (and yes, it's defined: at least 300 at-bats in the prior season) in the lineup, but not every team strictly hews to that requirement. Pitchers are restricted by pitch and inning counts, starters are limited to just three or four innings on the field, and by the seventh inning you'll be watching mostly players already ticketed for time at the Triple-A or Double-A levels.

So what? You're out in the sun at a glorious time of year partaking in America's Pastime. It's a great experience no matter if you're watching a starting MLB pitcher or a kid destined (in the short-term, at least) to be a Quad Cities River Bandit.

One more thing to note when scheduling your time: most spring-training games are played in the afternoon. Last year saw several MLB teams scheduling fewer night games, but some teams—the Yankees, Orioles, Astros, and Nationals—hosted several. Given that several teams train in the greater Tampa Bay area—Philadelphia, Detroit, New York, Toronto, Pittsburgh—you could hit an afternoon game and then head to Steinbrenner Field for the nightcap. Throw in a college game in Tampa or Fort Myers (we cover college facilities in this book as well), and you could schedule a spring trip with daily doubleheaders. Baseball nirvana.

HOW TO ORDER TICKETS

There's no one date when all MLB teams put spring-training tickets on sale: each team sets a sale date separately, sometimes with very little warning.

Unless you are lucky enough to score tickets the day they go on sale or buy a season ticket, you'll need to order them from teams and deal with the distinct possibility that popular games are sold out. Many of you will deal with the resale market—not the worst outcome.

Buying your ticket directly from the team will usually be the cheapest way to snare a ducat. With popular teams, the selection will be limited. Every team sells spring-training season tickets, bought mostly by locals and snowbirds, and the best tickets in any spring ballpark are controlled by these season-ticket holders. Indeed, MLB teams have put an emphasis on building a spring season-ticket base, cutting down the number of tickets available for any single game. Many of the best tickets to a game at a Steinbrenner Field or JetBlue Park have been sold for weeks before single-game seats go on sale, as season-ticket holders control the top inventory.

Still, tickets are available from a variety of sources. Most people assume that only MLB teams sell tickets, but that's not the case. MLB teams do sell most spring-training tickets, but there are usually some alternative ways to come up with ducats for a popular match.

For sheer convenience, however, your search for tickets should begin with the MLB teams. They're set up best to sell massive amounts of tickets in a short amount of time; the beginning of spring-training ticket sales can be a feeding frenzy, as tens of thousands of fans rush to obtain tickets for specific games.

There are four ways to order spring-training tickets directly from MLB teams: via telephone, via the Internet, in person, and via the U.S. Mail. We'll describe each.

- **Via the Internet.** The vast majority of spring-training tickets are now sold on the Internet. There are some pluses and minuses to this approach. On the one hand, you can bypass clogged phone lines and make your purchases directly, although Ticketmaster has implemented the equivalent of telephone wait times when you buy popular tickets online. New ticketing systems are sophisticated: many teams have systems where you can order specific seats or see a list of available seats within a section and select the ones you want. And yes, you'll also pay a ticketing fee for the convenience of buying tickets. But by using a credit card online you will receive an instant refund if a game is canceled: you don't even need to call in. Paperless tickets are very mandatory these days, and apps from ticket vendors are safe and secure methods for buying, managing, and transferring tickets.
- **Via telephone.** Many tickets are sold via phone sales. This can be a frustrating way of doing things, as you're likely to encounter some busy signals or long wait times when tickets first go on sale. Don't bother calling before the tickets are technically on sale: all you'll do is waste your time and irritate the ticket reps. They can't help you until the tickets are actually on sale; they won't call you back, and they won't put you on a secret list to be hauled out when tickets are on sale. When the tickets do go on sale—and you'll find a complete listing of when tickets go on sale at the *springtrainingonline.com* team pages—be prepared to call early in the day for popular games, like the Boston-New York matchups. You'll also pay a ticketing fee for the convenience of buying tickets.
- **In person.** Many teams sell spring-training tickets at their main ticket office at the major-league ballpark, the spring-

training ticket office, or local team stores. Three big advantages to buying tickets in person: you can usually get a good idea of the range of available tickets, you can request specific seats, and you won't need to wait too long in line. Plus, the major-league box office and the spring-training box offices are the only locations where you won't incur ticketing fees. One troubling trend we are seeing: many teams first put tickets on sale via online and phone sales and then don't open the spring-training box office until several weeks have passed by, some not until the team's reporting date. The days when tickets went on sale locally and online simultaneously are long gone. Also, we have noted that MLB teams are scaling back on team stores in malls and suburbs, places we'd recommend folks go to buy their tickets. But the New York Yankees still operate four Clubhouse Shops in Manhattan, and it may be more convenient for you to buy tickets in person at the West 42nd location than at Yankee Stadium.

- **Via U.S. Mail.** Some teams sell tickets via the mail. You send in your money for a certain price range, and you take whatever tickets the team decides to send you. Will you receive the best tickets in your price range? Depends on the whims of a ticket rep with the team. The advantage, however, is that these orders tend to be filled first, so you are virtually assured of receiving tickets to the game of your choice. Not every team offers this service, and we list addresses on *springtrainingonline.com* team pages if mail fulfillment is available.

INSIDER'S TIP

If you order tickets and plan on picking them up at the ballpark, make sure you have the confirmation number and an ID with you. Ticket-office personnel are instructed to make sure that the right person is picking up tickets. More than once have we waited in line in the Will Call line and cooled our heels while the party in front of us argued in vain with the ticket staff over disputed tickets. In general, the Will Call folks are accommodating. You can leave tickets there for other members of your group at no charge even if not purchased directly from the team, letting you enter the ballpark instead of waiting at the front gates for your friends.

INSIDER'S TIP
The current trend is toward paperless tickets, billed as a safety measure by many teams to prevent contact between a worker and a fan. This is somewhat disingenuous—teams use scanners at the gates, and it makes no difference if you're scanning in a bar code on a piece of paper or a phone screen —but paperless tickets do give MLB teams more control over tickets, and they certainly like control. But you can buy e-tickets anywhere on the aftermarket, and they'll work just fine.

In recent years, you could count on tickets being on sale at the spring-training offices in Florida or Arizona. Generally, this is still true, but not every spring box office opens when tickets go on sale. In 2024, most teams offered tickets for sale at the launch of sales season only online and via the phone. Weeks later, the sales office at the spring-training site would open for business and stay open through the start of spring training. Each team does it differently, and we note the specific dates and locations on *springtrainingonline.com* when they are released by MLB teams.

Teams also offer two more ways to obtain tickets that may fit your needs.

If you think you'll be attending many games, consider a season ticket. Season-ticket packages go on sale weeks before single-game tickets. Usually season tickets are the province of locals and brokers, but if you really, really want some tix for the Red Sox-Yankees games and realize that you have no chance of obtaining a good ticket via conventional means, spring for the season ticket and then try and sell tickets to some of the other games via eBay or StubHub.

Other teams offer a break to groups of 10 or more. Again, this won't apply if just you and your friends or family are heading to a game, but there may be opportunities where you could put together a group (via a church organization, an Internet chat site, etc.) that could buy discounted tickets to a game or two. These transactions require some interaction with a sales agent. At this time no team is offering discounted group tickets online during the course of spring training; you'll need to contact the sales office and talk to a human.

For instance, the New York Yankees offer discounts for groups of 10 or more at Steinbrenner Field and offer both discounted tickets and premium spaces with all-inclusive hospitality. The latter includes a dedicated personal account representative. These transactions require some interaction with a sales agent. Similarly, the Minnesota Twins offer group discounts to parties of 15 or larger— the larger the group, the greater the discounts. At this time no team is offering discounted group tickets online; you will need to deal with a live person.

INSIDER'S TIP

If you can, schedule a game on St. Patrick's Day. It's the only real holiday celebrated at the spring-training ballpark, and most teams do something to mark the occasion, whether it be green uniforms or food specials. You can also bet watering holes close to the ballparks will have some St. Patrick's Day drink specials as well. In 2025, St. Patrick's Day falls on a Monday, making for the end of an extended baseball weekend.

BUYING AT THE GATE

The nice thing about the Internet is that you can gauge ticket availability even if you have no intention of buying a ducat online. At some of the larger spring ballparks, there's very little chance of a game selling out. So you can roll the dice and buy your tickets at the gate. As a bonus, the ballpark ticket office is the place where you can take advantage of a senior discount. They're not offered by all teams, but we do note on *springtrainingonline.com* where they are offered. The same goes for military discounts: some teams offer them, some do not. So if you're willing to take a chance on your seat location, by all means buy tickets at the gate. We don't always recommend it (we like to know where we are sitting and rest easy knowing we'll be able to get into the game), but feel free to live dangerously.

WORKING WITH THIRD-PARTY RESELLERS

There is another way to obtain a single-game ticket: through a third-party reseller. Resellers used to be anathema to the baseball industry, until teams realized resellers should be embraced and encouraged—to an extent. Today every MLB team embraces the open market with official ticket partners that end up offering ducats through other resellers. They also put tickets on sale early, giving you peace of mind in your planning process. They're also not shy about telling the world about the availability of the tickets, so if you want to go to a game badly enough, chances are good one of them will step up with a ticket. We work with a very reputable vendor to offer tickets at *ballparkdigesttickets.com*; of course, we'd recommend you start there. Last spring we saw the market at work: for many games, like Boston Red Sox games early in spring training, we saw tickets sell *below* face value because the season-ticket holders were all committed to attending games later in March, not the final days of February. And by using a credit card online with a third-party reseller you are able to receive an instant refund if a game is canceled: you don't even need to call in.

WHERE TO STAY

If you lack friends or family in Florida, you'll need to arrange housing for your stay. There are a few ways to go.

The obvious choice is a hotel. Virtually every spring-training site is located in an urban or suburban area with easy access to a slew of hotels. You'll pay more to stay near the more popular ballparks; in our guides to each venue, we list the closest hotels to each ballpark and tell you if it's worth staying near the ballpark. (In many cases, it's not.) There are some baseball fanatics that insist on staying within walking distance of a spring-training facility, but they a) tend to spend the entire day at the facility and b) don't want to spring for the cost of a car.

In the chapters covering specific complexes, we list the local numbers for hotels located close to the ballparks, as well as the official hotel for every team (when there is one). Yes, fans—not just baseball Annies—still hang around hotel lobbies hoping for a glimpse of a star or a potential autograph opportunity. You won't be alone. But those chances for a glimpse of a star are exceedingly remote: most stars maintain private housing or own their Florida residences.

Only in rare situations will you be shut out of an affordable hotel room for spring training—provided you can be flexible about where you stay. In Lakeland, for instance, there are plenty of times where all the decent affordable hotel rooms in town are sold out during spring training. That doesn't mean you should avoid spring training; it means you should cast a wider net for hotel rooms in Winter Haven, Plant City, Tampa (which sits less than 35 miles from Joker Marchant Stadium), or Orlando (especially the abundance of Kissimmee/southwest Orlando/Disney World hotels located less than 45 miles from Publix Field) if you're set on seeing the Tigers at TigerTown. If your target is Fort Myers, your choices include Port Charlotte to the north and Naples to the south when it comes to alternative hotel selections.

You can also investigate a package deal involving a hotel. Some teams and hotels now offer package deals, which combine a hotel stay with tickets to a game or two.

But there are some alternatives to daily-stay hotels. The most prominent is a residence-sharing service like Airbnb or VRBO, where you can see the specifics of the rental before committing. There are plenty of listings for the likes of Tampa or Palm Beach during spring training. While they may not be the cheapest venues under the sun, you won't get that hotel feel when staying at someone else's residence. Depending on your viewpoint, that's either a good thing or a bad thing. Just beware the hidden fees: don't be sucked in by a cheap daily or weekly rate and then discover there's a sizable mandatory cleaning fee.

There are many folks who visit spring training in the comfort of their own RV. They're the ones setting up shop three or four hours before a game, grilling their pregame brats, watching the noontime news. Though you can't park overnight at a ballpark parking lot, most communities hosting spring training also have several RV parks, and some ballparks have special areas set up for RV parking. Alas, these these are becoming more scarce as areas around ballparks are developed. We note them throughout this book.

You don't even need to own an RV to use one for spring training: Companies like Cruise America rent RVs by the day or week from hundreds of locations across the United States. Today's RV is not like yesterday's RV. They have considerably more amenities (like showers, decent bathrooms, and air conditioning) and are more reliable than in the past. And RV parks can be amazingly upscale, with shaded parking, wireless networking, and more.

MAKING YOUR WAY TO THE BALLPARK: PLANES, TRAINS, AND AUTOMOBILES

Getting to the city hosting spring training is one thing. Making your way to your hotel room and the ballpark is another.

The ballparks of Florida spring training, in general, aren't easily accessible via public transit. In many Florida cities, save Tampa or Orlando, public transit is spotty or nonexistent. For Yankees or Red Sox fans used to hopping a bus or subway to the game, forget about it: ain't no subway running beneath the sands of Florida.

So, in most cases, you'll need to resign yourself to an inevitable cost of attending spring training: renting a car. Sure, you could drive your own car to spring training—and trust us, plenty of folks do just that, as evidenced by the large number of Michigan license plates in the Publix Field at Joker Marchant Stadium parking lot throughout February and March—but if you're committed to flying, you're going to be forced to rent a car.

There are some challenges to renting a car in Florida: they are highly taxed and tend to be on the expensive side, driving up the cost of travel. You should have no problem in obtaining a rental car at a large tourist-driven airport, like Orlando International, Tampa, Palm Beach, or Sarasota-Bradenton. (We love Sarasota-Bradenton: it's a small airport with quick access both to rental cars and ballparks.) The issue will be how much you pay for that rental.

INSIDER'S TIP

Depending on your destination, you will want to think about whether you rent from an agency located onsite or offsite. There are pluses and minuses to both. When you rent from an onsite agency, you walk out of the airport and right to your car; convenience is the big plus. When you rent from an offsite agency, you catch a shuttle bus to a rental-car building located outside the airport; a lower price is the plus here. If you're traveling with a family, spring for the onsite rental, as shuttle buses are a pain. In Orlando and Tampa, the major car-rental agencies are located onsite, either directly in the terminal or a short tram ride away.

INSIDER'S TIP
Consider an alternative to rental cars: ridesharing services like Uber and Lyft. The appeal: you can order a car at a specific place at a specific time, and you can be dropped off at or near the ballpark. (Most, but not all, spring-training ballparks have a designated dropoff area. But any smart driver in Tampa or Fort Myers can get you fairly close to the ballpark.) They definitely lessen the need for a rental car for those staying in more urban areas: you could certainly stay at a neighborhood hotel in Clearwater or Dunedin and then arrange a rideshare to and from the games.

ATTENDING A GAME: SOME GENERAL GUIDELINES

Now that you actually have a game ticket, a plane ticket, a hotel room, and a way to hit the training complex, you're all ready to actually attend a spring-training game. What will that Spring Training 2025 game look like? There are some things you should know:

- Most spring-training ballparks open at least two hours before game time, and we note pregame schedules for every team on team pages. (There's no uniform MLB schedule to when workouts start; teams set their own daily schedules.) This is usually the best time to score autographs: players are relaxed during their warm-ups and are willing to wander over to the stands and sign away. Some teams hold workouts for players not slated to be in the game. And, of course, you could head to the practice facility in the morning and try to score some autographs there. That's a much easier task, of course, when teams train at the same complex as the ballpark.

- Many of the ushers at spring-training games are volunteers, usually senior citizens living in the area. Don't hassle them: they're volunteering at a game because they love baseball. Some of them can be a little on the officious side, but remember their job is to make sure fans are in their proper seats. In Bradenton, almost 100 locals volunteer their services at Pittsburgh Pirates games.
- You're not always assured of seeing a superstar or even a famous player at a spring-training game. Visiting teams are notorious for leaving their best players at home. There is an MLB rule that each team must send four regulars on the road to play in an exhibition game, but that doesn't mean Ronald Acuña Jr. will regularly play in an away game.
- Don't be in a hurry to leave the ballpark once a game is done. Some coaches will hold a practice right after an afternoon game, either in the main ballpark or a practice field. (This doesn't happen as often as it once did, unfortunately.) Another bonus to remaining for entire games: players will usually sign on their way back to the clubhouses. So take your time. Wander the grounds. Take a stroll. Relax: this is the very essence of spring training.

"B" GAMES

You don't need to shell out the big bucks to see major leaguers in action during spring training.

If you're willing to put up with the lack of a few creature comforts like seatbacks, concessions, and restrooms, you can hit a "B" game held on a satellite field in a spring-training complex. These are pure practice games, usually held in the late morning or early afternoon. There's no scoreboard tracking the action or an announcer introducing the players, so you should know a little about the players to get anything out of the experience.

And you can't be too much of a purist. As said, these are true practice games: players bat out of order and wander in and out of the lineup depending on the situation.

But these games are also excellent places to see the real major leaguers work on their game: you're never going to be closer to a superstar working on specific skills. Hard-working players are legendary for using these games to work on their swings or on specific pitches.

In the past, teams held "B" games almost daily, but they seem to be going by the wayside. Call the team's local box office to see if a "B" game is scheduled for a given day (they are not subject to a published schedule), but your best bet may to be wander around a facility in the morning and see if there's any action on a field.

MINOR-LEAGUE GAMES

Another option during your spring-training trip: taking in a minor-league match. These games are played on satellite fields (at the spring complex when possible; at a larger offsite training facility if not) and are open to anyone wandering through the facility. Unlike "B" games, minor-league games are subject to a schedule: they begin a few weeks into spring training and feature all the full-season teams in an organization taking on all the teams from another organization. For instance, the Triple-A and Double-A teams from the Philadelphia Phillies will host the Triple-A and Double-A teams from the Detroit Tigers at the satellite fields at the Carpenter training complex next to BayCare Ballpark, while the two High-A and Single-A teams from the Tigers will host the two High-A and Single-A Phillies teams at Tiger Town. In the minors, there are four levels of teams in training camp (Triple-A, Double-A, High-A, and Single-A); if the Triple-A and Double-A teams are home, the High-A and Single-A teams will be away, and vice versa. Again, these games are run on a casual basis, and most of the better players will be with the parent team, but they offer a very intimate view of some of tomorrow's superstars. Schedules for these games are released after the beginning of the year; check *www.springtrainingonline.com* a complete list of minor-league schedules, or at least the schedules released by MLB parents.

INSIDER'S TIP
We've seen fewer and fewer MLB teams release MiLB schedules over the past five years. We've also seen MLB teams

arrange fewer and fewer MiLB games over the past five years, scheduling more camp days.

MLB added another layer of MiLB matches in 2024, scheduling Spring Breakout games. These games were created with the goal of showcasing future stars, with the MLB ballparks hosting a match between top prospects in a seven-inning exhibition game, either scheduled separately or with an MLB game. The tickets were affordable—$10 in many MLB ballparks as a separate game, free as part of a doubleheader—and gave fans another chance to take in some spring action, albeit with no MLB stars. These games are returning in 2025.

WEATHER

You can tell spring-training rookies by their beet-red faces and sunburned shoulders. If you've spent the last four months cooped up in a climate dominated by snow and ice, you're going to do the logical thing and bask for hours on end in the warm spring sun.

Don't.

Yes, you'll hear from everyone the importance of slathering on some sunscreen before hitting your first spring game. The advice is sound: even a mildly overcast day can scorch your skin to the painful point, and you don't want to ruin your trip with a bad sunburn.

Otherwise, you should plan on good weather for your spring-training sojourn and buy supplies accordingly. In general, you can expect highs in the upper 70s and lows in the middle 50s at the beginning of spring training, and highs in the lower 80s and lows in the lower 60s at the end of training camp. And it's almost a Florida cliché that you can expect some sort of rain in the late afternoon.

WHAT CAN I BRING INTO THE BALLPARK?

Forget about bringing much into the ballpark past a medium-sized bag. There's a uniform MLB policy regarding what you can bring into a ballpark. First, everything must fit within a backpack, cooler, or purse no larger than 16 inches by 16 inches by 8 inches. (Diaper bags are exempted from the size requirements.) Non-alcoholic beverages must be in sealed, plastic containers. Food must be stored in sealed, clear-plastic containers. If you're carrying any sort of backpack, purse, or larger bag, you will be asked to open it up for inspection. Most teams are pretty mellow about backpacks and oversized bags, even if you're bringing in some peanuts or snacks. The key is to have sealed water and food: it's a way to ensure you're not sneaking booze into the ballpark. Unless noted otherwise, every team in this guide conforms to these MLB guidelines.

So don't try to bring a six-pack of cans or bottles into the park. You can't bring Fido or Fluffy with you unless your dog is a certified service dog. Alas, you can't bring in sunscreen unless it's in a plastic container, so apply sunscreen in spray form in the parking area and leave it in the car.

There are also plenty of other items not allowed in a spring training ballpark. You can't bring in lawn chairs or umbrellas, but you can bring a seat cushion or a blanket if you want to sit in the berm. In general, firearms are not allowed, even if you have a permit for concealed carry.

Since we are talking about February and March in Florida, be smart and throw a raincoat or rain poncho into that backpack as well.

INSIDER'S TIP
Not every team hews to this policy, despite an effort from MLB to make it uniform. If a team does not follow this policy, we note it in the team chapter.

INSIDER'S TIP
Our strategy for keeping those bottles of water colder: throw them in the freezer the night before.

INSIDER'S TIP
Be prepared for a wait at the gates, as most teams have installed metal detectors, with guards checking bags. Unfortunately, metal detectors are a way of life in our modern world: We now expect them at any place people congregate—airports, stadiums, arenas—and now at spring-training ballparks. Most spring-training ballparks have installed next-

generation metal detectors that don't require you to empty
your pockets of keys or phones before entering.

WHAT IF IT RAINS?

If it rains, you'll be able to exchange your ticket for a ticket to a
future game. Some teams also refund unused tickets in case of game
cancellations due to weather. You will not be refunded any service
or parking fees, however.

FLORIDA AND THE GRAPEFRUIT LEAGUE

For many people, Florida is synonymous with spring training. Though MLB teams trained all throughout the South and the West between 1900 and 1940, after World War II baseball settled on Florida as home of spring training, with almost every major-league team save the modern expansion franchises spending some time in the warm Florida sun.

It's easy to see the allure of Florida, particularly going back to the days when major-league baseball's westernmost team was in St. Louis and most franchises were in the north and the east. (Remember: for decades, MLB's 16 teams were located in New York City, Boston, Philadelphia, Chicago, Baltimore/Washington, Detroit, St. Louis, and Pittsburgh.) For residents of Pennsylvania or New York or Massachusetts, there was nothing as magical as spring training, that sudden rush of warm air when departing from the train after a three-day ride, or the realization for the carbound that the snowline is firmly in the rear-view mirror and the outside temperature is fast approaching short-sleeve territory. Folks from Minnesota or Detroit still feel that rush today when they walk out of the airport and inhale that first whiff of scented spring air.

Over time Florida became fused with the National Pastime, providing us sustenance at the end of an arduous winter. And that's the power of the Grapefruit League: it provides a long, rich tradition at a time when Americans are increasingly in search of stability and meaning in their lives.

In this book, we'll cover the teams of the Grapefruit League. Our coverage will focus on four areas: Gulf Coast (spring home of the Boston Red Sox, Minnesota Twins, and Tampa Bay Rays), Sarasota and Manatee Counties (spring home of the Atlanta Braves, Baltimore Orioles, and Pittsburgh Pirates), Tampa/St. Pete (spring home of the Detroit Tigers, New York Yankees, Philadelphia Phillies, and Toronto Blue Jays), and the Palm Beach area (spring home of the Houston Astros, Miami Marlins, New York Mets, St. Louis Cardinals, and the Washington Nationals).

VISITING THE GULF COAST

The greater Fort Myers region on the Gulf Coast is the southernmost point for spring training, and three teams train in the general area: the Boston Red Sox and Minnesota Twins in Fort Myers and the Tampa Bay Rays in nearby Port Charlotte.

If you stay in Lee County or Charlotte County, you may feel a little isolated from the rest of spring training. Tourism types stress the isolation and the scenic seashore when they sell Fort Myers, Naples, and Port Charlotte as vacation destinations. It's a laid-back tropical area with relatively unspoiled beaches on the Gulf Coast, so you should not plan on lining up a series of frenetic activities aimed at keeping the kids occupied.

In terms of planning, Charlotte Sports Park is a useful bridge to CoolToday Park, spring home of the Atlanta Braves, in southern Sarasota County. Despite the apparent remoteness of Fort Myers, the three spring ballparks in Sarasota and Manatee counties are within a very doable day trip. And, if you're feeling truly ambitious, you can make the 125-mile trip up the coast to Tampa/St. Pete.

For the purposes of this section, we're discussing the entire Port Charlotte/Fort Myers/Naples area, with a special focus on Fort Myers. These cities along the Gulf Coast run the gamut of restaurants, hotels, and demographics. In the north, Port Charlotte has a more rural feel and offerings geared for the locals. Fort Myers is a thriving city with a solid downtown, relying heavily on the tourist trade with plenty of attractions. Naples, to the south, has many ties to the Twin Cities that make it feel like Minnesota South: many Minnesotans winter in Naples, and there are popular restaurants with ties to Minneapolis, like Campiello and D'Amico's The Continental. And Naples features the best shopping in the area, by far. We'll focus on Fort Myers because most baseball tourists set up shop there.

Just because the area is a little isolated doesn't mean it's unoccupied. Indeed, one of the dirty secrets of the area—especially when discussing Fort Myers and Naples—is how built up it really is. You will, unfortunately, spend a lot of time just getting from Point A to Point B because of the many locals and the influx of snowbirds in March. Add to that thousands of baseball fans and you have the recipe for congested roads, crowded restaurants, and hard-to-find affordable hotel rooms. Scenic, yes; bucolic, no. (Speaking of hotels: we will cover hotels in association with each spring-training complex.)

Still, you should be prepared for days of baseball, nature, shopping, and history. The Florida Everglades are located in the southern part of the area, stretching all the way to the eastern and southern coasts of the state. Sanibel and Captiva Islands are known for their long expanses of white beaches and mangrove forests, as well as many biking and hiking trails. In fact, over half of the islands are preserved as wildlife sanctuaries, and you could spend days wandering through the area in search of the perfect beach. The folks at the Lee County Visitor & Convention Bureau recommend the following beaches:

- **Boca Grande on Gasparilla Island** is known for the Boca Grande Lighthouse, still used to guide ships through the Boca Grande Pass. The lighthouse area also features a maritime museum.
- **Coya Costa State Park** requires a ferry-boat ride to a seven-mile-long island, but the remote location—no electricity and few buildings—makes it an attractive day trip, while some prefer staying overnight and setting up camp in a primitive cabin or in a tent on the beach. The area is also noted for its great shelling because of its remote location. Don't lose track of time: the last ferry leaves at 3:30 p.m.
- **Lighthouse Beach on Sanibel Island** is one of the easiest beaches to reach—it's the first one you reach after crossing the Sanibel tollway—but it's also the one where the parking lot fills rapidly. You can watch the dolphins from the white-sand beach.
- **Fort Myers Beach** is the most developed of the beaches in the area, so it's an attractive area for those who want to combine a stroll on the beach with a cocktail or two. Most of the services and restaurants are back to normal.

This is by no means an exhaustive list of beaches in the area; the best advice is to ask a few locals where they like to hang out—and hope they're gracious enough to give up their secrets. *Lee County Visitor & Convention Bureau, 800/237-6444;* **fortmyers-sanibel.com.**

Also recommended by the locals: the Six Mile Cypress Slough Reserve. A 1.2-mile boardwalk takes you into a nature preserve, where there are opportunities galore for wildlife viewing. Birders adore the conditions here. *Six Mile Cypress Slough Reserve, 7751 Penzance Blvd., Fort Myers; 941/432-2004;* **leegov.com/parks/parks.**

Open dawn to dusk daily; Interpretive Center open 10 a.m.-4 p.m. Tuesday-Sundays.

Another escape to nature: Manatee Park, a Lee County non-captive warm-water refuge for the Florida manatee. Manatees like warm water and gather here during the cooler winter months; the warm discharge from a nearby power plant is a draw for them. An educational visitor center provides background on manatees, while the grounds also features a butterfly garden. Best visited at the beginning of spring training. *Manatee Park, 10901 State Road 80 (Palm Beach Blvd.), Fort Myers; leegov.com/parks/parks/manateepark. Free to visit, but there is a parking fee.*

If you want a little of the sea without actually getting sand in your shoes, check out the Bailey-Matthews Shell Museum. While this may smack of the naked tourism found in backwater Florida, the Bailey-Matthews Shell Museum is actually a serious endeavor: it publishes the definitive academic journal on malacology (the study of mollusks), and while there's a little whimsy in the exhibits (you can see shell valentines created by the women of Barbados in the early 19th century for sailors to take home to their loved ones), most of the public area concerns the history of shells and mollusks. Don't miss the Great Hall of Shells. *Bailey-Matthews Shell Museum, 3075 Sanibel-Captiva Rd., Sanibel; 888/679-6450; shellmuseum.org. Open daily 10 a.m.-5 p.m. Adults, $23.95; youth (12-17), $14.95; kids (5-11), $8.95.*

Fort Myers is also known as the former winter home of both Thomas Edison and Henry Ford, with their estates located on the Caloosahatchee River. Inventor Edison started wintering in Fort Myers in 1885 and built a small estate, "Seminole Lodge," as a winter retreat and lab. Industrialist Ford followed suit in 1915 and built his own winter home, "The Mangoes," to be near his friend Edison. The two houses sit on 17 acres of riverfront property and are open for tours. The buildings are maintained in the style of the era, while a reproduction of Edison's original lab is open for showing as well. You can tour both homes as well as the lab and an adjoining museum, or you can just visit the museum and lab. It's also close to Terry Park if you're headed for a college-baseball game. Highly recommended. *Edison & Ford Winter Estates, 2350 McGregor Blvd., Fort Myers; 239/334-7419; edisonfordwinterestates.org. Open daily 9* *a.m.-5:30 p.m. Self-guided tours: Adults, $25; teen (13-19), $20; children (6-12), $15.*

Just down the road from the Twins training complex is Sun Harvest Citrus, a processing plant for Indian River citrus. Citrus processing isn't a very exciting activity—basically, oranges, grapefruit, and tangerines are sorted, washed, and packed—so the large store is the main draw. You'll jostle for free samples of juice and citrus, but it's worth a few sharp elbows, and you can load up on bags of fresh produce. The lines for the café can be a bit long, as the orange soft serve is a big hit. *Sun Harvest Citrus, 14601 Six Mile Cypress Parkway, Fort Myers; 800/743-1480; sunharvestcitrus.com. Open 9 a.m.-8 p.m. daily.*

FORT MYERS RESTAURANTS

There is a wide variety of restaurants in the greater Fort Myers area, ranging from your standard chains to some very unique offerings. Here we will focus on the unique offerings that will appeal to the entire family; in the team chapters we'll cover some options close to each ballpark.

Many of these restaurants are located on Captiva and Sanibel Islands. We've already extolled the virtues of these islands off Fort Myers on the Gulf Coast: At a time when parts of Fort Myers more resemble a parking lot than a laid-back Florida community, we've come to appreciate getting away from it all at Captiva and Sanibel Islands. Yes, the main drags on both islands can be a little crowded, but getting away from it all after a day of baseball is a very relaxing experience--and going to an isle location for a laid-back meal and a potentially scenic sunset will just enhance your spring-training experience.

You'll need to pay a toll to access Sanibel Island, but it's worth the money if you're seeking out a good restaurant or two. They're all of the same sort, really: slightly upscale with outside seating options. We've eaten at Traders Restaurant and Emporium (*1551 Periwinkle Way; 239/472-7242; traderssanibel.com*) and can recommend a meal there. But really, you can't go wrong at many of the restaurants on Sanibel Island, as long as you have a nice glass of wine or a fruity cocktail and a sunset in front of you. Just be sure establishments are open; the lovely Sanibel Island Cow is still closed, but not due to hurricane damage; a kitchen fire did the damage. From the same owners: Wickie's Lighthouse Restaurant (*362 Periwinkle Way, Suite 2, wickieslighthouserestaurant.com*).

We write a lot about celebrity restaurants in this book, but here's a first: a celebrity restaurant based on a fictional character. Many of you are familiar with Doc Ford, the Randy Wayne White creation who solves mysteries from his home on Sanibel Island. The Sanibel Island location (*2500 Island Inn Rd., 239-472-8311; docfords.com*) is open, billed as the personal hangout of White. Also open: Doc Ford's Rum Bar & Grille at Fort Myers Beach (*708 Fishermans Wharf, Fort Myers Beach; 239/472-8311; docfords.com*). The mini-chain also has two locations in St. Petersburg.

Take the kids to The Bubble Room Restaurant, where the décor is strictly kitsch: Christmas lights, over 2,000 movie stills, memorabilia from the 1930s, and a seven-foot-high Mickey Mouse from a 1930 Disney float. Oh, the place is known for the food as well, especially the seafood and the desserts (try the Orange Crunch Cake). No reservations, so be prepared to wait in line. *Bubble Room Restaurant, 15001 Captiva Dr., Captiva Island; 239/472-5558; bubbleroomrestaurant.com.* (Call ahead. It was still closed for repairs in 2024, with a fall opening date anticipated.)

Definitely more of a high-end experience: Harold's, a high-end farm-to-table restaurant with an ever-changing menu, though there are a few regulars worth seeking out, like the buffalo cauliflower appetizer and the scallops entree. It's frequently hailed as the best high-end dining experience in Fort Myers. *Harold's, 15250 S. Tamiami Trail, Suite 107, Fort Myers; 239/849-0622; haroldscuisine.com.*

The Mucky Duck is somewhat of an anomaly: a British-style pub in a converted beach house. But it's popular with the locals, who seem to enjoy playing darts and eating duck fingers (strips of duck-breast meat) after a day on the beach. No reservations. *Mucky Duck, 11546 Andy Rosse Lane, Captiva Island; 239/472-3434; muckyduck.com.*

March means NCAA March Madness, and many spring-training attendees make plans to catch broadcasts of their favorite teams at a local sports bar. We discuss sports bars close to training facilities in the Twins and Red Sox chapters, but one is worth a short drive from both: Fat Katz Sports Bistro. It's an upscale sports bar: yes, there is the requisite abundance of flat-screen TVs, but there is also a wide variety of menu items transcending the typical burger and fries. Try the banh mi or Cuban sandwich, and wash it down with house sangria. *Fat Katz Sports Bistro, 10080 Daniels Interstate Court, Fort Myers; 239/768-3541; fatkatzsportsbistro.com.*

Another sports bar on the south side of Fort Myers worth a look: Whiskey Creek Station. Yes, there's the requisite flat-screen TVs for catching the latest action, and yes, there's a requisite emphasis on seafood at the former Clancy's. Highly recommended: a grouper Reuben sandwich, the weekly prime rib special, and the Friday night fish fry. *Whiskey Creek Station, 11481 McGregor Blvd., Fort Myers; 239/482-3241; whiskeycreekstation.com.*

Roughly halfway between Hammond Stadium and JetBlue Park —in a ubiquitous strip mall—is Artisan Eatery, combining fast casual with upscale preparations. The emphasis is on sandwiches and flatbreads. Hit it at any time in the day: open for breakfast, lunch, and dinner. *Artisan Eatery, 8951 Daniels Pkwy., Fort Myers, 239/887-4844; artisaneatery.com.*

For cheap eats, the locals hit Farmers Market Restaurant, which specializes in Southern delicacies like biscuits, black-eyed peas, country-fried steaks, catfish, liver and onions, and fried chicken gizzards. If you know what meat and three means, you'll love the Farmers Market. *Farmers Market Restaurant, 2736 Edison Av., Fort Myers; 239/334-1687; farmersmarketrestaurant.com.*

Another outstanding breakfast and lunch spot: CRaVE, where the emphasis is one traditional breakfast offerings—in fact, breakfast is served until 4 p.m. A day that starts with huge pancakes, shrimp and grits, or a brisket omelet is a good thing. *CRaVE Restaurant, 12901 McGregor Blvd., Fort Myers; 239/466-4663; cravemenu.com.*

One more breakfast spot worth noting: Skillet's, a southwest Florida chain of home-cooking restaurants. There are five Skillet's in Naples and two more in Fort Myers. Open only for breakfast and lunch, Skillet's has the sort of offerings you'd expect: lots of diner food with egg, potato, pancakes/waffles, and grits. *skilletsrestaurants.com.*

The most convenient location for spring-training fans is the Fort Myers Skillets is at Daniels Parkway and Cleveland/Tamiami Trail Avenue. That location is not far from Hammond Stadium and the Twins camp, and farther afield of the Boston Red Sox camp. For many attending spring training in Fort Myers, it's inevitable that many will spend some time in this area, thanks to the large number of restaurants and shopping (Target, Total Wine) outlets in the area. The notable restaurants in this area include Blue Moon Pizza (*7381 College Pkwy., Fort Myers; 239/936-2583; bluemoonpizza.com*) and The Blue Pointe (*13499 SE. Cleveland Av., Fort Myers; 888/456-3463; bluepointerestaurant.com*) for seafood. The Bell Tower Shops are located at this intersection as well.

Closer to the Red Sox camp, but still convenient to Hammond Stadium: Two Meatballs in the Kitchen (*8880 Salrose Lane, Fort Myers; 239/489-1111; 2meatballs.com*), a traditional Italian spot with a heavy emphasis on seafood; and Origami (*8911 Daniels Pkwy., Fort Myers; 239/482-2126; sushiorigami.com*) for traditional sushi, ramen, and Korean bulgogi and BBQ.

Just down the road from Hammond Stadium on Six Mile Cypress Highway is Goldwater Oyster Market. There's a huge raw bar culture in Florida, and some of that is reflected in the Goldwater Oyster Market menu, which is definitely on the eclectic side. Pair the fresh offerings of the day with an upscale designer cocktail. *Goldwater Oyster Market, 5611 Six Mile Commercial Ct., Fort Myers; 239/220-5918; coldwateroystermarket.com.*

There's a little bit of the Key West spirit in the Fort Myers area, so it's no surprise that Jimmy Buffett reportedly wrote "Cheeseburger in Paradise" while dining at the Cabbage Key Restaurant, renowned for its cheeseburgers. You can't drive there: Cabbage Key on Pine Island Sound is accessible only via boat, helicopter, or seaplane, so a reservation is pretty much required. (Boats make the run to Cabbage Key from Punta Gorda, Captiva Island, and Pine Island.) *Cabbage Key, 239/283-2278; cabbagekey.com.*

An outstanding spot for seafood: The Dixie Fish Co., located on San Carlos Island. There are a string of islands off Fort Myers, including San Carlos Island and Fort Myers Beach, and Estero Island, that really exemplify the beachfront lifestyle, with plenty of great dining options, including The Dixie Fish Co., a beachfront fish house that began as a wholesale seafood clearinghouse in 1937 and eventually became a casual restaurant. The same folks own the larger and more polished Doc Ford's next door, but we prefer the more casual and historic Dixie Fish Company. *The Dixie Fish Co., 714 Fishermans Wharf, Fort Myers Beach; 239/233-8837; dixiefishfmb.com.*

Fancy's Southern Cafe has great Southern cuisine from the entire region. Here you'll find staples like *etouffee* with crawdads and andouille, chicken and waffles, and burgers topped with pimiento cheese. Add a side of collard greens or black-eyed peas and top it all off with red-velvet cake. Highly recommended. *Fancy's Southern Café, 8890 Salrose Lane, Fort Myers; 239/561-2988; fancyssoutherncafe.com.*

If you're a baseball fan, chances are good you're also a beer fan. A Venn chart of spring-training attendees and craft-beer enthusiasts would show a large overlap between the two groups, so a trip to a local brewpub is a must. We have a few favorites. Near JetBlue Park, Fort Myers Brewing Company features 10 or so house-brewed beers on tap at any given time, and with outdoor seating and food trucks daily, it's a good place to unwind most evenings. Ask for a taste of the chocolate peanut-butter porter if it's on tap. *Fort Myers Brewing Company, 12811 Commerce Lakes Dr., Fort Myers; 239/313-6576; fmbrew.com.* RipTide Brewing Company is close to downtown Naples and features upwards of 10 house-brewed beers as well as other craft beers. If it's your first visit, consider a themed beer flight to get a good feel for the house styles. The place definitely has a laid-back vibe, with couches for lounging, board games, and an outdoor patio. *RipTide Brewing Co., 987 3rd Av. N., Naples; 239/228-6533; riptidebrewingcompany.com.* Point Ybel Brewing Co. is known for some unusual brews, but with live music, Wednesday trivia night, and a laid-back atmosphere, Point Ybel Brewing Co. is perfect to end a day that includes some spring-training baseball. *Point Ybel Brewing Co., 16120 San Carlos Blvd., Fort Myers; 239/603-6535; pointybelbrew.com.* Palm City Brewing Co. has developed quite the reputation as a superior vendor of IPAs, along with a taproom heavy on the games and hospitality. Yes, millennials, this brew's for you. *Palm City Brewing, 7887 Drew Circle, Fort Myers; 239/362-2862; palmcitybeer.com.*

This is by no means an exhaustive listing of breweries and restaurants in the area. We'll cover more in our team chapters.

COLLEGE BASEBALL

There is plenty of college baseball in the Fort Myers area, and you could easily put together a day-night pro/collegiate doubleheader depending on how the schedules break. With the college baseball season beginning in late January and ending in May, you'll have plenty of opportunities to take in a game during your spring-training travels.

The Florida SouthWestern State College Buccaneers moved to a new on-campus ballpark. Not familiar with the Bucs? Florida South-Western—also known as FSW—is the old Edison Community College, now positioned as a state college. The move to an on-campus facility means the team doesn't play at City of Palms Park, spring home of the Boston Red Sox between 1993 and 2011. This will inevitably lead to more city discussions about the future of City of Palms Park. (The future of City of Palms is up for debate in Fort Myers. Soccer? Development? Who knows at this point.) Still, a decent level of NJCAA play makes a trip to the new facility worthy if you have some time to kill. (*fswbucs.com*)

Florida Gulf Coast University competes in the Atlantic Sun Conference and plays out of Swanson Stadium, a small (1,500 seats) on-campus facility. The Atlantic Sun is a decent baseball conference, with some good players coming out of the likes of New Jersey Institute of Technology, Stetson University, and USC Upstate. Atlanta Braves pitcher Chris Sale, who started the 2016 All-Star Game for the American League, attended Florida Gulf Coast, as did current major leaguer Richard Bleier. Swanson Stadium opened in 2004 and last renovated in 2012. *Swanson Stadium, 10501 FGCU Lake Pkwy. E., Fort Myers; fgcuathletics.com.*

We cover Terry Park, which hosts college and high-school tourneys throughout the spring, in its own chapter.

OTHER SPORTS

With all the Minnesotans living in the area, the success of the Florida Everblades is no surprise, as the team is one of the top draws in minor-league hockey. Hertz Arena holds 7,181, and crowds approaching that number aren't uncommon. The ECHL is a decent league, and the Everblades put on a good show. It's impossible to miss Hertz Arena: It's painted in the yellow color associated with Hertz. *Florida Everblades, Germain Arena, 11000 Everblades Pkwy., Estero; 239/948-7825; floridaeverblades.com.*

FLYING IN

Fort Myers is home to Southwest Florida International Airport (*flylcpa.com*), which is served by most major airlines, including Air Canada, Alaska, American, Breeze, Delta, Frontier, Southwest, Spirit, Sun Country, United, WestJet and, of course, JetBlue. Direct flights between Fort Myers and both Boston and Minneapolis/St. Paul are run by JetBlue and Delta, respectively. JetBlue flies seasonally from Worcester and Hartford to Fort Myers; Breeze flies from several New England destinations (Providence, Bangor, Manchester) to Fort Myers.

You may also want to consider flying into Tampa or Sarasota and then driving to Fort Myers if the fare is significantly cheaper. The drive from Tampa is 125 miles and 75 miles from Sarasota, but as Tampa Bay is home to several other spring-training facilities, you can combine several visits to games with the excursion to Fort Myers. Then again, if you're a Boston Red Sox fan, you probably don't give a darn about any other teams—the only reason you'd venture outside of Fort Myers would be to see the BoSox take on the likes of Pittsburgh in Bradenton.

JETBLUE PARK AT FENWAY SOUTH / BOSTON RED SOX

QUICK FACTS

- **Capacity**: 10,823 (9,909 seats, the rest in berm and SRO seating)
- **Year Opened**: 2012
- **Dimensions**: 310L, 379LC, 420C, 380RC, 302R
- **Local Airport**: Southwest Florida International Airport
- **Dugout Location**: Third-base side
- **Pregame Schedule**: Gates open 2.5 hours before gametime. For a 1:05 p.m. start, Red Sox BP runs from 10:30 a.m.-11:30 a.m.; visitors BP runs from 11:30 a.m.-12:30 p.m.; visitors infield runs from 12:30 p.m.-12:45 p.m. Add six hours for a 6:05 p.m. game time.
- **Practice Time**: 10 a.m., with gates opening at 9 a.m. Enter at the left-field corner of the ballpark, near the batting-cage building. You won't get run of the complex.
- **Phone**: 1-888-REDSOX6
- **Address**: 11500 Fenway S. Dr., Fort Myers, FL 33913.
- **Directions**: Daniels Parkway runs east/west through south Fort Myers and is also marked as County Rd. 876. The ballpark is on the eastern side of the city, north of the Fort Myers airport.

A LITTLE NEW ENGLAND ON THE GULF COAST

Boston Red Sox fans certainly love their team, and they certainly love spring training. With a great ballpark to match the great passion, it's no surprise that Red Sox ducats are in heavy demand—but most fans will find a game at JetBlue Park to be worth the effort.

Located on the outskirts of Fort Myers, near one of those ubiquitous Florida planned communities (Gateway) with the requisite designer golf course, JetBlue Park is one of the larger Grapefruit League ballparks, hosting almost 11,000 in seating and SRO spaces. The park is partially based on Fenway Park in some overt ways—yes, there is a Green Monster in left field, though this one is three feet higher than the original—and some subtle ways. These subtle ways make the ballpark unique in Florida spring training.

INSIDER'S TIP

With 11,000 fans able to cram into JetBlue Park, there's less of a crunch for tickets than when the Red Sox trained at City of Palms Park, where a capacity crowd of 7,700 made for some awfully tight quarters. Although it's still not easy to score a grandstand seat for many games, you can usually score a cheap ticket somewhere in the outfield area during the vast majority of exhibitions, unless the Yankees are in town.

We know that over the years many Red Sox fans have given up on attending spring training because of the lack of tickets, but with the luxurious capacity at JetBlue Park, scoring some ducats isn't the chore it once was. Though most games end up sold out, the after-market prices aren't too bad. (Indeed: last spring you could have scored an aftermarket ticket below list price at the end of January for February and early March games.) And the first game of spring training does not immediately sell out. The traditional college doubleheader against Boston College and Northeastern early in spring training has been scaled to a single game, alas, but the good news is that the single game does not sell out—most fans correctly deduce the chance of seeing more than one or two Red Sox stars in action are between slim and none, as you're basically watching future WooSox and Sea Dogs take the field against a college squad. Still, the Sox are the Sox, and we've found these games to be as delightful as many early-spring games.

It's one-stop shopping for Boston Red Sox spring training these days. All functions of training camp—and year-round player rehab, by the way, as well as rookie development—are in one location, with the entire Fenway South complex made up of JetBlue Park, a quad of practice fields, two other practice fields (including one with exact Fenway Park dimensions), and the Fen Walk, containing tributes to Red Sox greats. At one point the Red Sox were looking to build a replica of Fenway Park in Florida, complete with plenty of brick-work, but luckily that plan was dropped. Instead, fans now have a spring-training home with features based on Fenway Park, but is distinctly different.

For instance, the Green Monster in Florida is much different than the original in Boston, a design derived from ballpark confines in an oddly shaped site with a below-grade field. In Florida, the 211-foot-long Green Monster is a multilevel structure serving a variety of needs. On the ground level, it fronts the left-field clubhouse on the ground floor. The next level is also for team use, while the level above features 258 tiered seats in front of the Monster Bar. On the top level there's another open bar, with four tops, bar stools, and bar rails for 120 fans. The bullpens are located side by side in right-center field—again, just like Fenway Park—and there are two score-boards, one a manual board (originally installed at Fenway Park in 1976, entertaining fans for thirty-some years) and the other a videoboard. (Watch between innings: Because there's no space behind the Florida Green Monster manual board, an employee brings a ladder to the front of the scoreboard and replaces the numbers.) And, of course, the Red Sox play "Sweet Caroline" in the middle of the eighth inning and "Dirty Water" after a win. (Good for the Sox. We're not too elitist to admit we love singing along to "Sweet Caroline.")

The signature item to the ballpark: the white canopy covering most of the grandstand, which undulates like its inspiration, the cypress mounds (or groves) in the area. Cypress mounds are an important part of the local ecosystem: they provide shelter and shade for a host of animals and birds. Here, the canopy provides shade and shelter for spring-training fans. It doesn't run completely across the concourse: instead, it's broken into four sections, with three overlapping. During a game—especially on a clear, warm day—you'll appreciate the canopy, as it provides shade to the majority of fans in the grandstand.

There's also a subtler signature item to the ballpark construction: the building material found on the walls of the ballpark structure. The blocks are augmented with seashells, and when the surface is polished, it adds a unique sheen to the construction.

And one final thing to note: unlike Fenway Park, JetBlue Park has a berm. Perfect for spring training.

INSIDER'S TIP
In the past, the Red Sox put 200 or so tickets on sale the day of the game at 9 a.m. As you might expect, be prepared to queue early for these tickets. They are sold at the six ticket windows at the box office, directly behind home plate. These six windows also serve Will Call ticket holders.

INSIDER'S TIP
Before the game, stop by the Fan Information Booth at the concourse behind home plate and pick up a copy of the game notes distributed in the press box. Alas, the scoring insert now costs $1.

INSIDER'S TIP

The Red Sox do not conform with MLB guidelines regarding food in the ballpark: the rules state no outside food or drink allowed no matter how it is packaged. However, we've found the folks at the front gates to be a little more liberal than the rules indicate, and we've brought in peanuts and unopened water containers. Just be discreet; don't attempt to bring in a larger soft-sided cooler, for instance.

INSIDER'S TIP

The area is not served with great cellphone service. And with no WiFi, you may want to print out your electronic ticket, no matter what the BoSox say.

The Minnesota Twins also train in Fort Myers, making for a nice little rivalry when the teams square off multiple times during the first few weeks of spring training.

Attending a Red Sox game is one of the great events in the Grapefruit League. Yes, it can be a tad expensive to attend a game, but it's worth the money.

WHERE TO SIT

As we noted earlier in this chapter, Red Sox ducats can be one of the hardest gets in spring training, depending on the date and the opponent. You can plan and plan and plan and be ready to order tickets online the minute they go on sale, but odds are that you've been destined to fail for weeks and weeks. The vast majority of good seats in JetBlue Park are controlled via season tickets, so, basically, you really never had a shot at sitting right behind the dugout or even within 10 rows of the playing field.

But...as noted earlier, the move to JetBlue Park meant that more tickets are now available for games, so there are fewer sellouts at the new ballpark than at City of Palms Park, where the Red Sox would frequently sell every spring-training ticket within 15 minutes of being placed on sale. The move expanded the seating bowl by a couple thousand seats (while also increasing the season-ticket pool, natch), and the new ballpark configuration added a slew of berm, Green Monster, and SRO tickets. There's a proud tradition of SRO ticketing at Red Sox spring-training games, with fans crammed into most empty spaces (including, sometimes annoyingly, in the walkway separating the seating areas in City of Palms Park). The new berm seating is appropriate for families, and the Green Monster barstools provide a great view.

So, now that you know there is no direct way to obtain the best seats in the grandstand, you'll need to accept that any good seat for a Red Sox spring game must be purchased through the secondary-ticket market. We work with a third party via *ballparkdigesttickets.com*, and there are other services out there. The selection goes up considerably when you begin buying tickets on the secondary market, and here are some things to look for:

- Every seat in the JetBlue Park grandstand is a chairback, so no need to do a lot of work to avoid bleachers. If you do want bleachers, they're located in right-center field in Sections 231, 233, and 235.
- Yes, there are cupholders with every grandstand seat.
- The netting extends all the way down the line, past the far end of the dugout. This was done as part of MLB's mandate to install extended netting at every MLB park. The netting isn't very obtrusive: it's made from a finer mesh with smaller knots and colored green to blend into the field.
- If you require shade, most of the 200-level sections in the middle of the ballpark are shaded at the beginning of an afternoon game, as well as the back five rows of upper-grandstand sections down the left-field line. The back five or so rows in the lower bowl will be shaded as well. In addition, there are 258 seats within the third level of Green Monster that are partially shaded, but be warned you'll be sitting on a barstool. If you think you may need sunscreen—particularly those of us with pasty skin kept covered in a northern clime—head to the bullpen area before the game, where the Red Sox set up a sunscreen dispenser, or the top of the Green Monster, where there is a sunscreen dispenser next to the restrooms. There are also sunscreen dispensers outside the ballpark next to security entrances.

- SRO tickets are plentiful, but they're assigned to specific areas, and they will be checked. SRO tickets are sold for the Green Monster, Green Monster Deck, Right Field Picnic Area, and Left Field Deck. We'd recommend the Green Monster Deck as your first choice.
- Being a newer ballpark, JetBlue Park has a very small number of bad seats. Part of the outfield berm is blocked by the back bullpen wall, and a staircase blocks the end seats in rows 12 and 13 in Section 208.

INSIDER'S TIP

The numbering system for JetBlue Park seating is a little different than most spring facilities: even-number sections are to the left of home plate, odd-number sections are to the right of home plate. If you want to sit on the Red Sox side of the field, choose an even-numbered section. If you want a good view of the inside of the Red Sox dugout, choose an odd-numbered section. The 100-level seats are in the lower bowl; the 200-level seats are in the upper bowl.

One underrated way to score some good seating at JetBlue Park: putting together a group and reserving a group space. There are several within JetBlue Park, but they need to be ordered through the sales office and are not available online. There's certainly demand for group space, such as Babcock Ranch Porch, a private group space past right field that accommodates up to 125 people. Now, that's a pretty big group, but the team does offer smaller group spaces as well. Use the ticket line at the beginning of this chapter to investigate potential group spaces.

BALLPARK HISTORY

The Red Sox have trained at JetBlue Park at Fenway South since the ballpark opened in 2012.

THE SPRING-TRAINING BALLPARK EXPERIENCE

CONCESSIONS

There are two sets of concessions at JetBlue Park: inside the ballpark and outside, but all within the security entrances. (Same as Fenway Park: inside the ballpark and outside on Yawkey Way.) Taste of Fenway South is basically a tent city to the south of the ballpark, with one tent featuring food and another featuring drinks. You can find the requisite lobster rolls at the food pavilion's Maine Shack, as well as jumbo hot dogs and deli items. Worth seeking out: the bruschetta pizza from local firm Fine Folk Pizza. On the Beer Garden side, there are the obligatory craft and premium beers, as well as margaritas, daiquiris, and mixed drinks.

Inside the ballpark, enjoy a real Fenway Frank from Kayem (sans traditional split-top bun, alas), a foot long, cheesesteak, a lobster roll, maybe a familiar Italian sausage with peppers and onions. Another favorite from home: Del's Frozen Lemonade. There is a wide abundance of tap and canned beers available, including Massachusetts favorites Sam Adams Boston Lager, Rebel IPA, Sam 76, and Narragansett, as well as microbrews (Coors, Miller Lite), and Florida faves like Yuengling and Fort Myers Brewing's Gateway Gold.

The Red Sox do change up concessions annually. In 2024 new offerings included DonutNV selling hot mini donuts and larger cookie/brownie hybrids from Cookie Plug.

None of the concessions are particularly cheap—$4 for a bottled water—but such is the state of spring-training economics these days.

PARKING

Parking is adjacent to the ballpark. In 2024 the Red Sox overhauled the process, including prepaid parking in the ticket price. It was billed as a way to streamline the parking process, and it did, to an extent, but it also forced you to pay for parking to the BoSox and not to a third-party vendor. Still, anything that expedites entry to the ballpark is a good thing: Daniels Parkway was basically a parking lot 45 minutes before a Red Sox game in previous years.

With over 3,300 parking spots in the complex, you shouldn't worry about being shut out. Mark the location of your car in your parking app: there is no signage marking the parking sections. One nice touch: the team runs shuttles between the far reaches of parking and the ballpark as a fundraiser for a local charity, so throw a few bucks into the jar when you're saved the ordeal of a long walk on a hot day. And be patient when leaving the ballpark.

AUTOGRAPHS

Your best bets to score an autograph: immediately before the game next to the player entrance near Sections 110, 112, and 114 (located past the extended protective netting), or at a practice field when it opens in the morning. The Red Sox do not go out of their way to provide access for autograph seekers: no autograph alley, no designated spot for players to meet the fans.

There are six practice fields at the complex, and fans can wander through them during morning workouts. The major-league squad practices at Field #1, which is set up with Fenway Park outfield dimensions and a chain-link Green Monster. (You'll find this field right past the left-field area in JetBlue Park, on the opposite side of the complex from the main entrance.) The minor leaguers practice on Fields #3-#6, and these fields are named after former Red Sox greats: Felix Maldonado (#3), Eddie Popowski (#4), Lou Gorman (#5), and Johnny Pesky (#6).

If you want to ask a visiting player for an autograph, the easiest way is to wait until after the game and snare someone heading for the bus outside Gate E. You'll be roped to the side, but our experience is that most visiting players are happy to spend some time signing.

HISTORY

Only the Yankees approach the Red Sox when it comes to American League history, and there's plenty of it at JetBlue Park. First, long-time Red Sox fans will be glad to know the Ted Williams statue formerly gracing the main entrance at City of Palms Park greets you at JetBlue Park as well. Another Williams link: a red chair roughly located 502 feet from home plate—which puts it in the back of the outfield concourse—as a reminder of the longest home run hit by Williams in Fenway Park. Ovals commemorating retired Red Sox numbers are located both inside and outside the ballpark. And, of course, the right-field foul pole is dubbed the Pesky Pole. Johnny Pesky, in many ways, was Mr. Red Sox: He played for Boston for a decade (1942-1952) and lived up to the abbreviated name (his given name: John Michael Paveskovich), setting the table for the likes of Ted Williams and Dom DiMaggio. The lefty was definitely a singles hitter—only 17 homers in his career—but announcer Mel Parnell started calling it "Pesky's Pole" after a Pesky homer curled right around the right-field foul pole, located only 302 feet down the line. (Whether or not this is true is a matter of much conjecture in The Hub, but it doesn't matter: Pesky was a beloved figure amongst Red Sox fans, and it's suitable such a unique feature in Fenway Park— and JetBlue Park—be named for him.) Bring a Sharpie and sign the Pesky Pole.

FOR THE KIDS

This is really for the whole family, not just the kids. In 2024 fans had access to the Red Sox Showcase, featuring a batting cage, merchandise, a pitching machine, and a Green Monster backdrop for the selfie generation.

SELFIE SPOTS

Besides the Green Monster backdrop, there's an abundance of spots for a selfie at JetBlue Park, The Fen Walk features large tributes to players whose numbers have been retired—literally, with large numerals along the Fen Walk. (Speaking of Johnny Pesky: His #6 is on the Fen Walk.) You'll find fans taking selfies along the Fen Walk —and so should you.

Another hot selfie spot: the Ted Williams statue next to the Fen Walk. Teddy Ballgame, of course, is a Boston legend, and the statue is a popular gathering spot before the game.

One final option: the Wally bench in front of the ballpark, where a statue of team mascot Wally is installed on a bench, perfect for photos and selfies. Kids may not know who Ted Williams was, but they probably know Wally.

> **INSIDER'S TIP**
> Be warned that the Fen Walk, the Wally bench, and the Ted Williams statue are located outside the JetBlue Park gates. Keeping with MLB policies, folks are not allowed to leave the ballpark after entering, a rule that's sometimes strictly enforced. So make your plans to view this area before or after the game: you won't be allowed to reenter.

TOURS

Tours are available, but limited: you need a ticket for the day's game, and the pricing is $40 for adults for the VIP experience, $10 for a standard tour. Call the main ballpark line for further information.

IF YOU GO

WHAT TO DO OUTSIDE THE BALLPARK

The big advantage to City of Palms Park for many fans was its central location in the greater Fort Myers area and proximity to downtown Fort Myers. When JetBlue Park opened, there was little to attract you to the portion of Daniels Parkway east of I-75. Today, however, there is a growing assortment of restaurants and bars in the area. One of our strategies is to hit these establishments before the game for a snack and a brew. As noted earlier in this chapter, eastbound Daniels Parkway resembles a parking lot an hour or so before a game, and by avoiding this mess—while also shifting your approach to JetBlue Park to the east, a considerably less busy westbound approach—you can cut down the game-day stress.

Lucky for you, one of the best breweries in Florida is also less than two miles from JetBlue Park: Fort Myers Brewing Company. We discussed Fort Myers Brewing Company in our Fort Myers overview, and we can't stress what a sanctuary this place is before and after a game. While Fort Myers Brewing Company is located within

an industrial park, management has carved out an inviting environment, with plenty of games (like cornhole), outdoor seating, and 25
or so Fort Myers Brewing Company brews on tap, along with
several guest taps featuring other Florida microbrews. *Fort Myers
Brewing Company, 12811 Commerce Lakes Dr., Fort Myers; 239/313-
6576; fmbrew.com.*

INSIDER'S TIP
Fort Myers Brewing Company puts on a big St. Patrick's Day
bash, complete with live music and multiple food trucks.
We'd recommend combining a game with a Fort Myers
Brewing Company run if the BoSox are in town.

When JetBlue Park opened, there wasn't much near the ballpark
in terms of dining options. But this part of Lee County has seen
steady growth the past few years, and today there are plenty of
dining options before and after a game. A favorite in the Gateway
planned community is The Saucy Meatball (*12401 Commerce Lakes
Dr., Fort Myers; 239/800-7172; saucymeatball.com*), a red-sauce
Italian joint with ties to the popular Two Meatballs in the Kitchen in
Fort Myers, covered in our overview chapter. It's an especially good
choice after a day game because of its solid Happy Hour food and
beverage menu. We covered Fat Katz in our overview chapter as
well, and that sports bar has opened a sister establishment in Gateway: Skinny Dogz Brunchery (*11970 Fairway Lakes Dr., Fort Myers;
239/362-2693; skinnydogzbrunchery.com*), serving up a solid diner
menu of burgers, brats, and hot dogs, as well as breakfast items like
biscuits and gravy and pastries. It's open only for breakfast and
lunch. Speaking of sports bars: Twin Peaks (*16411 Corporate
Commerce Way, Fort Myers; 239/789-2506; twinpeaksrestaurant.com*)
bills itself as a sports lodge, combining ski-lodge decor with plenty
of large-screen TVs and local beers on tap. The food tends to be
better than found at a regular Florida sports bar, with standard
offerings like burgers and chicken wings augmented with unusual
choices like venison chili or Mom's Pot Roast. If you're looking
outside the Gateway development but want to stay close to the ballpark, check out Fine Folk Pizza (*11300 Lindbergh Blvd., 239/313-5155;
finefolkpizza.com*), with an upscale approach to pizza. Yes, you can
find your standard pepperoni pies, but you can also order fancier

pizzas and massive calzones. Also close to JetBlue Park: Casa Lupita (*13120 Westlinks Terrace #10, 239/479-5244; **casalupitafm.com**), with a Mexican menu bordering on the Tex-Mex side of things.

Many Red Sox fans head over to Hammond Stadium to watch the Minnesota Twins play, even if Boston isn't the opposing team, as the schedules are usually arranged so one of the two teams is in town. Red Sox fans also make the relatively easy drive to Port Charlotte to see the Sox in action against the Tampa Bay Rays. And, of course, many of the Boston faithful follow their team no matter how far the drive. In fact, we're so sure that readers of this book will follow the Red Sox on the road, we've put together this handy little chart so you can plan your drive from Fort Myers. Distance and driving time don't always add up in Florida. Taking the back roads can be an infuriating process, so it quite often takes less time to drive 140 miles than it does 109 miles when you're comparing a freeway route versus back roads.

Fort Myers to: / Distance / Time
Charlotte Sports Park (Rays) / 51 miles / 55 minutes
North Port (Braves) / 68 miles / 1.2 hours
Sarasota (Orioles) / 83 miles / 1.5 hours
Bradenton (Pirates) / 95 miles / 1.75 hours
Jupiter (Cardinals/Marlins) / 109 miles / 3 hours
West Palm Beach (Astros/Nationals) / 128 miles / 2.3 hours
Port St. Lucie (Mets) / 133 miles / 3 hours
Clearwater (Phillies) / 135 miles / 2.25 hours
Tampa (Yankees) / 138 miles / 2.25 hours
Dunedin (Blue Jays) / 138 miles / 2.5 hours
Lakeland (Tigers) / 150 miles / 2.5 hours
Fenway Park / 1,424 miles / 22.5 hours

Since many Red Sox spring games are now televised, you should be able to find a bar with a Red Sox game on the dish when the team is on the road. Several bars in Fort Myers and tonier Naples market to Boston expats:

- Stevie Tomato's Sports Page is exactly what you'd expect from the name: a sports bar with plenty of TVs to watch and plenty of beers on tap for consumption. This is probably the closest sports bar to JetBlue Park, so if you're staying near the ballpark and the airport, you'll be close to Stevie Tomato's. *Stevie Tomato's Sports Page, 9510 Market Place Rd., Fort Myers; 239/939-7211;* **stevietomato.com**.

- Foxboro Sports Tavern markets to Boston sports fans with plenty of Boston sports on big-screen TVs and lots of references to Boston sports teams on the walls. The owners took advantage of a COVID-19 shutdown to implement some sorely needed renovations. *Foxboro Sports Tavern, 4420 Thomasson Dr., Naples; 239/530-BEER (2337);* **foxborotavern.com**.
- Landsdowne Street is another hangout for Boston sports fans of all stripes. *Landsdowne Street, 24851 S. Tamiami Trail, Bonita Springs; 239/495-3800;* **lansdowne-street.com**.

If you're in Fort Myers for an extended period, you may want to head downtown. Imagine a great bar crawl in (probably) warmer weather that you've been experiencing at home. If some March Madness and maybe a Red Sox away game are on your agenda, there's the Hideaway Sports Bar (*1418 Dean St., Fort Myers; 239/337-9966*). Patio De Leon, a historic plaza, features a range of dining and drinking establishments. Plus, there's the raucous atmosphere and live music at The Cigar Bar (*1508 Hendry St.; 239/337-4662;* **worldfamouscigarbar.com**). We cover more Fort Myers hotspots in the previous chapter, but in general you can't go wrong by heading downtown and wandering around.

WHERE TO STAY

Be warned: hotel rooms are on the expensive side during spring training, and chances are pretty good you'll be discomfited when paying more than $250 for what would be a $125 room in almost any other circumstance. Shop around and jump on any bargains: it's a very competitive market within the greater Fort Myers area, though you can save a whole lot of money if you're willing to drive in from Port Charlotte or Naples.

The Doubletree Fort Myers at Bell Tower Shops (*13051 Bell Tower Dr., Fort Myers; 239/482-2900;* **hilton.com**) had been billed as the official hotel for Red Sox spring training in past years, and you'll find plenty of Red Sox ties there. If nothing else, it's a convenient spot to stay during spring training: the Bell Tower Shops, located at Daniels Parkway and Cleveland Avenue/Hwy. 41, features plenty of restaurants and bars, with many more just a short distance away. Within the Doubletree: Shoeless Joe's, a sports bar with an extensive menu (*shoeless-joes.com*).

There are a number of hotels within two or three miles of the ballpark: airport hotels usually catering to business travelers. These include the Comfort Inn and Suites Airport (*10081 Intercom Dr., Fort Myers; 239/939-5002; comfortinn.com*), Springhill Suites Fort Myers Airport (*9501 Marketplace Rd., Fort Myers; 239/561-1803; marriott.com*), La Quinta Inn & Suites Fort Myers Airport (*9521 Market Place Rd., Fort Myers; 239/466-0012; lq.com*), Hampton Inn Fort Myers Airport I-75 (*9241 Marketplace Rd., Fort Myers; 239/768-2525; hilton.com*), Baymont Fort Myers Airport (*9401 Marketplace Rd., Fort Myers; 239/454-0040; baymontinns.com*), Quality Suites Airport (*3651 Indian Paint Ln., Fort Myers; 239/768-0005; qualityinn.com*), Holiday Inn Express and Suites (*14567 Global Pkwy., Fort Myers; 239/327-0198; ihg.com*), and Home2 Suites (10400 Aircraft Ct., Fort Myers; 239/208-5454; *hilton.com*). We would not recommend walking to the ballpark from any of these hotels—not because of any issues with the hotels, but because there's really no good and safe way to walk from a hotel to the ballpark. We are talking borderline rural environment here, not an urban environment with nice sidewalks and a walker-friendly ethos.

RV PARKS

There are no RV parks with daily availability within walking distance of the ballpark. Several RV parks are located within a close drive: Cypress Trail RV Resort (*5468 Tice St., Fort Myers; 239/333-3246; cypresstrailrv.com*), Cypress Woods RV Resort (*5551 Luckett Rd., Fort Myers; 888/29-6637; cypresswoodsrv.net*), Blueway RV Village (*19370 S. Tamiami Trail, Fort Myers; 888/634-4080; covecommunities.com*), Woodsmoke Camping Resort (*19551 S. Tamiami Trail, Fort Myers; 239/267-3456; woodsmokecampingresort.com*), and Calusa Cove RV Park (*19421 Santa Elena Dr., Estero; 239/357-7098; calusa-cove-rv-park.com*). There are other RV resorts closer to the beaches as well.

SPRING TRAINING HISTORY: BOSTON RED SOX

The Boston Red Sox have trained in the following locations: Charlottesville, Va. (1901); Augusta, Ga. (1902); Macon, Ga. (1903-1906); Little Rock (1907-1908); Hot Springs, Ark. (1909-1910); Redondo Beach, Cal. (1911); Hot Springs, Ark. (1912-1918); Tampa (1919); Hot Springs, Ark. (1920-1923); San Antonio (1924); New Orleans (1925-1927); Bradenton (1928-1929); Pensacola, Fla. (1930-1931); Savannah (1932); Sarasota (1933-1942); Medford, Mass. (1943-1944); Atlantic City (1945); Sarasota (1946-1958); Scottsdale (1959-1965); Winter Haven (1966-1992); and Fort Myers (1993-present).

HAMMOND STADIUM / MINNESOTA TWINS

QUICK FACTS

- **Capacity**: 9,300 (including 8,730 fixed seats)
- **Year Opened**: 1991; renovated 2014-2015
- **Dimensions**: 330L, 405C, 330R
- **Tickets Line**: 800/33-TWINS (800/338-9467)
- **Local Airport**: Southwest Florida International Airport
- **Dugout Location**: Third-base side
- **Pregame Schedule**: Gates open three hours before game time. Twins batting practice, 10:15-11:15 a.m.; visitors batting practice, 11:15 a.m.-12:15 p.m.; Twins infield, 12:15-12:30 p.m.; visitors infield, 12:30-12:45 p.m. Add six hours to each figure for a 7:05 p.m. game.
- **Address**: 14100 Six Mile Cypress Parkway, Fort Myers, FL 33192.
- **Directions**: Hammond Stadium is part of the Lee Health Sports Complex, which also houses the team's training fields and minor-league complex. From I-75, take Exit 131 (Daniels Parkway). Head west (toward Fort Myers) for about three miles and turn left on Six Mile Cypress Parkway. Go south and the ballpark and training complex are on your right.

THE PERFECT ANTIDOTE TO A MINNESOTA WINTER

For Minnesota Twins fans understandably filled with discontent after a long winter filled with snow, cold, and seasonal affective disorder, there's nothing more precious than walking through the gates of Hammond Stadium and seeing their beloved boys in action. Of all the sites in the Grapefruit League, Hammond Stadium may be the most revered—if only because it presents a stark contrast to the weather at home in March, historically the snowiest month in Minnesota.

Lee Health Sports Complex (yes, the name is new as of 2024) and Hammond Stadium in Fort Myers have been the spring-training home of the Minnesota Twins since 1991 and will be for the next 30-some years after a $48.5-million renovation in 2014-2015 that saw an overhaul of Hammond Stadium and more. It's a facility designed for the entire organization, with five full fields (including one devoted to the Florida Complex League Twins), two half fields, a year-round player dorm, workout facility, and a ballpark that also serves as the home of the Fort Myers Mighty Mussels (Single-A; Florida State League).

There's a strong sense of place at the complex, which begins the minute you drive in from Six Mile Cypress Parkway. As you enter, you'll see the ballpark and parking to the right and training fields to the left. All the streets within the complex are named for Twins greats, a welcoming sight for Minnesota snowbirds who undoubtedly are disoriented by the lack of snow on the ground. (You'll know them by their pasty skin.) Palm trees line the sidewalks leading to the ballpark, enhancing the tropical experience.

Every part of Lee Health Sports Complex underwent some sort of renovation in the last decade, and the facility saw more repairs cleaning up from the damage caused by Hurricane Ian. It already was a unique facility, featuring a facade designed to invoke the feeling of Louisville's Churchill Downs. The renovations took the bones of what was already a decent ballpark and added a 360-degree concourse, upgraded seating options, outfield bars, expanded concourses, improved restrooms, a new retail store, and more. After Hurricane Ian, repairs and cleanup took place throughout the complex.

Twins fans are passionate and annual attendees; season ticket sales are strong, and there are frequent sellouts—especially when a strong draw like the Boston Red Sox is visiting. There is no escaping the presence of Red Sox Nation at Hammond Stadium: Red Sox fans will take in a Twins game if the Red Sox are out of town, and during a Red Sox/Twins matchup, there's almost an even split between the loyalties in the stands. Of course, Minnesota fans are much too polite to ever confront the Red Sox Nation, so a laid-back vibe is always present.

When the Twins moved spring training in 1991 to Fort Myers, the training complex was located out in the country: the land beyond the outfield wall formerly was pastureland for cattle. Today there is development all around the ballpark, and Fort Myers is a bustling city on the rise.

Gone are the narrow concourses filled with concessions; the single burger grill has been moved and expanded to two outfield locations. Seating behind home plate is gone, replaced by a wide entrance off the concourse designed to give fans a "wow" experience as they enter the seating area. The expanded entryway also has two additional benefits: it allows some sorely needed breeze into the ballpark, and it offers a shaded area for fans seeking temporary respite from the sun. The air-conditioned team store is designed to be open year-round; beside it is a casual seating area next to a beer stand and other concessions. Walk down the concourse toward left field and you'll have an overhead view of a workout field. Before he was sidelined by health issues, this is where former Twins manager Tom Kelly schooled youngsters on the fundamentals of the game, and it is still a prime spot for viewing workouts. Next to that vantage point: a large bar featuring beer, wine, and mixed drinks.

If you keep walking around the outfield concourse, you'll encounter the boardwalk, comprising some 42,000 square feet and 1,236 seats. You'll be treated to a variety of seating areas (four tops to semi-shaded box seats to the left-field berm), lots of bar rails, and concessions ranging from the aforementioned burger grills to beer stands to other specialty points of sale. Behind the center-field batter's eye is a concession stand, flanked by restrooms. One of the interesting things about the renovation is that it added capacity for 1,300 more fans while simultaneously making the ballpark feel less crowded. Even during a sellout, Hammond Stadium doesn't feel packed: fans mill around the ballpark, watching a few innings here, a few innings there, with traffic disbursed throughout. The old Hammond Stadium felt cramped; the new one feels airy.

The expansion of the concourses also allowed for new seating to be added to the grandstand, and the upper level now provides a shaded group sky deck (there are six new party/group areas in all) as well as a drink rail. These seats, accessible from steps leading from the main concourse, are some of the best in the house: they provide a great view of the action while being totally shaded. They're now reserved seating, but well worth the money in terms of comfort.

Look beyond the right-field concourse for a potential glimpse of Florida wildlife in the pond. An alligator has been known to drop in occasionally, but you're more likely to see one of the many turtles living there.

Interestingly, much of what makes the complex work for the Twins is behind the scenes and won't ever be seen by fans. Chief among them: a state-of-the-art player development academy. Player acquisition these days is now a global effort, as MLB teams draft and sign many players from the Caribbean and South America. For these young men, transitioning to professional baseball and life in the United States can be a wrenching experience.

The player facility is designed to address that transition. The Twins, who funded the $6 million construction cost, call it a player development academy, but it wouldn't look out of place on most college campuses. It includes a modern design featuring dorm-like housing built around a courtyard, a group multimedia/game area (complete with big-screen TVs, game consoles, domino tables, and more), conference rooms named for Twins greats, 24-hour security, and a large cafeteria with the capacity to feed 150 players and coaches. These days, it's all about nutrition for developing players; in the old days dinner would have been some burgers and shakes, but these days it's all about nutritionally correct meals with proper portions, healthy snacks—and no pop. That's why the Twins set up a system of individual nutrition plans for every player, offered in the spacious, modern cafeteria space. The player development academy runs year-round (save for a short Christmas break), so as to accelerate player development in a focused environment.

The player development academy also features a plush auditorium large enough to seat all Twins players and coaches in camp at a given time—with a capacity of 192. The team also uses it for press conferences and other events.

When the decision was made to renovate Lee Health Sports Complex and Hammond Stadium, the Twins agreed to a lease extension through 2045, not a surprise when you consider the team rarely moves spring-training facilities. The team has trained in Florida since their days as the Washington Senators: 1936 to the present, except for the war years of 1943-45, when the team trained in College Park, Maryland. Most of those years were spent training in Orlando's Tinker Field—1936 through 1990—while their minor-league teams trained in nearby Melbourne from 1964-1989 and Fort Myers' Terry Park in 1990. The minor- and major-league camps were combined at the Lee Health Sports Complex in 1991. (We discuss Tinker Field in the Orlando chapter.)

INSIDER'S TIP
The ballpark was named for Bill Hammond, the assistant director for Lee County who was a prime mover in attracting the Twins to Lee County.

INSIDER'S TIP

The Boston Red Sox also train in Fort Myers, just six or so miles to the east. As a result, you will see many Twins/Red Sox scrimmages and games during spring training.

INSIDER'S TIP
A highlight of spring training at Hammond Stadium is the annual Minnesota Day, where fans display flags in the parking lot proclaiming their Minnesota point of origin, complete with some tailgating.

INSIDER'S TIP
At times the southern end of Fort Myers resembles a huge traffic jam, with everyone moving more slowly than you'd expect. City planners didn't do a very good job anticipating the growth in the market, so as a result you find traffic snares everywhere. It takes longer to get around the area than you'd expect no matter the time of the day, so give yourself plenty of time to get to and from Hammond Stadium.

BALLPARK HISTORY

Lee Health Sports Complex has been the home of the Twins for its entire history, while Fort Myers has been home to several major-league clubs in its spring-training history. Nearby Terry Park is possibly the oldest surviving spring-training ballpark site in Florida; we discuss it in a following chapter.

The Single-A Fort Myers Mighty Mussels play regular-season games at Hammond Stadium, while the rookie-level Florida Complex League Twins play on an adjoining practice field. It is a busy year-round complex, what with extended spring training and other rehab activities. The only time baseball isn't being played here is during a two-week Christmas break.

THE SPRING-TRAINING BALLPARK EXPERIENCE

WHERE TO SIT

The best seating in the ballpark is purchased by season-ticket holders. These folks gather in Sections 108-114, behind the Twins dugout, comfortably ensconced in chairback seats. Because so many tickets are controlled by season-ticket holders, you won't have much selection unless you hit the aftermarket.

Still, you have a wealth of options when it comes to seating options. Before we get into them, we have one huge recommendation: *bring your sunscreen to the ballpark,* and make sure you meet MLB standards by buying sunscreen in a plastic container. Many of the Hammond Stadium seats are in the sun. For a Minnesotan cooped up for months, that transition to the Florida spring is a jarring one, and before you've had that first beer, be sure to lather up. By the time you realize you are sunburned, it's too late.

Now, having said that, you can plan a Hammond Stadium trip to mitigate the sun's impact on your pale skin. There are basically three sections to the ballpark. The bottom of the grandstand, in the 100-numbered seats, features comfortable chairback seats. The top of the grandstand, in the 200-numbered seats, is also populated with chairback seats. And then there is the boardwalk, with an abundance of seating options.

With the comfy seating, any seat in the grandstand is now good. If you want shade, buy a seat in the back of Sections 208-213, as the last five rows are shielded by the press-box/suites level. Earlier in this chapter we discussed the upper-level shaded seating down the first-base line. And the right-field outfield areas are shaded as well.

If you find yourself overwhelmed by the sun, there are plenty of spots to seek refuge. In the right-field corner there's a small team store next to a canopied seating area: this is a popular spot before the game but usually abandoned once action starts. Canopies provide shade at the two large bars down the left-field line and in right field. The right-field bar is probably better when it comes to providing a view of the ballpark from the shade: you can belly up on the far side and keep an eye on the action. There is also shaded seating next to the main team store, but you won't see the game.

CONCESSIONS

Go hungry. The boardwalk area is a good bet for fulfilling your spring-training dietary needs. The traditional Hammond Stadium grills have been relocated there, with a selection of freshly prepared and nicely priced hamburgers, cheeseburgers, brats, and hot dogs. Here we discuss offerings of the recent past; the Twins do a good job in bringing in new vendors every spring. A variety of beer stands offer a variety of beers, including a Leinenkugel stand in the left-field corner. The two aforementioned bars offer a variety of Minnesota and Florida microbrews as well as a full selection of macrobrews, wine, and mixed drinks. If you want Florida micro-brews, you have access to a wide selection from Bury Me Brewing, Fort Myers Brewing, Islamorada, and Scotty's Bierworks. If you look hard, you can find cans of Summit Extra Pale Ale and Saga IPA at some stands.

For those missing that Minnesota angle, the Taste of Twins Territory in the third-base concourse offers a variety of hometown offerings, ranging from a pretty good take on cheese curds and a pancake bacon burger to poutine and Killebrew root beer. Yes, there are ties to former Twins great Harmon Killebrew—the Killer and his family launched the root-beer business—and it's a fine root beer if you consider yourself a root-beer connoisseur.

You'll also find more good options in back of the grandstand, including hot dogs, brats, burgers, pizza, cheese curds, poutine, and more. With the expansion of Hammond Stadium came the addition of many more specialty food carts, so take the time to walk through the concourse and evaluate your options before committing to a purchase.

AUTOGRAPHS

The practice fields are usually open to fans before games begin, with workouts beginning at 10 a.m. Once games start, the best place to find players is during batting practice and immediately before a game, next to the dugout.

It's rare you have a chance to snare a player unless they're on a practice field or on the field: the clubhouses are in the grandstand and connected to dugouts. Similarly, fans have little access to visiting players: the team bus pulls into a restricted area next to the clubhouse.

PARKING

Parking costs $15 and is located next to the ballpark. As you enter the ballpark, attendants will politely guide you to an open parking spot. Take a second to orient yourself. Don't go right to the front entrance, but figure out where the central walkway to the ballpark is located and head there. This palm-tree-lined walkway features a sign showing the distances to the Twins' farm teams, and it's a popular spot for photos. Walk to the ballpark, where you'll end up at another scenic spot: a large fountain in front of the Hammond Stadium main entrance. The main ticket office—including Will Call —will be to your left.

If you don't want to take the scenic tour, there are shuttles running between parking areas and the box office before and after the game.

SELFIE SPOTS

There are three great spots for selfies at Hammond Stadium. First: the aforementioned tree-lined walkway in the parking lot, where you can get a photo of the sign showing the distances to the Twins' farm teams. Second: in front of the large fountain at the end of the tree-lined walkway, in front of the ballpark. Third: Next to the ticket office, where you can capture the huge TC Twins logo in the background.

IF YOU GO

WHAT TO DO OUTSIDE THE BALLPARK

Fort Myers is in southwestern Florida, far away from the madding crowds of Tampa or Orlando. The closest foes for the Twins are the Boston Red Sox (who also train in Lee County) and the Tampa Bay Rays (who train in Port Charlotte). It's 125 miles up the coast to Tampa/St. Pete, but less than that to North Port (spring-training home of the Atlanta Braves), Bradenton (spring-training home of the Pittsburgh Pirates), or Sarasota (spring-training home of the Baltimore Orioles). All in all, it would be simple to create a spring-training trip with a daily Twins fix. For most of the spring schedule, the Twins stick to the Gulf Coast and Tampa Bay, with an occasional foray to the Palm Beach area.

We cover many of the local hotspots in our Fort Myers overview. You can sometimes find Twins players—usually rookies and minor leaguers—at Potts Sports Café (*6900 Daniels Pkwy., Fort Myers; 239/768-5500*). It's a typical Florida sports bar; virtually every restaurant touts their wonderful grouper sandwich, and Potts is no different. Even if no Twins are on the premises, it's a good place to stop after the game.

If something a little lighter is more to your liking, head west from the ballpark on Six Mile Cypress Parkway to Tamiami Trail; there are many, many good and fast-food restaurants both north and south of the parkway. Within two miles of the ballpark are safe chain bets like Glory Days Grill (*5056 Daniels Pkwy., Fort Myers; 239/690-3287; **glorydaysgrill.com***), Bonefish Grill (*14261 S. Tamiami Trail, Fort Myers; 239/489-1240; **bonefishgrill.com***), and the local outpost of the Florida Duffy's Sports Grill chain (*13721 S. Tamiami Trail, Fort Myers; 239/590-8631; **duffysmvp.com**). On the high end is Harold's (*15250 S. Tamiami Trail, Fort Myers; 239/849-0622; **haroldscuisine.com**), the favorite of local foodies.

You won't starve if you head out of the ballpark and north onto Tamiami Trail, unless you're forever stuck in traffic—one of the unfortunate realities of March in Fort Myers.

WHERE TO STAY

There's nothing within easy walking distance of the ballpark, due to its location on a fairly major throughway. The Twins have stayed at a few different hotels in the past few years. In 2024 the team hotel was the Drury Inn & Suites Fort Myers Airport FGCU (*9950 University Plaza Dr., Fort Myers; 239/267-1340; **druryhotels.com**).

Hotels closest to the ballpark include Fairfield & Suites Inn (*7090 Cypress Terrace, Fort Myers; 239/437-5600; **marriott.com***), Homewood Suites (*5255 Big Pine Way, Fort Myers; 239/275-6000; **hilton.com***), and Doubletree (*13051 Bell Tower Dr., Fort Myers; 239/482-2900;*

hilton.com). The last two hotels are located in the Bell Tower Shops area, which features a host of restaurants, bars, retail, movie theaters, and grocery stores. (We discuss the restaurants in this area in our Fort Myers overview chapter.) It's a good place to center your spring-training travels.

SPRING TRAINING HISTORY: MINNESOTA TWINS

The Minnesota Twins/Washington Senators have held spring training in the following locations: Phoebus, Va. (1901); Washington, D.C. (1902-1904); Hampton, Va. (1905); Charlottesville, Va. (1906); Galveston, Texas (1907); Norfolk, Va. (1910); Atlanta (1911); Charlottesville, Ga. (1912-1916); Atlanta (1917); Augusta, Ga. (1918-1919); Tampa (1920-1929); Biloxi, Miss. (1930-1935); Orlando (1936-1942); College Park, Md. (1943-1945); Orlando (1946-1990); Fort Myers (1991-present).

The team trained at Tinker Field during the Orlando years. We cover Tinker Field in our Orlando chapter.

TERRY PARK

Though the Boston Red Sox and Minnesota Twins are relatively recent transplants to the Fort Myers area when it comes to spring training, the area has hosted preseason squads for more than a century, mostly at Terry Park.

Terry Park was named for Dr. Marshall Terry and his wife, Tootie McGregor Terry, who turned a cow pasture into the Fort Myers Yacht and Country Club in 1906. That venture didn't work out, and the land was donated to Lee County. In 1914, the American Association's Louisville Colonels set up spring training at the Country Club grounds, utilizing a small clubhouse and large playing field. The Colonels practiced twice a day, charging 25 cents for admission, and played host to the Philadelphia A's and the St. Louis Browns.

The Louisville Colonels never returned, but by 1923 Fort Myers was ready to make another pitch for spring training and approached Philadelphia A's owner/manager Connie Mack, guaranteeing $6,000 and a new 1,500-seat ballpark if he moved spring operations there from Montgomery, Alabama. The shrewd Mack knew a good deal once he saw it. He sent down ballfield specs and began play at the new wooden grandstand in 1925.

In those days, spring training was a considerably more fluid proposition than it is today, and stars didn't necessarily play every day with their own teams. In 1925, for instance, Babe Ruth suited up for the A's in an exhibition match against the minor-league

Milwaukee Brewers. Around 5,000 fans crammed into the 1,500-seat ballpark—a figure even more impressive when you consider at the time the total population of Fort Myers was 6,774. In 1927, Mack threw batting practice to inventor Thomas Edison, who was 80 years old at the time. Edison made good enough contact to smack the ball to Ty Cobb, who feigned surprise at the ferocity of the hit. Olympic star Babe Didriksen pitched an inning against the Brooklyn Dodgers in 1934, and the barnstorming House of David team played a memorable game against the A's in 1935.

The original Terry Park wooden grandstand burned down in 1943—a not-uncommon fate for wooden sports structures—but by 1954 a new 2,500-seat steel grandstand was erected, and the Pittsburgh Pirates set up shop in 1955. In a nice move, the Pirates' first game was against the Philadelphia A's, with the 92-year-old Connie Mack throwing out the first pitch. The Pirates left after spring training 1967 for Bradenton, replaced by the expansion Kansas City Royals. Over the years the Royals were a steady attraction, but spring training was changing. By 1987, the Royals were ready to move on to a state-of-the-art complex in Haines City. (So much for state of the art: the Haines City complex has already been leveled, while Terry Park lives on.)

In many ways the Terry Park complex is more popular than ever before. The grandstand was rebuilt in 2004 in a slimmed-down 1,000-seat configuration, and around 2,000 games are played at the four-field complex each spring and summer. If you visit today, you'll probably see a game of some sort, as many colleges schedule games there in February and March. You will probably have some downtime if you're in the area to see a Red Sox, Twins, Rays, or Braves game, and there's something grand about watching baseball played on a field where Jimmy Foxx, Roberto Clemente, George Brett, and Bob Feller spent serious time in the course of their long and illustrious careers. Highly recommended.

Terry Park, 3410 Palm Beach Blvd., Fort Myers. Palm Beach Boulevard (also marked as Highway 80) runs northeast from downtown Fort Myers. The ballpark complex is located on the south side of Palm Beach Boulevard; there's a small field for parking west of the ballpark. Virtually every game in February and March is free and open to the public.

CHARLOTTE SPORTS PARK / TAMPA BAY RAYS

QUICK FACTS

- **Capacity**: 7,000
- **Year Opened**: 1986; renovated 2009 and 2024
- **Dimensions**: 343L, 384LC, 414C, 384RC, 3434R
- **Ticket Line**: 888/FAN-RAYS
- **Local Airport**: Southwest Florida International Airport
- **Dugout Location**: First-base side
- **Practice Time**: 10 a.m. Enter the practice fields in the walkway next to the parking lots to the roped-off areas.
- **Pregame Schedule**: Gates open two hours before gametime. Rays batting practice, 10:15-11:15 a.m.; visitors batting practice, 11:15 a.m.-12:15 p.m.; visitors infield, 12:20-12:30 p.m. Add six hours for an evening game.
- **Address**: 2300 El Jobean Road, Port Charlotte, FL 33948
- **Directions**: From the north and I-75, take Exit 179 at Toledo Blade Road and turn right (west). Drive for 6.5 miles and then go right on El Jobean Road (SR 776). Drive two miles; the ballpark will be on your left. From the south, take I-75 to Exit 170. Head west on Kings Highway (under freeway) and turn right on Veterans Boulevard, which turns into FL-776 and El Jobean Road.

AN OLD-TIME FLORIDA SPRING-TRAINING EXPERIENCE

After a March 2023 training season spent at Disney's Wide World of Sports and the Trop, the Tampa Bay Rays returned to Port Charlotte in 2024, with Charlotte Sports Park repaired after extensive water damage from Hurricane Ian.

The move to Port Charlotte may only be temporary—the Rays openly sought a new training facility in Pasco County, only to see state funding vetoed by Gov. Ron DeSantis—but if you're a hardcore spring training fan, it's still a good temporary measure, as a game at Charlotte Sports Part is a throwback experience.

It's also a temporary measure for another reason. When the Rays moved to Port Charlotte in 2009, there wasn't much of anything near the ballpark. Today, the gap between Port Charlotte and the Charlotte Sports Park is seemingly closing by the day, with plenty of development to the east. We were at the 2024 reopening of Charlotte Sports Park and encountered an unexpectedly high level of traffic to and from the game.

Too bad, as the core Charlotte Sports Park experience hearkens to a time when a spring-training ballpark existed less as a tourism exercise and more as a player-development exercise. Though the ballpark is fairly modern—a 2009 renovation upgraded the former spring home of the Texas Rangers—the experience is not. Or, rather, it doesn't need to be: it's really your choice.

In a way, the Rays and Charlotte County anticipated and pioneered the whole social-space movement during the 2009 renovation of Charlotte Sports Park. The renovation kept the basic grandstand design intact but eschewed fixed seating down each line and center field, opting instead for plenty of four tops in the 19,000-square-foot Baseball Boardwalk ringing the playing field. You are right on top of the action and the bullpens. The Boardwalk contains group seating areas and a Tiki bar, as well as space for other concession and beer stands. Many fans just buy the cheapest ticket possible and then spend all day lounging on the boardwalk. (Which may or may not have enough space for all. If there are two groups occupying most of the seating areas, you will not have much space—or drink-rail availability—to spread out).

The result: fixed seating for the hardcores (yeah, just try scoring a good seat at a Rays game) and plenty of social space in the outfield for the party crowd. The fan base in Port Charlotte is largely made up of locals, but there are enough folks driving down from the greater Tampa Bay area to keep things interesting. A game there has turned into one of the better spring events in Florida, as Charlotte Sports Park features suites, a 360-degree concourse, and family picnic areas down each line.

On the player side, there are plenty of goodies as well, including a 40,000-square-foot clubhouse, full-size major-league practice field, one half field, and four full-size minor-league practice fields. In addition, there's parking for 1,500 cars. It is quite the Florida experience: alligators patrol the ponds surrounding the ballpark.

INSIDER'S TIP

There are several ponds surrounding the ballpark, complete with the requisite alligator warnings, but our favorite spot to view an alligator is while safely standing on the boardwalk behind the left-field bullpen, where we often see the wild gators lounging in the sun.

The Tampa Bay Rays have had the unfortunate luck of always operating under another team's shadow, especially in spring training. While Al Lang Field was a historic venue, it wasn't the best setup for the Rays in terms of actual training: the team worked out at a separate complex and played games on the St. Petersburg waterfront.

Even though the Atlanta Braves are training in southern Sarasota County and the Rays training in northern Charlotte County, the actual driving distance between the two facilities is only 15 minutes or so. That set up a natural rivalry between the Rays and the Braves, and it also sets up a four-team cluster in North Port, Port Charlotte, and Fort Myers.

BALLPARK HISTORY

Charlotte Sports Park was formerly the spring home of the Texas Rangers from 1986 through 2002, when the team shifted operations to Surprise, Arizona. In 2007, it served as the home of the best-drawing team in the independent South Coast League, the Charlotte County Redfish.

THE SPRING-TRAINING BALLPARK EXPERIENCE

CONCESSIONS

The food operations at Charlotte Sports Park were scaled back in recent years: what was once an abundance of delights from local and varied vendors is now a lineup of ballpark staples at multiple stands. Not much variety.

At Home Stand Concessions located on the main concourse behind Sections 202-203 (on the first-base side) and Sections 217-218 (on the third-base side) you'll find the usual offerings: hot dogs, brats, burgers, beverages, and more. There are picnic tables as well.

Also on the main concourse: the Hot Corner Grill, located behind Section 214.

Additional concessions stands can be found next to the Tiki Bar in left-center field (featuring Philly cheesesteaks) as well as along the third-base line. If you're a beer fan, Charlotte Sports Park offers a variety of brews, with offerings from the likes of Yuengling, Fort Myers Brewing, Goose Island, Big Storm Brewing, and Fat Point Brewing throughout the ballpark. Speaking of the Tiki Bar: the selection of beer there is usually better than at the concourse stands. Also available at the Tiki Bar: an oversized margarita or a rum punch bucket. It's a bucket containing basically two-and-a-half drinks, with as many straws as you'd like. When you need a handle to carry your cocktail, you may need to evaluate some life choices.

INSIDER'S TIP
The Rays are more restrictive than MLB guidelines in what's allowed in the ballpark: no water or food containers.

PARKING

Parking is plentiful at a large lot next to the ballpark and at the county fairgrounds across the highway. It will cost you $10. Overflow parking is located in the Expo Center lots across the highway. The Harley-Davidson dealership next door offers a parking deal if you want to dine before the game and walk over.

AUTOGRAPHS

It's fairly easy to get an autograph at Charlotte Sports Park before a game, no matter if you're a Rays fan or at the ballpark to snag the signature of a visiting player. Clubhouses for both teams are beyond the right-field boardwalk, which means everyone enters the field from the same right-field corner gate. Usually players from both teams will stop for signing down the right-field line, next to the berm area. The same goes after the game when both teams are leaving the dugouts.

INSIDER'S TIP
Players will sometimes stop after they leave the batting cages

outside the ballpark, which are located outside the right-field corner and next to the walkway leading to the cloverleaf practice fields.

INSIDER'S TIP
Workouts are not a particularly good time to seek autographs. The Rays rope off the practice fields; you won't have any access at all to Fields 1-4—the cloverleaf—and you'll have limited access to Field 5. Plus, if the Rays are practicing in the actual ballpark, you can expect it to be closed to fans. Let's just say there are lots of ropes cutting off access to any player. (Coaches, on the other hand, are another matter. They'll stop to chat and sign. Remember, the polite way to address a coach is as "coach.")

WHERE TO SIT

Rays spring-training games at Charlotte Sports Park were formerly automatic sellouts. That's not the case in more recent years, even before the age of COVID-19, but the best seats in the ballpark are controlled by season-ticket holders, especially the prime tickets in the shade. So, while there are seats available down the line in Section 101 or 115, you may not want to sit there.

That leaves you to spend time in Sections 213-218 or Sections 201-206. (Again, forget about anything right behind home plate, unless you go through a ticket reseller.) There are some advantages to Sections 201-206, particularly the sweet spot of Sections 202-204: you're behind the Rays dugout (in such a small ballpark, being in the back of the grandstand isn't a huge tragedy), and you're likely to be in the shade, as the generous roof covers all the seating in Sections 201-206, save the first few rows. (In comparison, only the last few rows of seats in Sections 213-218 are covered by the roof at the start of an afternoon game.) These are perhaps the best tickets at this price range in the entire Grapefruit League.

INSIDER'S TIP
If you can, buy tickets in the first five rows of sections 106 or 110; these seats provide a direct view in the Rays dugout.

They're largely controlled by season-ticket holders, so you will need to buy them through a ticket reseller.

We'd urge you to consider buying a berm ticket if you don't snare a seat in Sections 202-206. The massive boardwalk features plenty of four tops, picnic tables, and drink rails: if you're at the ballpark with a group, you'll probably have a better time interacting in a social situation than sitting in the grandstand. As a bonus, the berms provide good access to bullpen views (visitors in left, Rays in right). But be warned: they do not provide very good angles to the action, they're down the lines, and, in the case of left field, they curl around the foul pole. However, these SRO tickets are still a solid deal.

INSIDER'S TIP
There are no bleachers at Charlotte Sports Park. Every seat is a chairback seat with cupholder.

In general, there's not much shade at Charlotte Sports Park past the grandstand. A canopy down the third-base line provides some needed shade if you get overheated on the boardwalk. And several picnic areas are shaded as well. But if you have a deep aversion to the sun, plan ahead: the regulars know where every shaded seat is located, and they reserve those seats with season passes.

FOR THE KIDS

A playground is installed down the third-base line. Alas, you will not be able to see the game while the kids burn off some energy.

SELFIE SPOT

The center-field Tiki area is popular with the selfie crowd; you can get the bar and the grandstand in the action.

IF YOU GO

WHAT TO DO OUTSIDE THE BALLPARK

The Atlanta Braves train in North Port, less than 15 miles from Charlotte Sports Park. The Boston Red Sox and the Minnesota Twins train in nearby Fort Myers. In addition, the Baltimore Orioles train in Sarasota, up the freeway, and the many teams training in the Tampa-St. Pete area are at most a two-hour drive away.

Port Charlotte is located on the northern part of the Fort Myers metro and is considered to be the more working-class area: while Naples and Lee County attract the bigger-buck residents, most of Port Charlotte's main drags are made up of strip malls and big-box retailers. If you're coming down from Tampa-St. Pete or up from Fort Myers, don't expect a scenic drive in Charlotte County.

Like most Florida cities on the Gulf Coast, Port Charlotte is oriented toward the waterfront, and it's there you'll find restaurants and nightlife. Nearby Punta Gorda and Fisherman's Village feature a more upscale nightlife scene as well.

A Harley-Davidson dealership has been located next to the ballpark since the Rays moved in, and next to that dealership is the Twisted Fork, a hopping place on gamedays. It's a country music/biker/hot rod kinda place—it's what you would expect from a bar/restaurant that's part of a Harley complex. Recommended for pre- or post-game drinks and snacks. *Twisted Fork, 2208 El Jobean Rd., Port Charlotte; 941/235-FORK; twistedfork.net.*

You will also find an abundance of decent spots at the intersection of Tamiami Trail and El Jobean Road, including Metro Diner (*1720 Tamiami Trail, Port Charlotte; 941/220-6291; metrodiner.com*) and Zoe's Sweet Kitchen (*1101 El Jobean Rd., Port Charlotte; 941/743-9637; zoessweetkitchen.com*), recommended for breakfast and lunch. We'd also recommend All-Star Sports Grill (*2360 Tamiami Trail, Port Charlotte; 941/743-4140; allstarsportsgrill.com*), a traditional sports bar with plenty of big-screen TVs. Mostly, however, you'll find a slew of decent chain restaurants in that area, including Buffalo Wild Wings, Hooter's, and Culver's.

There are also a number of great restaurants in the area should you decide to stay in a local hotel. A fave: Visani Restaurant and

Comedy Theater (*2400 Kings Hwy., Port Charlotte; 941/629-9191; visani.net*). The theater features a host of musical acts and standup comedy (Chris Kattan, Tammy Piscatelli, Kevin Hart, and John Heffron have graced the stage), while the food is Italian steakhouse. Prime Serious Steak (*19655 Cochran Blvd., Port Charlotte; 941/627-8325; primeseriousssteak.com*) lives up to its name with great steaks and a decent wine list.

WHERE TO STAY

There is very little within walking distance of the ballpark, much less a hotel. Most chains are represented in downtown Port Charlotte, which is a little more than three miles west of the ballpark, while other accommodations can be found along I-75. And as the Rays do not designate a team hotel, you're not bound to staying in the area. There are several chain hotels at the I-75-Kings Highway (Exit 170) interchange.

RV PARKS

The closest RV park is Harbor Lakes RV Park, located less than four miles down El Jobean Road from the ballpark. It's a larger RV park with lots of activities. *3737 El Jobean Road, Port Charlotte; 877/570-2267; rvonthego.com.*

SPRING TRAINING HISTORY: TAMPA BAY RAYS

Tampa Bay trained at historic Al Lang Field in downtown St. Petersburg from 1998 through 2008. Al Lang Field is amongst the most historic venues in Florida. We cover Al Lang Field, now Al Lang Stadium, in its own chapter.

COOLTODAY PARK / ATLANTA BRAVES

QUICK FACTS

- **Capacity**: 8,000 (6,200 seats, 1,800 SRO/berm)
- **Year Opened**: 2019
- **Dimensions**: 335LF, 385LC, 400C, 375RC, 325RF
- **Ticket Line**: 800/745-3000
- **Local Airport**: Sarasota-Bradenton International
- **Dugout Location**: First-base side
- **Workout Schedule**: Practice begins at 9:30 a.m.
- **Pregame Schedule**: Gates open two hours before game time. Braves batting practice, 10:10-11:10 a.m.; visitors batting practice, 11:10 a.m.-12:10 p.m.; Braves infield, 12:10-12:25 p.m.; visitors infield, 12:25-12:40 p.m. Add five hours to each figure for a 6:05 p.m. game.
- **Address**: 18800 W. Villages Pkwy., Venice, FL 34287
- **Directions**: West Villages Parkway is located directly off Tamiami Trail (Hwy. 41), a major throughway running from the Everglades and north to Bradenton. From the north (Sarasota), take I-75 south to exit 191 (North River Road) and follow it to West Villages Parkway. From the south (Fort Myers/Naples), take I-75 north to take I-75 south to exit 191 (North River Road), head west on Tamiami Trail, and then to West Villages Parkway.

MOVING SOUTH TO NORTH PORT

With the opening of CoolToday Park at the end of spring training 2019, the Atlanta Braves became the second team currently training in Sarasota County, joining the Baltimore Orioles. In the process, the Braves and CoolToday Park became the latest cog in a string of Florida spring-training ballparks in western coastal areas, beginning with Dunedin and Tampa to the north and Fort Myers in the south.

Featuring a modern design, CoolToday Park tends to be very vertical from the outside but surprisingly light and airy inside. Part of this design has to do with the quirks of building in Florida, where you're never too far above the water line, so the only option is building up. Some Florida ballparks, such as CACTI Park of the Palm Beaches, deal with this need to build up with plenty of ramps, sloped berms, and gradual approaches to a concourse level. At CoolToday Park, the decision was made to divide the ballpark into separate areas, building up from there and asking patrons to walk up to a raised concourse level.

Once there, the 360-degree concourse provides a lovely view of the surrounding area (Florida is a pretty flat state, so being up a story-plus provides a great perch). An added bonus to the raised and open concourse: It allows in some breezes sorely needed on a hot day. The concourses are wide, allowing for easy access throughout the ballpark. A sellout crowd makes the ballpark feel busy, but not jammed.

As the ballpark improved over the years, so did the area around the ballpark. CoolToday Park was built as the centerpiece of a planned community, Wellen Park, and since opening the area has been built up. This part of North Port is largely built up with residences, but there is commercial development around Tamiami Trail. That includes a Publix grocery store and other businesses at the corner of West Villages Parkway and Tamiami Trail.

INSIDER'S TIP
One of the big issues with CoolToday Park has to do with its location, with the main (and formerly only) route to the ballpark via West Villages Parkway, off Tamiami Trail. Access is better now that the Wellen Park (formerly the West Villages) development to the northeast of the ballpark is open, as well as other back roads to the west. The alternatives: head south from North Port Fire Station 86 (19955 Preto Blvd.) and take Preto Boulevard and Playmore Road to West Villages Parkway, or head south from the Tamiami Trail Costco (11700 Mezzo Dr.) and head south to Playmore Road. We can't guarantee access to these alternate routes—local traffic officials would likely love to see all incoming traffic funneled to West Villages Parkway—so use your GPS to map the fastest and least-busy route.

It is tempting to compare CoolToday Park with The Stadium (formerly Champion Stadium), the previous spring home of the Braves. Such a comparison really isn't fair: at Disney's Wide World of Sports, the Braves were strictly a tenant, with limited workout facilities and little say over how the ballpark was run for spring training. There is a Disney way of doing business, and a spring-training game at The Stadium was a Disney experience, not a Braves experience.

But there's one comparison to The Stadium worth noting. The Braves' presence at The Stadium had diminished over the years, to the point where there was little in the ballpark to remind fans they were at the spring home of the Braves. That's certainly not true at CoolToday Park, where there are plenty of reminders you are at an Atlanta Braves spring-training game. Large murals of Braves greats like Greg Maddux, Warren Spahn, and Tom Glavine wrap the exterior towers.

The other showcase for the complex that fans won't see: a 62,400-square-foot clubhouse for both the major-and minor-league staffs, as well as the Florida operations staff. This is the sort of facility the Braves never had at Wide World of Sports, but this sort of facility is now utilized by virtually every MLB team in Florida and Arizona. The complex also features seven diamonds (four for major leaguers, three for minor leaguers), 11 batting cages, and 63 pitching mounds. Pregame workouts take place at these diamonds, as do "B" and minor-league games.

BALLPARK HISTORY

CoolToday Park was built as spring home of the Atlanta Braves. Also playing there: the Rookie-level Florida Complex League Braves.

THE SPRING-TRAINING BALLPARK EXPERIENCE

CONCESSIONS

The Braves run concessions at CoolToday Park, and there are plenty of points of sale on the ballpark concourse. Most feature ballpark standards like hot dogs, burgers, Chick-Fil-A, brats, Italian sausage, popcorn, and beer.

There are some concession stands worth a hike. The Braves Smokehouse BBQ, located on the grandstand's Terrace Level, serves barbecue favorites like pulled pork and brisket, as well as a fried bologna sandwich. Also on the grandstand second level: Greenfields, featuring build-your-own salads and frozen yogurt. (Despite this being a restricted area for suite holders and groups, head to Customer Service for a pass allowing you access to the Terrace Level to visit the concessions there.) Next to each other down the third-base line: Fish Camp and the Chicken Coop. Fish Camp offers fried fish served with hush puppies and fries in a tackle box, while Chicken Coop offers fried chicken with boom boom sauce, fried pickles and fries. The Sausage Shack, natch, serves sausages and sides. Other specialty stands offer tacos, street corn, Papa John's Pizza, and craft beers.

The Tiki Bar is located down the left-field line; you can belly up to the bar or buy a drink and hang out in the area. If you're hungry, order a half-pound burger as well. The best beer selection, we found, was the Craft Beer Bar near Section 117.

PARKING

As of now parking in the area is limited to lots at the ballpark. The price: $10 for cars and $20 for RVs. Ridesharing services like Uber and Lyft serve the ballpark, dropping off and picking up customers in a designated area.

AUTOGRAPHS

Braves players signed autographs at the near end of the third-base dugout, between the sections of netting.

WHERE TO SIT

CoolToday Park borrows a lot from Truist Park in terms of operating philosophy, set up like its MLB big brother, with plenty of discrete seating areas with a variety of offerings. If shade is what you seek, we have some recommendations. In Sections 106-111, shade covers seating all the way from the concourse to the first few rows. In Sections 112-113, the shade extends down 8-9 rows at the start of a 1:05 p.m. game.

Or you can buy a $20 SRO ticket and make a beeline for the open drink rails under the grandstand, on the concourse.

There are half-moon four tops extending from foul territory into fair, with drink rails to the back. There is a small berm space in the left-field corner. The Budweiser Bench is located in left-center field, below the scoreboard. A Centauri Super Suite sits at field level, beneath the wraparound concourse. Two Terrace areas on each end of the grandstand's second level are ticketed separately and feature access to an air-conditioned space and a full-service bar. The corner Left Field Lounge is a multilayer group area with a dedicated menu and waitstaff. Four group areas sit on the concourse, between the dugouts and between the grandstand seating and the concourse. And there are drink rails surrounding the entire seating bowl.

At opening CoolToday Park featured extended netting to the far ends of the dugouts, encompassing Sections 107-117.

SELFIE SPOTS

A tribute to Braves' retired numbers can be found outside the ballpark, as the team's retired numbers—#44 (Henry Aaron), #3 (Dale Murphy), #6 (Bobby Cox), #10 (Chipper Jones), #21 (Warren Spahn), #29 (John Smoltz), #31 (Maddux), #35 (Phil Niekro), #41 (Eddie Mathews), #47 (Glavine), and #42 (Jackie Robinson)—are memorialized on the front plaza. Be warned that these tributes are not inside the ballpark perimeter, so plan on visiting before or after the game: if you leave, you will not be allowed reentry, per MLB rules.

IF YOU GO

HOTELS

Right now there is no hotel within five miles of the ballpark, so be prepared for a drive to the facility and paying for parking there. We expect some new hotels at some point (again, delayed development at play), but until then, you'll need to stay a little farther afield.

Once past that five-mile mark, there are plenty of chain hotels in nearby Port Charlotte, Venice, or the rest of North Port. You could go old school and stay at a Florida resort on the Gulf. These aren't necessarily the fanciest accommodations, but the vibe is decidedly retro. If this appeals to you, check out the small, intimate and adult-only Seafarer Beach Resort (*8520 Manasota Key Rd., Englewood; 941/474-4388; seafarerbeach.com*), Pearl Beach Inn (*7990 Manasota Key Rd., Englewood; 941/473-2361; pearlbeachinn.com*), Sun Coast Inn (*2073 S. McCall Rd., Englewood; 800/633-8115; suncoastinn.com*), or Manasota Beach Club (*7660 Manasota Key Rd., Englewood; 941/474-2614; manasotabeachclub.com*). These are modest family-run estab-

---

lishments, perfect if you're a little tired of the hustle and bustle of the modern world. If you're looking for a more upscale hotel experience, you'll want to cast a net farther afield to Sarasota, with its mix of luxury resorts and lodgings, like The Westin Sarasota (*100 Marina View Dr., Sarasota; 941/217-4777; westinsarasota.com*).

RV PARKS

There's no RV park within walking distance of the ballpark, but there are several within a relatively close drive, including Myakka River RV Resort (*10400 S. Tamiami Tr., Venice; 941/488-0850; myakkarv.com*) and Encore Ramblers Rest (*1300 North River Rd.; 941/493-4354; thousandtrails.com*).

WHAT TO DO OUTSIDE THE BALLPARK

CoolToday Park is the centerpiece of a larger development in Wellen Park that includes a neighborhood shopping center between the ballpark and Tamiami Trail. Being part of a Florida planned development, The Marketplace (*wellenpark.com*) development features the mandatory Publix grocery store as well as a variety of retailers and restaurants, including a Dunkin', Fuji Noodles, and a Bocca Lupo Italian restaurant. As the Wellen Park development grows, so will the ancillary offerings. (Opening nearby in recent years: a Costco, Ace Hardware, and a small downtown Wellen development.) But as of now, don't expect to spend much time in the general area of the ballpark before or after a game. North Port is still a growing area—Wellen Park now has 7,500 homes but is expected to grow beyond 22,000 residences by the time all is said and done—and once the population arrives, expect the services and entertainment to follow in the area.

Since you're coming to Florida to watch baseball, you'll be interested in the other training camps in the area. Port Charlotte (Tampa Bay Rays) is a very short drive away—just 12.5 miles. Both Sarasota (Baltimore Orioles) and Bradenton (Pittsburgh Pirates) are an easy drive, as are the teams training in Fort Myers. A longer trip, but still very doable, could involve a drive to Tampa Bay, where several teams train: Tampa (New York Yankees), Clearwater (Philadelphia Phillies), and Dunedin (Toronto Blue Jays).

FLYING IN

The most convenient airport will be Sarasota-Bradenton International Airport, just 35 miles away. (Southwest Florida International Airport is farther afield, on the southeast side of Fort Myers.) We find it to be small enough to be convenient but large enough to be accessible from other larger markets. Delta flies several times daily from Atlanta (including a handy morning flight that arrives around 10 a.m., giving you plenty of time to fly in for an afternoon game), which means you are probably a non-stop or one stop from your home market. Other airlines serving Sarasota-Bradenton International Airport: Air Canada, Allegiant, American, Breeze, Frontier, JetBlue, Southwest, Sun Country, and United. But Sarasota-Bradenton International Airport is small enough where the rental cars sit in a parking lot right outside the airport, making it easy to pick up a vehicle quickly. *6000 Airport Circle, Sarasota; 941/359-2770; srq-airport.com.*

If flying in and out of Sarasota-Bradenton International Airport is not convenient (and it may not be: flights there tend to be a little pricier and many airlines do not offer daily service), your best bets are Southwest Florida International Airport in Fort Myers, which has boomed in recent years, and Tampa International Airport. Both are a little farther afield, but both are served by many more flights on a daily basis than is Sarasota-Bradenton International.

SPRING TRAINING HISTORY: ATLANTA BRAVES

The Atlanta Braves have trained at the following sites since the team's entry in the National League as the Boston Beaneaters: Norfolk, Va. (1901); Thomasville, Ga. (1902-1904, 1907); Charleston, S.C. (1905); Jacksonville (1906); Augusta, Ga. (1908-1912); Athens, Ga. (1913); Macon, Ga. (1914-1915); Miami (1916-1918), Columbus, Ga. (1919-1920); Galveston, Texas (1921); St. Petersburg (1922-1937); Bradenton (1938-1940, 1948-1962); San Antonio (1941); Sanford, Fla. (1942); Wallingford, Ct. (1943-1944); Washington, D.C. (1945); Fort Lauderdale (1946-1947); West Palm Beach (1963-1997); Orlando (1998-2019); and North Port (2019-present).

ED SMITH STADIUM / BALTIMORE ORIOLES

QUICK FACTS

- **Capacity**: 7,484, plus berm and SRO seating
- **Year Opened**: 1989; renovated in 2011
- **Dimensions**: 333L, 400C, 339R
- **Ticket Line**: 941/893-6312
- **Local Airport**: Sarasota
- **Dugout Location**: First-base side
- **Workouts**: 9:30 a.m.
- **Pregame Schedule**: Gates open two hours before game time. Orioles infield, 10-10:10 a.m.; Orioles batting practice, 10:15-11:30 a.m.; visitors batting practice, 11:30 a.m.-12:30 p.m.; visitors infield, 12:30-12:40 p.m. Add five hours to each figure for a 6:05 p.m. game.
- **Address**: 2700 12th St., Sarasota, FL 34237
- **Directions**: From North: Exit I-75 at University Parkway (Exit 213). Go west on University to Tuttle Avenue. Turn left onto Tuttle. Ed Smith Stadium will be located on your right at the intersection of Tuttle and 12th Street. From South: Exit I-75 at Fruitville Road (Exit 210). Go west on Fruitville to Tuttle Avenue. Turn right onto Tuttle. Ed Smith Stadium will be located on your left at the intersection of Tuttle and 12th Street.

THE ORIOLES IN SARASOTA: AN INSTITUTION

There's no mistaking Sarasota's Ed Smith Stadium as anything other than the spring home of the Baltimore Orioles, and a game there still stands out as a noteworthy Grapefruit League event. Designed with loving attention to detail, ranging from the atrium baseball-bat chandelier in the grand entry to the oriole weathervane, a spring game at Ed Smith Stadium is a particularly fulfilling trek for an Orioles fan and a great experience for anyone else.

Go back to 2009, when the Baltimore Orioles were looking for a new spring home after deciding a mouldering Fort Lauderdale Stadium wasn't in the team's future. The city of Sarasota, meanwhile, was looking for a tenant to replace the Cincinnati Reds at Ed Smith Stadium. At that time, Ed Smith Stadium was a very, very basic facility, with plenty of exposed concrete and many food concessions located outside the ballpark walls along the sidewalk. It was a limited ballpark on a small footprint—literally built on a dump, no less.

But then something amazing happened: people with vision joined forces to not only bring the Orioles to Sarasota, but did it in such a manner that ballpark whiz Janet Marie Smith, then in the employ of the Orioles, could oversee a renovation that turned one of the Grapefruit League's most depressing facilities into a grand celebration of Sarasota, spring training, and Florida. The Orioles have maintained that enthusiasm with constant upgrades to Ed Smith Stadium, whether it be a concessions upgrade or some new form of Orioles memorabilia on display.

The renovation kept the good parts of Ed Smith Stadium and overhauled the weaknesses. On the plus side, Ed Smith Stadium has always been a very intimate ballpark. You're never really far from any action as there's little foul territory, so the first few rows are very close to the action. The whole complex occupies a relatively small footprint in Sarasota, so it's easy to get around, with easy access to players and facilities.

The renovation put a shiny new Spanish Mediterranean veneer over the concrete bones of Ed Smith Stadium, transforming Ed Smith's brutalism into a very nice Florida-themed design featuring light stucco and decorative clay and tile elements. In many ways, it's the opposite of the team's regular-season home, Oriole Park at Camden Yards: while Oriole Park is retro with plenty of exposed steel beams and brickwork, Ed Smith Stadium is Florida to its core, with a design that perfectly fits into Sarasota.

Today Ed Smith Stadium features a second-level concourse, dramatic entryway (complete with that unique overhead bat-and-ball chandelier), extended canopy, berm seating, expanded clubhouses, picnic area, and 7,100 seats reclaimed from Oriole Park at Camden Yards. The 2011 renovation cost $31 million, and that included upgrades to the adjacent Sarasota Sports Complex—featuring four-and-a-half practice fields and 35,000 square feet of clubhouses and office space—as well as renovations to the run-down facilities at the minor-league Buck O'Neil complex at Twin Lakes Park (6700 Clark Road). The issue of the playing fields and clubhouse conditions at Twin Lakes Park was a contentious one before renovations; other MLB teams refused to send their minor-league squads there for spring-training games, so a renovation of the entire facility was needed.

INSIDER'S TIP
The minor-league complex was named for one of the great men in baseball, Sarasota native Buck O'Neil, who spent his

youth working in area celery fields before embarking on a baseball career that included stops in the Negro Leagues and the distinction as the first African-American coach in MLB after joining the Chicago Cubs staff in 1962. He was also one of the classiest men ever to don a pro-baseball uniform.

Despite occupying a very small footprint, it's a delight to wander Ed Smith Stadium. There are two main entrances to the ballpark—one down the third-base line, nearest the closest parking lots, and one behind home plate—and we'd recommend entering from behind home plate to get the full effect, even if it means walking the perimeter of the ballpark. That entrance is a grand statement, with team store on the left, deli restaurant on the right, and an Orioles team tribute in front of you. You'll head to your seats after walking through a covered concourse.

You can either take your seat in the grandstand or head to the Left Field Pavilion to an open seating area with its own food and beer service. Seating there truly exemplifies the Florida baseball experience: you can relax and take in the game in a low-key atmosphere with access to a nearby bar. Ed Smith Stadium went from being a blah experience to a great example of Sarasota finery.

BALLPARK HISTORY

Ed Smith Stadium opened in 1989 as the spring-training home of the Chicago White Sox. When the ChiSox moved spring operations to Arizona, the Reds moved to Ed Smith Stadium from Plant City in 1998 and stayed through the 2009 season. The Baltimore Orioles began training there in 2010.

Major-league teams have trained in Sarasota since 1924. The New York Giants, Boston Red Sox, and Chicago White Sox played there in past spring-training camps. Most of those teams trained at downtown's Payne Park (referring both to the ballpark and the park surrounding it), which opened in 1924 and was torn down in 1990. The White Sox trained at Payne Park before moving to Ed Smith Stadium; the Red Sox trained there between 1933 and 1942 and again after World War II between 1946 and 1958. There still is Payne Park near downtown Sarasota, but there's no baseball diamond or any remnants of the old ballpark past a historical marker where the

ballpark stood. (Set your GPS for 2001 Adams Lane if you want to
visit the marker.)

The New York Giants' arrival in Sarasota in spring training 1924
was noteworthy. The team had won three pennants and two World
Series in the three prior seasons, cultivating a national following
that extended far from the Polo Grounds. Entertainer John Ringling
(who we'll discuss later) was friends with John J. McGraw, the
Giants' colorful manager, and that connection helped land spring
training for Sarasota. Those were boom times for Florida real estate,
and McGraw decided to dabble with other local investors on a new
development, Pennant Park. The plan was for baseball-centric housing, with streets named for famous players. But a 1926 hurricane
and a subsequent collapse of the Florida real-estate market killed
those plans—and led the Giants to shift spring training away from
Sarasota, as McGraw did not want to face his angry investors.

THE SPRING-TRAINING BALLPARK EXPERIENCE

WHERE TO SIT

The renovation of Ed Smith Stadium dramatically upgraded seating
options at the ballpark: the recycled Oriole Park seats are in much
better shape than the old weather-battered blue seats, and the
changes acknowledged the fact that many fans like wandering the
ballpark during a game. At an Orioles game, you have access to
many different types of seating at many different price points.

For starters: there are plenty of areas in the ballpark where you
can just hang out on a bar stool at a drink rail and watch the action.
The Left Field Pavilion—Sections 127, 128, and 129—consists of four
tiers of tables flanked by five rows of drink rails. (Bring your
sunglasses; you'll be dealing with the sun during part of a day
game.) Similarly, the second-level concourse features drink rails and
space to hang out with friends; it's a group area on the cheap, with
some shade to boot.

If being near the Orioles' dugout is important, buy tickets in
Sections 101-105 or 201-205. The dugout is on the first-base side of
the diamond, and these are the sections immediately adjacent.

If you desire shade and don't want to spring for the lounge seating, go for the back eight rows of the upper grandstand on the first-base side. As the game progresses, the shade will creep into the rest of the bowl seating. Just be warned that when compared to newer spring-training facilities, there's a shortage of shaded seating at Ed Smith Stadium. Bring in that tube of sunscreen or lather up in the parking lot.

CONCESSIONS

The Orioles did a nice job of bringing the flavors of Maryland to Sarasota. Over the years Ed Smith Stadium was not known as a place with high-level grub—highlights were Big Red Smokies and Marge's Hamburgers, with any decent food disappearing from the premises during the final days of the Reds.

But the Orioles improved concessions as part of the ballpark updates. The Birdland Concessions stands in the now-covered concourse sell the usual ballpark fare as well as angus-beef hot dogs, fried shrimp, and Maryland delicacies like crabcake sandwiches. Café 54, located behind home plate, is a sit-down area selling sandwiches (featuring Boar's Head meats), paninis, fish and chips, flatbreads, and wraps. The grill near the Left Field Pavilion is your place for meat: brats, bison burgers, pit-beef sandwiches, and steak sandwiches. (If you are not a meat lover, don't worry: other stands offer vegan hot dogs and vegan burgers.) We'd recommend Boog's BBQ, a mainstay at Oriole Park, as well as the pit beef, the Maryland version of barbeque: it's top roast grilled over charcoal, thinly sliced, and served medium rare. And you can find a notable selection of craft beers at different stands in the concourse.

Speaking of BBQ: Boog's BBQ first opened on Eutaw Street at Baltimore's Camden Yards on Opening Day in 1992. A two-time World Series Champion (1966 and 1970) and four-time All-Star, Boog Powell played 14 seasons with the Orioles. He won the 1970 American league MVP and ranks third in Orioles history in home runs (303), fourth in RBI (1,063), and fifth in games played (1,763) and total bases (2,748).

Powell's son, J.W. Powell, operates the Left Field Pavilion stand at Ed Smith Stadium.

INSIDER'S TIP

The Orioles follow the standard limitations when it comes to what can be brought into the ballpark: food in clear baggies, sealed plastic bottles of water, and smaller bags/backpacks. No glass or aluminum bottles.

AUTOGRAPHS

The Orioles enter the ballpark from a right-field clubhouse. Your best bet is to set up shop between Sections 101 and 105 to snare players before the game. In general, the Orioles are not known for signing a lot of autographs. If you're looking to catch the attention of a visiting player, stake out a spot next to the third-base dugout.

INSIDER'S TIP

If you come out to the ballpark for practices, be warned the Orioles do not usually train at Ed Smith Stadium, but rather at the four practice fields comprising the Sarasota Sports Complex to the east of the ballpark. Minor leaguers train and play scheduled games at Buck O'Neil Baseball Complex at Twin Lakes Park (6700 Clark Road). It's named for Sarasota native O'Neil, the former Negro Leagues player who became the first African-American Major League coach during his time with the Chicago Cubs. He later became an eloquent ambassador for the game after appearing on Ken Burns' *Baseball* documentary series.

PARKING

There's plenty of parking in nearby lots for $12 per car; the city runs the largest one across from the ballpark, and most parking attendants in the area will point you to an entrance on the north side of 12th Street. You can also try to score a free spot in the surrounding neighborhood, but be warned: you will be towed from parking lots of local businesses.

As there are only two main entrances to the ballpark (one at home plate, the other past the left-field corner), you don't need to worry much about where you park, as most of the spots are oriented toward those two entrances.

SELFIE SPOTS

The rotunda entrance, featuring a bat-and-ball chandelier, is a popular spot for selfies, as is the left-field patio. So is the oversize Oriole bobblehead, located down the right-field line.

IF YOU GO

WHERE TO STAY

There's really nothing within walking distance of Ed Smith Stadium, but since the ballpark is less than two miles away from Sarasota-Bradenton Airport and downtown Sarasota, any of the area hotels—Homewood Suites, Aloft Sarasota, Comfort Inn, Hotel Indigo, Hampton Inn—will do you fine. But you could very easily stay in Tampa or St. Pete and head down to Sarasota for the day.

WHAT TO DO

Sarasota is only 65 miles outside of Tampa-St. Pete and close to Bradenton, so you're in the midst of spring-training nirvana. Sarasota County sports two spring-training venues, with the Atlanta Braves in North Port—though, interestingly, at the opposite end of the county. Ed Smith Stadium is only 25 minutes or so from LECOM Park, spring home of the Pittsburgh Pirates, 40 minutes from Cool-Today Park, and 50 minutes from Charlotte Sports Park, spring home of the Tampa Bay Rays. Other spring-training cities within easy driving distance of Sarasota include Lakeland (Detroit Tigers), Tampa (New York Yankees), Clearwater (Philadelphia Phillies), and Dunedin (Toronto Blue Jays). In addition, the Baltimore Orioles' minor leaguers practice at Buck O'Neil Baseball Complex at Twin Lakes Park (6700 Clark Road, Sarasota; about 11 miles from Ed Smith Stadium). You can expect your spring training trip to be filled with lots of baseball in the Tampa/St. Pete area.

Farther to the south you'll find two additional teams training in the greater Fort Myers area: the Minnesota Twins and Boston Red Sox.

Outside of baseball spring training and a generally elevated social scene, Sarasota is also known as the former winter home of the Ringling Bros. and Barnum & Bailey Circus and one of its founders, John Ringling. Ringling and his brothers grew up in Baraboo, Wisconsin, and began their own small circus in 1884, charging a penny per performance. They were successful, and by 1907 they were in position to buy the Barnum & Bailey Circus, creating an entertainment giant. In 1927, Ringling moved the circus's winter headquarters down to Sarasota and set up his personal winter base there as well. Despite his roots in the circus—a solidly lower- and middle-class entertainment—Ringling saw himself as a patron of the arts and spent the millions generated by his circus on a collection of European masterworks and a palatial Sarasota winter estate. Overspent, actually: during the Great Depression, Ringling lost control of the circus to creditors, although his nephew John Ringling North continued to run the circus until 1967. After that, the circus went through a series of owners and moved away from a tent show to an arena spectacle, eliminating the need for colorful wagons and parades to announce the presence of the circus in town. The circus shut down entirely in 2017, marking the end of an era, but emerged in 2023 as a scaled-down arena event sans performing animals.

Upon Ringling's death, his estate passed through to the state of Florida, which set up The Ringling. It encompasses four distinct facilities, as well as an extensive education center:

- The Ringling Museum of Art, which features Ringling's outstanding collection of 17th-century Baroque paintings, including pieces by Rubens, Van Dyck, and Velazquez. The museum is housed in the largest building on the estate.
- The Ringling Circus Museum, which features surprisingly little memorabilia from what was arguably the most famous and noteworthy circus in America. (In his bequest leaving the estate to Florida, Ringling did not include any circus memorabilia and clearly wanted his legacy to be his extensive art collection.) Kids expecting to be wowed with death-defying feats and marvelous circus acts may be a little disappointed.
- Cà d'Zan Mansion, the palatial winter home of John and Mable Ringling. The Venetian Gothic mansion was

designed to be reminiscent of two of Mable Ringling's favorite hotels and overlooks Sarasota Bay. The residence, with 32 rooms and 15 baths, is an opulent mix of Barcelona terra cotta, English veined marble, and Flemish tapestries. The house can be accessed only via a scheduled tour.

- The Historic Asolo Theater was built in Italy in 1798, deconstructed in the 1940s and then transported to Sarasota, reopening after a renovation in 2006.

When there, take the time to walk the Bayfront Gardens, comprising some 66 acres of tropical fauna imported from around the world. It also features plenty of highly decorative spaces.

The Ringling, 5401 Bay Shore Rd., Sarasota; 941/359-5700; ringling.org. Adults, $30; students/children 6-17, $5; children under 6, free. Additional costs for access to Cà d'Zan Mansion and guided tours.

For those who don't want to mess with art during spring training, there's another Sarasota museum worth a visit: the Sarasota Classic Car Museum, located (conveniently) across the street from The Ringling. The collection features over 100 automobiles, including John Lennon's Mercedes Roadster, Paul McCartney's Mini Cooper, the original Batmobile, and a rare Cadillac station wagon. *Sarasota Classic Car Museum, 5500 N. Tamiami Tr., Sarasota; 941/355-6228; sarasotacarmuseum.org. Adults, $19; seniors, $17; military, $14; children (6-12), $12; under 6, free.* (Note that as of this writing the museum was temporariy closed until a move to a new location. Check the website closer to your trip for updates.)

Also next to The Ringling: the Powel Crosley Estate. In his time, Powel Crosley Jr. was one of America's most famous inventors and innovators, bringing cheap radios and auto parts to the masses. As owner of the Cincinnati Reds, he instituted regularly scheduled radio broadcasts on his WKRC-AM station and, with the aid of Westinghouse, brought night games to Major League Baseball. Redland Field was renamed to Crosley Field as a branding move when he bought the Reds. Along the way, he also created the first line of compact cars, launched daytime soap operas to promote products, and formed the first radio superstation, WLW, reaching receivers from coast to coast. In Sarasota, he built Seagate in 1929-30, a 11,000-square-foot, 21-room, 10-bedroom winter retreat. As with everything connected with Crosley, innovation was involved: Seagate was built using a steel frame clad with stone, rather than a wood frame—the better for the estate to survive fires and hurricanes. Crosley sold the estate in 1948, and in 1991 it was purchased by the state of Florida. Today, the Powel Crosley Estate is an event center, used for meetings, weddings, and holiday parties. It's not open to the public on a daily basis, but open houses are offered throughout the year, and there's usually an open house in February or March. *Powel Crosley Estate, 8374 N. Tamiami Tr., Sarasota; 941/729-9177;* **bradentongulfislands.com/crosley-estate***.*

For those from a land-locked clime, a visit to an aquarium is a must during a Florida trip. In Sarasota, the appropriate visit would be the Mote Marine Laboratory, which combines a research mission with public exhibits on marine life, including a shark tank and a touch tank where both kids and grownups can handle mollusks, crabs, and rays. *Mote Marine Laboratory, 1600 Ken Thompson Parkway, Sarasota; 941/388-4441;* **mote.org***. Adults, $29; children (3-12), $21.*

The Sarasota Jungle Gardens began life as an impenetrable swamp and then developed in the 1930s into a tropical paradise. To do so, its owners imported a slew of tropical trees, plants, and flowers from around the world. (You probably couldn't get away with such an extensive import of non-native foliage today.) Many of these plants and trees are still thriving: you can wander through the grounds and find exotic species like the Australian Nut Tree, a Bunya Bunya Tree, Banana Trees, and a Peruvian Apple Cactus. Individual habitats feature birds of prey, reptiles, and birds of the rainforest. *Sarasota Jungle Gardens, 3701 Bay Shore Rd., Sarasota; 941/355-5305;* **sarasotajunglegardens.com***. Adults, $24.99; children (4-16), $14.99.*

And, of course, you can just wander around the countryside: Sarasota County boasts 35 miles of beaches and six barrier islands. Siesta Key combines scenic beaches, fine dining, and family activities into one destination. Siesta Beach is a classic white beach, made up of 99 percent pure quartz, while Turner Beach is well-regarded by shell collectors.

SARASOTA RESTAURANTS

Sarasota is very artsy, very old money, and the atmosphere translates into a laid-back nightlife. In terms of restaurants, Sarasota is an oasis when it comes to good restaurants in Florida; really, there are great dining establishments along the Gulf Coast, and they almost all seem to be clustered in Sarasota. In fact, four are located in the aptly named Grand Slam Plaza strip mall right across the street from the ballpark.

- One of Sarasota's best restaurants is Antoine's (*1100 N. Tuttle Av., Sarasota; 941/331-1400; antoinessarasota.com*), featuring French-based fine dining, with an emphasis on seafood. That means mussels in garlic sauce and scallops. Don't let the strip-mall location fool you.
- Also in the Grand Slam Plaza: El Patio Latino, which specializes in Peruvian cuisine focused on lamb, chicken, beef, and fish. With outposts in Barcelona, Spain, and Lima, Peru, El Patio Latino offers a very cosmopolitan experience. Again, don't let the strip-mall location fool you. *El Patio Latino, 1100 N. Tuttle Av., Suite 5, Sarasota; 941/955-5093; elpatiolatino.com.*
- Also in the Grand Slam Plaza: Mariscos Azteca, a Mexican restaurant specializing in fresh seafood dishes like ceviche and shrimp. *Mariscos Azteca, 1100 N. Tuttle Av., Suite 8, Sarasota; 941/210-3873; mariscosazteca.com.*
- Finally, you have one last noteworthy offering in the Grand Slam Plaza: Siam Gulf, specializing in Thai and Japanese cuisine. We always recommend grabbing a bite or three as the ballpark, especially at Ed Smith Stadium, but it's tempting to take in an inexpensive lunch featuring stir fry or sushi rolls. *Siam Gulf, 1100 N. Tuttle Av., Suite 1, Sarasota; 941/312-4605; siamgulfsarasota.com.*

We'd also recommend these places a little farther afield than across the street from the ballpark.

If all you crave is a beer, a mile east of the ballpark is The Shamrock, near downtown Sarasota. There's a wide selection of beers on tap, ranging from Irish stouts and lagers to local microbrews, but be warned that a) it's a cash-only bar and b) it's a small neighborhood joint and c) no WiFi and d) the patrons don't care about baseball or March Madness basketball. This is a soccer hangout, but if you can live with that, it's a good place to relax after an afternoon in the sun. It's also known for its St. Patrick's Day festivities. *The Shamrock, 2257 Ringling Blvd., Sarasota; 941/952-1730.*

Marina Jack Dining Room, on the downtown waterfront, features several restaurants and lounges specializing in (what else?) seafood. A salt-water aquarium will entertain the kids, while the adults will enjoy the late-night atmosphere of the Deep Six Lounge. *Marina Jack, 2 Marina Plaza, Sarasota; 941/365-4232; **marinajacks.com**.*

One unassuming spot in downtown Sarasota is worth a stop: Owen's Fish Camp (*516 Burns Court, Sarasota; 941/951-6936; **owensfishcamp.com***). At Owen's Fish Camp, stick with whatever is the freshest; we've had the fish camp basket and can recommend it, but there's usually something good to find among the catches of the day (the sea scallops are always a safe bet). The sides do shine: black-eyed peas and sausage, grits, and collard greens are all tasty.

Close by: Made Restaurant (*1990 Main St., Sarasota; 941/953-2900; **maderestaurant.com***), featuring local/Southern comfort cuisine. Yeah, we're talking meat loaf, tater tots, and the inevitable fried chicken. But it's always a good day when there's good fried chicken for dinner. Also downtown: Boca-Sarasota (*19 S. Lemon Av., Sarasota; 941/256-3565; **bocasarasota.com***), with a farm-to-table menu that stresses local offerings in season.

Also close by downtown, but technically in Longboat Key and worth the drive: Dry Dock Waterfront Grill (*412 Gulf of Mexico Dr., Longboat Key; 941/383-0102; **drydockwaterfrontgrill.com***) and its waterfront views. There are the inevitable grouper bites on the menu, but there's a much wider selection of local specialties as well. Ask to sit close to a window on the second story.

For something more upscale, Peruvian ceviche is the highlight menu item at the Selva Grill (*1345 Main St., Sarasota; 941/362-4427; **selvagrill.com***). Ceviche—raw fish, marinated in citrus juice and seasonings—is the perfect item for a seaside restaurant, and the Selva Grill is renowned for its many nightly selections.

Finally, one more seafood restaurant of note: the Crab & Fin, which features fish and caviar from around the world. It's also worth a drive because of its location: St. Armands Circle, located on the island of Lido Key and relatively close to the ballpark. St. Armands Circle was originally planned by John Ringling to be a world-class tourist destination, and although he died before the project was launched, St. Armands Circle has developed into an attractive mix of upscale restaurants, shops, and hotels. True, it is touristy—Tommy Bahama has an outpost here—but you are a tourist during spring-training season, after all. *Crab & Fin, 420 St. Armands Circle, Sarasota; 941/388-3964; crabfinrestaurant.com*). Some solid St. Armands Circle alternatives: Shore (*465 John Ringling Blvd., Suite 200, Sarasota; 941/296-0301; dineshore.com*), within the Shore store, and Speaks Clam Bar (*29 N. Boulevard of Presidents, Sarasota; 941/232-7633; speaksclambar.com*).

Sarasota has evolved into a brewpub nirvana. Our favorite: Big Top Brewing Co. (*975 Cattlemen Rd., Sarasota; 941/371-2939; bigtopbrewing.com*), where a circus theme fits in with Sarasota history. That means beers like Hazy Sky Wire, and Conch Republic Key Lime, along with a surprisingly tasty Hawaiian Lion Porter. Don't let the strip-mall location fool you: Brew Life Brewing (*5767 S. Beneva Rd., Sarasota; 941/952-3831; brewlifebrewing.com*) is a top-notch microbrewery utilizing many unusual ingredients.

FLYING IN

The most convenient place to fly in will be Sarasota-Bradenton International Airport. We find it to be small enough to be convenient but large enough to be accessible from other larger markets. Southwest flies direct from Baltimore BWI, including an early morning flight arriving in Sarasota around 10 a.m., giving you plenty of time to hit the ballpark for an afternoon game. (If you just want to make a day of it, there's a 7:25 p.m. nonstop back to Baltimore BWI on Southwest as well.) Delta flies daily from Atlanta, which means you are probably a non-stop or one stop from your home market. Other airlines serving Sarasota-Bradenton International Airport: Air Canada, Allegiant, American, Breeze, Elite, Frontier, JetBlue, Southwest, Sun Country, and United. But Sarasota-Bradenton International Airport is small enough where the rental cars sit in a parking lot right outside the airport, making it easy to pick up a vehicle quickly. *6000 Airport Circle, Sarasota; 941/359-2770; srqairport.com.*

If flying in and out of Sarasota-Bradenton International Airport is not convenient (and it may not be: flights there tend to be a little pricier and many airlines do not offer daily service), your best bets are Southwest Florida International Airport in Fort Myers, which has boomed in recent years, and Tampa International Airport. Both are a little farther afield, but both are served by many more flights on a daily basis than is Sarasota-Bradenton International.

SPRING TRAINING HISTORY: BALTIMORE ORIOLES

The Baltimore Orioles have trained at the following sites (including their years as the St. Louis Browns): St. Louis (1901); French Lick, Ind. (1902); Baton Rouge (1903); Corsicana, Texas (1904); Dallas (1905-1906); San Antonio (1907, 1919, 1937-1941); Shreveport (1908, 1918); Houston (1909-1910); Hot Springs, Ark. (1911); Montgomery, Ala. (1912); Waco (1913); St. Petersburg (1914); Houston (1915); Palestine, Texas (1916-1917); Taylor, Ala. (1920); Bogalusa, Ala. (1921); Mobile, Ala. (1922-1924); Tarpon Springs, Fla. (1925-1927); West Palm Beach (1928-1936); Deland, Fla. (1942); Cape Girardeau, Mo. (1943-1945); Anaheim (1946); Miami (1947); San Bernardino, Cal. (1948, 1953); Burbank, Cal. (1949-1952); Yuma, Az. (1954); Daytona Beach, Fla. (1955); Scottsdale (1956-1958); Miami (1959-1990); Sarasota (1989-1991); St. Petersburg (1992-1995); Fort Lauderdale (1996-2009); and Sarasota (2010-present)

LECOM PARK / PITTSBURGH PIRATES

QUICK FACTS

- **Capacity**: 8,500
- **Year Opened**: 1923; rebuilt after World War II, renovated in 1993 and 2013
- **Dimensions**: 335L, 370LC, 400C, 370RC, 335R
- **Tickets Line**: 877/893-2827
- **Local Airport**: Sarasota
- **Dugout Location**: First-base side
- **Practice Schedule**: When pitchers and catchers report, the team trains at Pirate City, located about five miles away from LECOM Park at 1701 27th St. E. (Roberto Clemente Memorial Drive), with morning workouts beginning at 9:30 a.m. daily.
- **Pregame Schedule**: Gates open two hours before game time. Pirates batting practice, through 11:15 a.m.; visitors batting practice, 11:15 a.m.-12:15 p.m.; Pirates infield, 12:15-12:25 p.m.; visitors infield, 12:25-12:35 p.m.; grounds crew, 12:35-1 p.m. Add six hours for a 7:05 p.m. game.
- **Address**: 1611 9th St. W., Bradenton, FL 34205
- **Directions**: LECOM Park is on the corner of 17th Avenue West and 9th Street West. From St. Petersburg: Go over Skyway Bridge to Exit 5 (19 South); continue on 41 South.

Make a right turn on 17th Avenue West; continue to
LECOM Park. From Sarasota: Take Route 41 North to
Cortez Road, then go straight on Business 41 and turn
right onto 17th Avenue West. From I-75: Exit at Route 64;
go west on Route 64 to Ninth Street West; turn left to
ballpark.

LECOM PARK: OLD MEETS NEW IN BRADENTON

It's the oldest spring-training location still in use, with the site
hosting MLB exhibitions since 1923. True, what's there isn't the
same facility as fans experienced in 1923—during the World War II
years, the original old ballpark was dismantled and the site used for
wartime equipment staging—but even taking that into account,
nostalgia is key to the modern LECOM Park experience.

Many old-timers remember the former McKechnie Field as the
past spring home of the Milwaukee/Atlanta Braves. That's going
back quite a ways—1968 or so—but it's not hard to envision the
greats of old taking the LECOM Park field. This is where Roberto
Clemente gracefully patrolled the outfield, where Willie Stargell
engaged the fans, and where Henry Aaron awed onlookers with his

sheer power and determination. It is the very essence of spring training: A neighborhood ballpark serving up an authentic baseball experience.

The Pirates have been training in Bradenton and playing games at LECOM Park since 1969. The original ballpark opened in 1923, and the Boston/Milwaukee Braves trained there in 1938-1940 and 1948-1962.

Let's take a short stroll down memory lane to see how much LECOM Park—and spring training—has changed over the years. In 1958, the World Champion Milwaukee Braves ventured to their spring-training grounds in Bradenton. Then known as Braves Field, the ballpark consisted of a small grandstand behind home plate (complete with elevated press box), open bleachers down the first-base line, two sections of covered seating down the left-field line, a keyhole infield, and plenty of parking on an adjacent street and field. A wooden home-run fence would have not held up well against running catches, and neither would any player running into it—remember, this was before the widespread use of padded outfield walls. A chain-link fence would have been a serious upgrade.

But, in a way, you can see the roots of today's LECOM Park in that very rudimentary Braves Field layout. LECOM Park's use of three distinct grandstand structures behind home plate hearkens back directly to the old grandstand sitting behind home plate in 1958. Today, when you attend a Pirates spring-training game, you can sit in the grandstand, think about those Braves fans taking the train from Milwaukee years ago, and marvel at how similar the experiences are.

Today's LECOM Park is the result of three major remodels, one due to weather damage and two due to the need for upgraded facilities. Over the years, the grandstands were upgraded and rebuilt, while the outfield area was totally revamped with a 360-degree concourse, outfield bar, drink rails, group areas, and new left-field covered bleacher seating. The concessions in back of the grandstand were upgraded and expanded, with plenty of places to relax with a cold one before the game. These days many fans are looking to experience the game from all sorts of ballpark angles, and today's LECOM Park provides that experience.

And, in recent years, the player experience was upgraded as

well. In 2015, a new 3,500-square-foot team workout facility was added to the LECOM Park grounds. While upgrades to the fan experience are certainly treasured by Pirates officials, the addition of the workout facility—most of which will never be seen by fans— was a big deal as well. These days teams are in the business of training players year-round, whether it be MLB players on rehab or future MLB players on the Bradenton Marauders squad needing nutritional assistance. It's an arms race when it comes to player development and attracting free agents. You can see the workout facility and the new agility field from the outfield boardwalk on the right-field side.

With these improvements, you'll want to plan a visit to Bradenton for a Pirates game. It's close enough to Tampa Bay that you can go on an impulse. However, be sure to buy your tickets in advance. In the past the Pirates were not a hot spring-training draw, but with the ballpark renovations, you see far more full houses than in the past, especially on weekends. Yinz gonna love it.

INSIDER'S TIP
This is the fifth name for the ballpark: City Park (1923–1926), Ninth Street Park (1927–1947), Braves Field (1948–1961), McKechnie Field (1962–2017), and LECOM Park (2017-present). Many fans still think of it as McKechnie Field, named for Hall of Famer and former Pirates manager Bill McKechnie, who wintered in Bradenton. LECOM stands for Lake Erie College of Osteopathic Medicine, buyer of the naming rights. The home clubhouse is now named for McKechnie.

INSIDER'S TIP
Minor-league baseball returned to McKechnie Field in 2010 when the Pirates fielded a team in the Florida State League: the Bradenton Marauders. There had not been minor-league ball at the ballpark since the Bradenton Growers played in 1926.

With all the improvements, the overall comfort level in LECOM Park is very high. Seating is divided into three basic areas. The three grandstands are totally shaded (a press box sits above the center grandstand, while canopies shade the other two): in late February it can be a little chilly at a game when a cool breeze wafts into the grandstands.

The permanent structure in back of the grandstand is built in a Florida Spanish Mediterranean style, highlighted by white stucco. The design is like most spring-training facilities: there are box seats on the field side of a wide concourse, and bleacher seats on the other side of the concourse. The Pirates sell box, reserved bleachers, and general-admission seats.

INSIDER'S TIP

Though spring-training operations have been professional-ized in recent years, the Pirates still stay close to their roots by working with the Bradenton Pirates Boosters, who work the concession stands and the front-gate turnstiles. They're also responsible for putting up flags beyond the outfield fence near the batters' eye commemorating historic land-marks in Pittsburgh Pirates history: the black flags commem-orate National League titles, the gold flags represent World Series championships, and white flags honor divisional champion teams.

The outfield seating is where the action is. LECOM Park sports a wraparound 360-degree concourse, and many fans will start in their grandstand seats before making their way to the outfield. In left field, covered bleachers are a draw, while in right field drink-rail seating, a group area, and four tops dominate the proceedings, offered on a first-come, first-served basis. The aforementioned Tiki bar provides some needed shade to fans bellying up for a bucket of beer.

Be warned the Pirates don't actually train at LECOM Park, at least not at the beginning of spring training. When pitchers and catchers report, the team trains at Pirate City, located about five miles away from LECOM Park at 1701 27th Street East (Roberto Clemente Memorial Drive), with workouts beginning at 9:30 a.m. daily. When spring-training games begin, the Pirates shift morning workouts to LECOM Park, while the minor-leaguers continue to work out at Pirate City.

Pirate City is a prototypical spring-training facility, with five playing fields and a two-level dorm. The fields are named for icons in Pirate baseball history—the Waner brothers, Pie Traynor, Honus Wagner—while the infield facility is named after Bill Mazeroski. If you really want to get close to a player, this is the place to do it. You can watch the games on the practice fields; they feature small wooden bleachers and the odd picnic table. The occasional "B" games are held here, usually at 10 a.m., as well as minor-league matchups, which usually begin at 1 p.m. And there's plenty of free parking.

THE SPRING-TRAINING BALLPARK EXPERIENCE

CONCESSIONS

When it comes to variety, some of the best dining in the Grapefruit League is at LECOM Park. Most the concessions are in back of the grandstand. Highly recommended is the jumbo hot dog: it's meaty, big, and delicious. Also recommended: orange-swirl ice cream from Mixon Farms.

The center-field Tiki bar is one of the most popular spots in the ballpark, totally filled well before the first pitch. In the past fans could find dedicated stands offer Southern Tier, Yuengling, and Leinenkugel beers, while brews from the likes of Cigar City Brewing, Goose Island, Iron City, Sam Adams, and Fat Tire could be found throughout the ballpark, including the Craft Beer Korner. (Look for new offerings this spring as well.) Better yet, stake out a shaded spot at the Yuengling plaza bar before the game and watch the fans enter the ballpark.

Several concessions stands offer a wide variety of ballpark foods, including Cracker Jack, gator bites, pork chop sandwiches, and fried fish sandwiches. (It's not easy finding Cracker Jack at ballparks these days!) Adirondack chairs lend to the laid-back environment if you're lucky enough to snare one.

INSIDER'S TIP
The food stands behind the grandstand can sport some awfully long lines. Head to center field, where several small booths offer a variety of high-end food offerings, such as

gator bytes, grouper tacos, and cheesesteaks. If you head for the outfield seating, there are plenty of other points of sale to serve you, either on the right-field side in the form of the Tiki bar or standalone booths on the left-field side.

WHERE TO SIT

As noted, there are three main seating areas between the foul poles. We'd recommend buying a ticket for a seat on the first-base side, but these tickets can be hard to snare. First, the Pirates' dugout is on the first-base side, so everyone wants to sit where there's a good view of the hometown heroes—including plenty of season-ticket holders. Second, this section is totally in the shade when the game starts. As the sun moves, more of the home-plate grandstand seating enters the shade.

There are also bleachers down each line, and while they're totally in the sun for most of the game, they're also popular with folks and families who want to spread out. Bring the sunscreen when you attend a LECOM Park game, as it's very likely you will be spending some good amount of time in the sun if sitting here.

As you will if you decide to head to right field and the drink-rail seats. Again, these seats have great views of the action—you're basically on top of the right fielder—but they go fast. If you want a respite from the sun, head to the covered left-field bleachers, which are set off from the field (a walkway runs between them and the playing field). Technically, they're sold as a separate ticket, but we crashed the shade on a crowded day and no one complained.

AUTOGRAPHS

Players sign autographs before games at an Autograph Alley down the right-field line. You can also try luring a player to the edge of the seating area before a game; the bullpens are also a good place to corner a player. (The Pirates' bullpen is down the first-base line.) Another good place for autographs, though, is Pirate City: fans have a lot of access to players there, and a more casual atmosphere means more autograph opportunities.

PARKING

There is limited $12 parking next to the ballpark, with valet parking offered for $20. We try to park at a lot maintained by the Bradenton Boys & Girls Club, accessible from West Ninth Street. A golf cart runs between the lot and LECOM Park. You'll be able to find some street parking within walking distance of the ballpark, including spots sold by locals for $10 within two blocks. Or you can park a little father afield for $5—Motorworks Brewing, which we discuss a little later, offers gameday parking for $5, well worth the cost if you plan on a brew or two before/after a game.

INSIDER'S TIP
Bradenton has revised parking rules for the adjacent Village of the Arts neighborhood in recent years, limiting parallel parking to one side of 11th, 12th, and 13th avenues. We know that parking in the Village of the Arts is a popular activity, so check the street signs carefully before leaving your car and walking to the ballpark.

SELFIE SPOTS

There's no exterior focal point for selfies. Inside, a popular spot for selfies is also one of the most popular spots in the ballpark: the right-field deck. You see a lot of selfies from there with either the grandstand or the center-field Tiki bar in the background.

IF YOU GO

WHAT TO DO OUTSIDE THE BALLPARK

Bradenton is only 65 miles outside of Tampa-St. Pete and close to Sarasota, so you're in the midst of spring-training nirvana. With the arrival of the Atlanta Braves in southern Sarasota County, you have another option of a spring-training facility 50 minutes or so away, depending on traffic. Spring-training cities that are within easy driving distance of Bradenton include Tampa (New York Yankees), Clearwater (Philadelphia Phillies), Dunedin (Toronto Blue Jays), and

Sarasota (Baltimore Orioles). You can expect your trip to spring training to be filled with lots of baseball in the area.

The area around the ballpark has changed dramatically over the last 15 years or so. There's always been an artsy vibe in the city, evidenced by the Village of the Arts (*villageofthearts.com*) directly adjoining the ballpark area. But there's now also a hipster millennial vibe, as evidenced by the rise of brewpubs and trendy restaurants. You can view both trends near the ballpark.

Across the street from LECOM Park: Magnanimous Brewing (*803 17th Av. W., Bradenton; 941/747-1970; magnanimousbrewing.com*), launched in 2022 in the old Darwin Brewing space. It's Florida, so you can enjoy outdoor seating, but be warned the place fills up quickly, especially on a game day. No food, but most nights feature food trucks.

Down the street from LECOM Park is Motorworks Brewing, a brewpub set up inside a 1920s-era automobile dealership. The old Hudson Motors dealership is now a taproom and brewery, with a 13,000-square-foot patio (billed as the largest beer patio in Florida) built around a massive oak tree. Really, you can't go wrong inside or out, and the promise of 30 craft beers always on tap is a powerful enticement. Many folks pay the $5 parking fee at Motorworks, do the 10-minute walk to the ballpark, and then head back for a beer or two after the game. Drop by for a tour; stay for a brew. *Motorworks Brewing, 1014 9th St. W., Bradenton; 941/567-6218; motorworksbrewing.com.*

In back of Motorworks Brewing is another typical Village of the Arts restaurant: Birdrock Taco Shack, housed in yet another charming cottage. You can go mainstream taco, such as carnitas tacos, or go with something out of the ordinary, like Korean BBQ short rib tacos or Peking duck tacos. It's a small space, but the patio rocks, as does the sangria. (Plan on a post-game visit; the place doesn't open until noon.) *Birdrock Taco Shack, 1213 13th Av., Bradenton; 941/545-9966; birdrocktacoshack.com.* Open for dinner just a few blocks from the ballpark is the highly rated Ortygia (*1418 13th St. W., Bradenton; 941/741-8646; ortygiarestaurant.com*), specializing in Sicilian cuisine with some Mediterranean twists.

Located in the nearby Village of the Arts: Arte Caffe, an Italian cafe and bakery in one of many lovely cottages in the area. It's charming and intimate. *Arte Caffe, 930 12th St. W., Bradenton; 941/750-9309; artecaffebradenton.com.*

One other brewery is close and definitely worth the short drive. 3 Keys Brewing & Eatery (*2505 Manatee Av. E., Bradenton; 941/218-0396; 3keysbrewing.com*) is known for its waffle sandwiches, tacos, and a wide variety of brews (sours, wheats, ales, lagers). Plan on a post-game visit; the place doesn't open until noon.

Downtown Bradenton isn't too far from the ballpark, so consider a run to O'Bricks Irish Pub and Martini Bar (*427 12th St. W., Bradenton; 941/896-8860; obricks.com*), especially if you're in Bradenton on near St. Patrick's Day. Yes, we know the aesthetics of an Irish pub (throw down another Harp!) and a martini bar (cool, baby, cool) are totally different, and at O'Bricks the Irish pub feel comes through strongest. But the food is good and the Happy Hours notable. In general, the dining offerings in downtown Bradenton are much more elevated and diverse than in past years. Oak & Stone (*1201 1st Av. W., Bradenton; 941/357-4306; oakandstone.com*) offers designer pizzas, a wide variety of craft beers, and outdoor seating overlooking the waterfront. If you're seeking a more refined dinner experience, consider Château 13 Restaurant & Wine Bar (*535 13th St. W., Bradenton; 941/226-0110; chateau-13.com*) for a great wine selection and a fixe prix menu; check the website for hours. Similarly high end is Jennings Downtown Provisions (*417 12th St. W., Bradenton; 941/896-5450*), with an emphasis on high-end wines and small plates.

Bradenton is still a smaller citrus town—home to the main Tropicana orange-juice plant—so there are not many attractions near the ballpark, as much of the surrounding area is a quaint neighborhood marketed as an arts district. Those looking to soak up some sun should head to Longboat Key and Anna Maria Island, both of which are known for their sandy beaches and relaxed atmospheres.

Bradenton is also known for its manatees. The Bishop Museum of Science and Nature features several at its Parker Manatee Aquarium, home to several manatees undergoing rehabilitation before being released back into the wild. You can view them in the specially designed 60,000-gallon aquarium. *The Bishop Museum of Science and Nature, 201 10th St. W., Bradenton; 941/746-4131; bishopscience.org. Adults, $25; seniors, $23; youth (5-17), $16; children (0-5), free.*

Alas, one of our favorite spring-training destinations is gone: the Mixon Fruit Farms retail store is closed. No more orange swirl after a Pirate City workout.

WHERE TO STAY

Bradenton is in the southern portion of Tampa Bay, so you could stay anywhere in the Bay and have easy access to the ballpark. Don't bother trying to stay at the team hotel: the Pirates don't have one.

If you decide to stay in Bradenton, there are four hotels within a few miles of the ballpark:

- Hampton Inn & Suites Downtown Historic District, 309 10th St W., Bradenton; 941/746-9400; *hilton.com*.
- SpringHill Suites, 102 12th St. W., Bradenton; 941/226-2200; *marriott.com*.
- Courtyard by Marriott Bradenton Sarasota/Riverfront, 100 Riverfront Dr. W., Bradenton; 941/747-3727; *marriott.com*.
- Bradenton-Days Inn, 3506 1st St. W., Bradenton; 941/746-1141; *wyndhamhotels.com*.

There are also some motels within walking distance of the ballpark. We would not recommend them.

FLYING IN

The most convenient airport will be Sarasota-Bradenton International Airport. We find it to be small enough to be convenient but large enough to be accessible from other larger markets. Delta flies daily from Atlanta, which means you are probably a non-stop or one stop from your home market. Other airlines serving Sarasota-Bradenton International Airport: Air Canada, Allegiant (flying direct from Pittsburgh, Harrisburg, Philadelphia, and Allentown), American, Breeze, Delta, Frontier, JetBlue, Sun Country, and United. Sarasota-Bradenton International Airport is small enough where the rental cars sit in a parking lot right outside the airport, making it easy to pick up a vehicle quickly. *Sarasota-*

Bradenton International Airport, 6000 Airport Circle, Sarasota; flysrq.com.

The largest airport in the region is Tampa International Airport, located on the north side of the bay opposite Bradenton. Many will find it more convenient to fly into this much larger airport.

SPRING TRAINING HISTORY: PITTSBURGH PIRATES

The Pirates have been training in Bradenton and playing games at LECOM Park since 1969. Other spring-training bases: Selma, Ala. (1900); Thomasville, Ga. (1900); Hot Springs, Ark. (1901-14; 1920-1923); Dawson Springs, Ky. (1915-17); Jacksonville, Fl. (1918); Birmingham, Ala. (1919); Paso Robles, Cal. (1924-34); San Bernardino, Cal. (1935; 1937-1942; 1946; 1949-52); San Antonio (1936); Muncie, Ind. (1943-45); Miami Beach, Fla. (1947); Hollywood, Cal. (1948); Havana, Cuba (1953); Fort Pierce, Fla. (1954); Fort Myers (1955-1968); Bradenton (1969-present). The Bradenton Growers of the Florida State League played at McKechnie Field in the 1923, 1924, and 1926 seasons.

TAMPA / ST. PETERSBURG

The Tampa/St. Pete area was one of the first in the nation to wholeheartedly embrace spring training: from Tarpon Springs to the north and Bradenton to the south, Tampa Bay cities have played host to dozens of teams in February and March for over a hundred years. For cities in the greater Tampa Bay region, spring training was an extension of what the region did well—promote unique tourism in a backwoods kind of way. Spring-training news in the 1920s and 1930s was equal parts baseball and kitsch, a time when legendary sportswriter Damon Runyon would spend more time chronicling the habits of a newly acquired alligator than the home-run exploits of Babe Ruth—much to the chagrin of Ruth.

Today's Tampa Bay bears little resemblance to the sleepy area originally hosting spring training for virtually every older MLB franchise at some point, and the ballparks are considerably more polished and professional than the rickety, wooden grandstands once seating fans looking for the latest spring phenom. Five teams play their spring games in the Tampa Bay area: New York Yankees (Tampa), Toronto (Dunedin), Philadelphia (Clearwater), and Detroit (Lakeland).

For today's baseball fans, Tampa Bay is still spring-training nirvana. Because of the high concentration of teams in the area (and many more in the region), you could take in a game a day and merely scratch the surface of spring training Tampa Bay style. And with teams like the New York Yankees and Philadelphia Phillies scheduling several night games each spring, it's easy enough to put together your own day-night doubleheaders, especially if you're willing to check out a college game in Tampa.

Of course, one cannot live on hot dogs and Single-A-bound rookies for long, and at some point, you'll need to venture past the ballpark and your hotel room and take in the local sights. As a major metropolitan area, Tampa/St. Pete has a lot to offer.

First, an explanation of the geography of the area. Greater Tampa Bay is really a set of cities, with Tampa to the northeast and St. Petersburg to the southwest. Tampa and St. Pete are the largest cities in the area and contain the vast majority of attractions. Clearwater and Dunedin are in the northwest quadrant of the Bay and comprise a fast-growing area. Lakeland, while not truly part of the Tampa-St. Pete metro area, is close enough to make for a short drive to and from the big city, though it certainly stands on its own as a separate entity. Similarly, Bradenton is a short drive from Clearwater and St. Petersburg.

Though it can feel a tad sprawling at times, it's relatively easy to get around Tampa Bay: none of the ballparks are too far away from the main freeways (I-4, I-275) or the Courtney Campbell Causeway, so you should easily make it to your ballpark of choice from anywhere in the area, if you avoid rush-hour traffic.

TAMPA ATTRACTIONS

Tampa/St. Pete has turned into a business center for Florida and the southern United States, and it lacks some of the more colorful roadside attractions found in the likes of Orlando. Perhaps that's why spring training has always been popular in the area. There's little competition for the attention of fans in March: no House of Mouse on the horizon, and relatively few tourist traps. In general, the Tampa/St. Pete area has evolved into a fairly sophisticated market, and a very trendy one to boot.

There's plenty for the family to do during February and March besides taking in a ballgame. If you're bringing the kids to spring training, take them to Busch Gardens, located eight miles north of downtown Tampa. Busch Gardens is a theme park built around a zoo, various rides, and an adjacent water park. It's a large place, so plan on spending a full day there. If you've not been there in recent years, you'll be surprised by upgrades (it seems like there's a new roller coaster annually) and a new emphasis on conservation. *Busch Gardens Tampa Bay, corner of Busch Boulevard and 40th Street, Tampa; 888/800-5447; **buschgardens.com**. Adults and children, $138.99 and up, depending on date of visit and whether you buy tickets online (yes, there are huge discounts when buying in advance online, with tickets as low as $69.99).*

If you want to see African animals in a little more affordable milieu, there's ZooTampa at Lowry Park in Tampa. The zoo features animals of all sorts, ranging from local flamingos, panthers, and alligators to Indian rhinoceroses, Komodo dragons, and Angolan Colobus monkeys. *ZooTampa, 1101 W. Sligh Av., Tampa; 813/935-8552; **zootampa.org**. Adults, $47.95; children (3-11), $37.95.*

The downtown Florida Aquarium is one of the leading attractions in Tampa and the perfect place to see the wide ecological variety of Florida wildlife in a single visit. The aquarium isn't one large tank, but rather a series of habitats organized by theme: wetlands, bays and beaches, coral reef, and more. This allows you to see a greater variety of wildlife in a wide range of habitats. Freshwater and saltwater wildlife are featured as well as mammals and amphibians that live in a wetland environment, such as otters and turtles. Among the wildlife on display: American alligators, turtles, sharks, stingrays, snook, octopus, sea horses, goliath grouper, and otters. Kids will also enjoy the Explore-A-Shore outdoor play area, featuring a two-story pirate ship and water jet sprays. For an additional fee, you can tour the Bay and look for some of the 400 bottlenose dolphins inhabiting the area. *Florida Aquarium, 701 Channelside Drive, downtown Tampa; 813/273-4000; flaquarium.org. The zoo uses variable pricing depending on day of the week: Adults, $34.95 and up; seniors (60+), $29.45 and up; children (3-11), $31.20 and up.*

Speaking of downtown Tampa: it's now one of the trendiest parts of the city, along with neighboring Hyde Park. The Tampa Riverwalk area alongside the Hillsborough River is a happening spot, particularly on the north end of the Riverwalk near Water Works Park. At night, the Riverwalk is a lively mix of bars and restaurants, including some of the best in Tampa. We'd highly recommend Ulele (*1810 N. Highland Av., Tampa; 813/999-4952; ulele.com*), a restaurant/brewery next to Water Works Park. The restaurant features fresh Florida cuisine cooked on a barbacoa grill and is insanely popular, while the Ulele Spring Brewery sports a 15-barrel system offering fresh-brewed lagers and ales. Yes, the food is worth the wait (make your reservations as early as you can!), but if you are famished or have impatient kids, head to the nearby Heights Public Market at Armature Works. The Armature Works building was once the repair and storage facility for the Tampa Electric Street and Railway Company, but it's been redeveloped as a social center/food hall/coworking space for Tampa's waterfront community, exemplified by the Riverwalk. The Heights Public Market sports an open floor plan and plenty of distinct offerings, ranging from the Butcher n' Barbeque (BNB) cured and house-smoked meats to The Fold fresh pizza. There is something for everyone at the Heights Public Market, and on a lovely Florida evening, there's nothing better than a cocktail and a bite on an outside patio. *Heights Public Market, Armature Works, 1910 N. Ola Av., Tampa; 813/250-3725; armatureworks.com.* A few blocks away is the Hidden Springs Ale Works, known for producing beers with some extreme and unusual flavors, such as a cheesecake-inspired sour ale, vanilla stout, and pineapple upside down cake. It's a small space in a nondescript building, but it's a great casual neighborhood spot. *Hidden Springs Ale Works, 1631 N. Franklin St., Tampa; 813/226-2739; hiddenspringsaleworks.com.*

Those more in a mood to party will want to head to Ybor City,

Tampa's Latin Quarter. Once home to numerous cigar factories, Ybor City is now a shopping and entertainment oasis. Located on 7th Avenue East between 15th and 20th streets, Ybor City's larger buildings can be seen from the freeway and the area is well-marked on the freeway, while a streetcar runs every 15-20 minutes from downtown Tampa. The center of the Ybor City Historic District is (appropriately enough) Centro Ybor, bounded by 7th and 8th avenues and 16th and 17th streets. It's a good place to begin your visit, and although the chains have moved into the area, there's definitely enough local color to go around when you combine Florida weird with the laidback Ybor City vibe in hotspots like Tampa Bay Brewing Company (*1600 E. 8th Av., Tampa; 813/247-1422; tbbc.beer*). It seems like everything is taken to an extreme in Ybor City, and the flavors pushed in Tampa Bay Brewing offerings, such as strawberry, pumpkin, and kumquat, are certainly extreme.

The cigar craze has peaked in most of the world, but in Tampa it's still a prime pursuit, and you can find plenty of folks—women included—puffing away on a stogie and hanging out at one of the dozen or so cigar vendors and restaurants/bars. A good place to start is Ybor City State Museum (*1818 9th Av., Tampa; 813/247-6323; ybormuseum.org*), which details the history of cigar manufacturing in the area. You can still buy hand-rolled cigars in Ybor City: there are several such vendors in the district. *Centro Ybor Visitor Information Center, 1600 E. 8th Av., Tampa; 877/9-FIESTA; ybor.org.*

Also located in Ybor City: The Tampa Baseball Museum at the Al López House. López is a Tampa and Ybor City native who spent 19 years as a catcher with several times and appeared twice in All-Star games. He then entered the managerial ranks and won pennants both with the Cleveland Indians (1954) and the Chicago White Sox (1959); his "Go-Go Sox" ended up losing in the World Series to the Dodgers. The Hall of Famer was revered in Tampa: a former spring-training ballpark used by the White Sox (and later the Reds) located at the current Raymond James Stadium site was Al López Field. The museum is housed in his childhood home and run by the Ybor City Museum Society. It's only open on Thursday, Friday, and Saturday, 10 a.m.-4 p.m., so plan ahead. *Tampa Baseball Museum at the Al López House, 2003 N. 19th St., Tampa; 813/400-2353; tampabaseballmuseum.org. $12 adults; $10 seniors and students; $6 children.*

Also located in Ybor City: Coppertail Brewing (*2601 E. 2nd Av.,*

Tampa; 813-247-1500; coppertailbrewing.com). At Bad Monkey (*1717 E. 7th Av., Tampa; 813/280-9971; badmonkeyybor.com*), you can combine a microbrew with a cigar while watching March Madness games on a big screen, or you can literally rent a tap and pay only for the beer you pour. But beer is not the only adult beverage in Ybor City: you'll also find wine bars and tequila bars and more.

Elsewhere in Tampa is the Cigar City Brewing brewhouse. Cigar City beers are now distributed across much of the United States, but it's still best known as a Tampa original, offering great beers like Jai Alai IPA and Maduro Brown Ale. The tasting room is open seven days a week, 11 a.m.-11 p.m., with tours offered Wednesday-Sunday. And the location can't be beat: between the airport and downtown Tampa, near Hyde Park and Steinbrenner Field. *Cigar City Brewing, 3924 W. Spruce St., Tampa; 813/348-6363; cigarcitybrewing.com*. There are also microbreweries close to the ballparks, which we cover in our Dunedin and Clearwater chapters.

Back on the local beer scene: Yuengling, with a new Draft Haus located at the old Stroh's Brewery location. No brewery tours are offered at the Yuengling Brewery, alas, but you may enjoy a visit to the new Draft Haus if you're in the USF area (more on USF baseball later). With plenty of Yuengling brews on tap (some 88 taps are available) across five bars and plenty of big screens for March Madness action, there's a little something for everyone, whether it be a traditional lager or a seasonal bock. *Yuengling Draft Haus & Kitches, 11109 N. 30th St., Tampa; 813/488-6444; yuengling.com*.

And, of course, there are the beaches. Truth is, it's a little chilly to be swimming in the ocean in February or March, but that shouldn't stop you from taking a walk on one of the many public beaches in Tampa Bay. One popular destination is Clearwater Beach, an island outside of Clearwater. It has the prototypical white beaches along with some amenities (cabanas and umbrellas for rent), as well as concessions and a slew of restaurants. We use this merely as an example and discuss it more in our Clearwater chapter; it's hard to go wrong with any beach on the Gulf side of the Tampa Bay area. *Clearwater Beach, 100 Coronado Dr., Clearwater Beach; 727/447-7600*.

Given Tampa Bay's central presence in spring-training history, there are plenty of landmarks to visit before and after games. We'll cover them throughout this section, but one is worth noting here: Al Lang Stadium, home of spring training in St. Pete from 1916 through spring 2008, when the Tampa Bay Rays ended the run with one final March at the quaint waterfront ballpark. Though a 1977 "renovation" largely replaced the charm of an old wooden grandstand with a concrete monstrosity, Al Lang Field was a must-visit for generations of spring-training aficionados. At one point the city was ready to tear down the ballpark, but it's been kept alive with minor-league soccer. We cover it in its own chapter after the end of this chapter.

TAMPA BAY HOTELS

Hotels in Tampa tend to be concentrated near the airport, in downtown, and along the waterfront on the north side of the Bay, off the Courtney Campbell Causeway (which connects Tampa and Clearwater). They also tend to pop up close to some spring-training headquarters; for instance, there are several newer hotels close to the Phillies' spring-training headquarters in Clearwater.

We'll cover specific hotel recommendations on the team pages. But if you plan on visiting multiple venues in the Tampa Bay area, a central location would make sense unless you plan on jumping from hotel to hotel. In Tampa, there are two centrally located hotel clusters: the airport area and the Rocky Point Island area. We're not going to list all of the airport hotels, for they are legion and corporate in their facelessness. (One tip: the Avion Park area is both close to the airport and convenient to all parts of Tampa. We cover it in the Steinbrenner Field chapter.)

Rocky Point Island has a little more character, as most of the hotels are on the waterfront and there are many restaurants nearby. Rocky Point Island is bisected by the Courtney Campbell Causeway, which connects Tampa and Clearwater, and is located on the north side of Tampa Bay. Fans attending spring training in any of the area sites—Dunedin, Clearwater, Tampa, and Lakeland—will find Rocky Point Island to be a convenient headquarters. And, as many spring-training fans know, there are a few watering holes on Rocky Point Island that make an evening sunset a delight when viewed from the party deck.

Hotels on Rocky Point Island include:

- Hampton Inn, 3035 N. Rocky Point Dr., Tampa; 813/289-6262; *hamptoninn.com*.

- Holiday Inn Express and Suites Rocky Point Island, 3025 N. Rocky Point Dr., Tampa; 813/287-8585; *ihg.com.*
- Doubletree Guest Suites, 3050 N. Rocky Point Dr. W., Tampa; 813/888-8800; *hilton.com.*
- The Godfrey Hotel and Cabanas, 7700 W. Courtney Campbell Causeway, Tampa; 813/281-8900; *godfreyhoteltampa.com.*
- Westin Tampa Bay, 7627 W. Courtney Campbell Causeway, Tampa; 888/627-8647; *westintampabay.com.*
- Chase Suite Hotel, 3075 N. Rocky Point Dr., Tampa; 877/433-9644, 813/281-5677; *chasehoteltampa.com.*
- Sailport Waterfront Suites, 2506 N. Rocky Point Dr., Tampa; 813/281-9599; *providentresorts.com.*

TAMPA BAY RESTAURANTS

Spring-training traditionalists tend to flock around the same restaurants every year; it's part of the ritual, and we cover many these places in the team chapters. Tampa Bay is a pretty good restaurant area, and while we won't cover every notable dining establishment here, we will touch on some places we think are worthy of special attention. (We will also cover notable restaurants near each of the spring-training ballparks.)

There's no better day in Tampa than an afternoon at the ballgame and dining at a top-notch restaurant, especially sitting on a deck and taking in a lovely sunset. In the last several years we've been drawn to Hyde Park for many a post-game meal when attending spring training in the Tampa Bay area. There's something for everyone at the various Hyde Park eateries. Be prepared to wait in line at Goody Goody Burgers (*1601 W. Swann Av., Tampa, 813/248-3000; goodygoodyburgers.com*), which is packed shortly after opening until close. The focus is on burgers, but there are plenty of other options for those not interested in a traditional diner burger and milkshake. More eclectic, with an emphasis on contemporary American: On Swann (*1501 W. Swann Av., Tampa; 813/251-0110; onswann.com*), where the selections range from a notable hot chicken to lamb meatballs to luscious scallops. Again, a very popular spot; reservations recommended. For plenty of tasty small plates and a great outdoor seating area, try Bartaco (*1601 W. Snow*

Av., Tampa; 813/258-8226; bartaco.com). The drinks are stiff and tasty, and it's great fun to put together your own plates with a variety of tacos and sides.

Bern's Steak House, also located in Hyde Park, is a Tampa institution for red-meat eaters. Yes, the decor is somewhat alarming, but the steaks are among the finest in the world. Plan to make a full night during a Bern's experience and savor every step of the way, beginning with a leisurely cocktail or a selection from the award-winning wine list. (There is a dress code: if you're not decked out in business casual or nicer, you will be asked to dine in the more casual lounge.) The menu is a work of art, featuring long and loving descriptions of the various offerings. Begin your meal with a properly prepared Caesar salad (featuring plenty of anchovies) or one of the three versions of steak tartare (or, for a change of pace, go for the Chateaubriand Carpaccio) and then follow with a main course of steak. Order a side veggie raised on Bern's organic farm. Top it off with a fine Armagnac and something sweet in the Harry Waugh Dessert Room. The place is an institution; enjoy and don't worry about the bill. *Bern's Steak House, 1208 S. Howard Av., Tampa; 813/251-2421; bernssteakhouse.com.* The Bern's folks are also involved in a modern restaurant, Haven; worth a visit for a fine cocktail/wine list and a more progressive menu. *Haven, 2208 W. Morrison Av., Tampa; 813/258-2233; **haven-tampa.com**.*

There are many other good steakhouses in the Tampa area besides Bern's—Charley's, Eddie V's, 1200 Steakhouse, Rococo Steak—but locals recommend Fleming's, located a little over a mile from Steinbrenner Field. Again, this is a traditional steakhouse, pure and simple, with an emphasis on service. Some may dislike the place because it's part of a chain, as Fleming's is the high-end offering from Outback Steakhouse. But this is the hometown Fleming's, and obviously the one where most attention is paid. You might also see a Yankee or two. *Fleming's Prime Steakhouse, 4322 W. Boy Scout Blvd., Tampa; 813/874-9463; **flemingssteakhouse.com**.*

For those staying in Clearwater or at an aforementioned Rocky Point Island hotel, there is a nearby Duffy's Sports Bar. Those who read through this entire book will see many references to Duffy's: it's an affordable Florida sports-bar chain with good food and great beer selections. The Tampa location, close to Steinbrenner Field, is no exception. *Duffy's Sports Grill, 1580 N. Dale Mabry Hwy., Tampa; 813/875-7340; duffysmvp.com.*

Ferg's Sports Bar & Grill is a huge downtown-area St. Pete sports bar; the converted garage features a slew of outdoor decks and some pretty decent food. It's mostly known as a pre- and post-game hangout for Rays fans attending games at Tropicana Field. *Ferg's Sports Bar & Grill, 1320 Central Av., St. Petersburg; 727/822-4562; fergssportsbar.com.*

Walter's Press Box Sports Emporium is the prototypical sports bar, with 40 TV screens scattered throughout the premises. This is the place to go if you want to check out some NCAA basketball tournament action in a March visit. It's also a convenient locale if attending a game at Steinbrenner Field. *The Press Box, 222 S. Dale Mabry Hwy., Tampa; 813/876-3528; pressboxsports.com.*

You've got to love a sports bar named the Dog Saloon. It may appear to be a dive bar, but don't be fooled: the food is good, the drinks are strong, and the TVs feature all manner of sporting events. *The Dog Saloon, 3311 W. Bay To Bay Blvd., Tampa; 813/832-8211.*

The Bay Street area of International Plaza is close to the Yankees' training facilities and features a wide range of (mostly chain) restaurants appropriate for the whole family, including The Cheesecake Factory, Capital Grille, Ocean Prime, Bar Louie (a good place to catch some March Madness action, by the way), and more. It can be quite the zoo, as the open-air layout and many outdoor seating areas create a very festive atmosphere. But it's still a top-notch gathering area. The mall also features a slew of upscale shops. Again, it's close to Steinbrenner Field and relatively convenient for those attending Phillies and Blue Jays spring training as well. *International Plaza/Bay Street, 2223 N. West Shore Blvd., Tampa; 813/342-3790; shopinternationalplaza.com.*

We mentioned Ybor City earlier in this chapter, and there you'll find a Tampa institution: Columbia Restaurant, dating to 1905 and launched in Ybor City by Cuban immigrant Casimiro Hernandez, Sr. His descendants still own and run the Columbia Restaurant, billed as Florida's oldest restaurant and the largest Spanish restaurant in the world, occupying an entire city block. It's the American dream writ large: Hernandez launched the Columbia Restaurant as a small cafe serving strong coffee and Cuban sandwiches to Tampa's cigar factory workers, all the while gradually expanding the restaurant. You can find outposts of Columbia Restaurant throughout Central Florida, but the Ybor City location is the mothership. Start your dinner with a mandatory 1905 Salad (prepared tableside, of course) and partake of the many Cuban specialties on the menu, including an iconic Cuban sandwich. Reservations highly recommended. *Columbia Restaurant, 2117 E. 7th Av., Tampa; 813/248-4961; columbiarestaurant.com.*

TAMPA GOLF

Tampa is not necessarily known as a golfing nirvana. As a matter of fact, Tampa has a reputation of lacking first-class golf courses open to the public, especially freestanding courses that aren't surrounded by housing. While this reputation has changed somewhat in the last ten years, golfers who want to combine a round with a spring-training game may need to do a little work in terms of driving and scheduling to secure a tee time at a good facility.

Here are a few course suggestions to get you going—but be prepared to deal with many water hazards no matter where you play.

If you're interested in lodgings near the Phillies' or Blue Jays' camps in Clearwater or Dunedin, respectively, consider a stay at the Innisbrook Golf Resort, located just up Hwy. 19 in Palm Harbor (close to Tarpon Springs). The Tampa Bay Championship is played at the resort's Copperhead Golf Course, but if your game is not up to the PGA level you can always take in one of three other courses on the resort (Island, Highland North, Highland South). It's a place to take the whole family, with six resort pools, featuring two water slides and a cascading waterfall. Guests at the resort have priority when reserving tee times. Plus, the courses have been overhauled in recent years. *Innisbrook Resort and Golf Club, 36750 U.S. Hwy. 19 N., Palm Harbor; 800/456-2000; innisbrookgolfresort.com.*

The TPC Tampa Bay was designed by Bobby Weed and is a fairly open, flat course (when designing it, Weed actually removed about half the trees to create a more spacious layout), though definitely on the longer side and with plenty of banks for television purposes. *TPC Tampa Bay, 5300 W. Lutz Lake Fern Rd., Lutz; 813/949-0090; tpctampabay.com.*

The Eagles Golf Club features two 18-hole courses: The Lakes (where there's water on virtually every hole) and The Forest, which features a more rolling design edged by dense forests. *The Eagles Golf Club of Tampa Bay, 16101 Nine Eagles Dr., Odessa; 877/446-5388; eaglesgolf.com.*

Bardmoor Golf and Tennis Club has hosted PGA and LPGA events in the past and has won awards for "Tampa Bay's Favorite Public Golf Course" from the *Tampa Bay Times. Bardmoor Golf and Tennis Club, 8001 Cumberland Rd., Largo; 727/392-1234, ext. 209; bardmoorgolf.com.*

Finally, there's Mangrove Bay, a 72-hole championship-level course maintained by the city of St. Petersburg. You'll need to work a little to snare a tee time, as reservations are taken only up to seven days in advance. *Mangrove Bay, 875 62nd Av. NE., St. Petersburg; 727/893-7800; golfstpete.com.*

OTHER SPORTS

Amalie Arena, located in downtown Tampa, is home to the NHL's Tampa Bay Lightning. A Lightning game tends to be a great show; the team is usually quite competitive (winning the Stanley Cup in 2022) and the presentation top-notch. The arena has been upgraded a few times in the past several seasons, yielding plenty of upscale seating experiences. One great potential itinerary would have you staying downtown Tampa and taking in spring-training games during the day and a Lightning game at night. The area around the arena is getting to be built up with restaurants, bars, office space, and housing, and there are plenty of bars in the general area. Or you can go hungry: an all-inclusive ticket to a special suite-level space offers great food and a good seat to the game. *Amalie Arena, 401 Channelside Dr., Tampa; 813/301-6500; amaliearena.com.* Close by: The legendary Hattricks (*107 S. Franklin St., Tampa; 813/225-4288; hattrickstavern.com*), hailed by many as the best sports bar in the bay. Go for the Shake & Bake wings.

College baseball is popular in the area, and a baseball purist will want to check out a game at the University of Tampa or the University of South Florida, where there are often night games for a nice accompaniment to an afternoon major-league game. Interestingly, the newest ballpark in Tampa is the home of the Bulls, USF Baseball Stadium, located northeast of downtown Tampa. The ballpark opened in 2011 and replaced Red McEwen Field, a small ballpark housing the Tampa Yankees for the first two years of that team's existence. The new ballpark seats 3,211 (1,500 in the grandstand) and is considerably more comfortable than Red McEwen Field. It's actually two facilities in one: the USF softball team plays on one side, and the man's baseball team plays on the other, with a walkway down the middle where concessions are located. If you can, head there on a night when both squads are in action. We did in 2020 and were blown away by the experience: the men's game was interesting in terms of a high level of college play, but women's college softball is a great experience both in terms of skill and atmosphere. The crowds are rowdy and the players lead the cheers. Highly recommended. *USF Baseball Stadium, 11899 Bull Run Dr., Tampa; gousfbulls.com. The ballpark is located near the corner of Bull Run and Elm Dr. on the USF campus. Follow the signs to the MUMA Basketball Center/Sun Dome; the ballpark is next door. Parking adjacent to the ballpark.* If you head that way, there's a Miller's Ale House (*2012 E. Fowler Av, Tampa; 813/210-8280; MillersAleHouse.com*) close by. No beer at USF games, so an Ale House run after a game is in order, especially if there's a little March Madness action on tap.

The University of Tampa is located across the channel from the core of downtown Tampa, at one of the most picturesque campuses anywhere. University of Tampa Baseball Field is a small ballpark next to Pepin Stadium (the former Plant Field site), but the Spartans program is solid, with plenty of NCAA tourney appearances in recent years, including championships in 2013 and 2015. Both Lou Piniella and Tino Martinez played here as well. A strong schedule in the Sunshine State Conference means you're likely to see some good baseball from both teams, and the ballpark is nice by D-II standards, with exposed bleacher seating close to the action. Downtown Tampa makes a nice backdrop during a night game. Several attractions and neighborhoods, such as Hyde Park, are close to the campus— making central Tampa a great place to centralize your spring-training trip. The University of Tampa Baseball Field is located at the corner of Cass Street and North Boulevard, at the northwest corner of the University of Tampa campus off downtown Tampa. Parking adjacent to the ballpark. (*tampaspartans.com*)

INSIDER'S TIP

If you attend a University of Tampa game, give yourself time to walk around the campus. The main building on campus was once the grand Tampa Bay Hotel, a former base for teams in Tampa for spring training, and pictures from that era can be found throughout the building and the Henry B. Plant Museum. The Tampa Bay Hotel was built to impress: the minarets atop the towers would have been seen from a good distance (especially for those visitors arriving by boat), and the huge porches were ideal for lounging. Plant Hall is the large building.

A short walk from Plant Hall is the John H. Sykes College of Business building. In front is a historic marker celebrating the site of what some say is Babe Ruth's longest home run, a 587-foot shot coming when the Babe was a babe with the 1919 Boston Red Sox. Given the sometimes questionable accuracy of records from that era, we're not going to go out on a limb and definitively argue the historic veracity of such a claim. But it is interesting to see the marker and imagine the spring-training atmosphere when Plant Field was a baseball destination and the Tampa Bay Hotel team headquarters. A more genteel time, to be sure.

INSIDER'S TIP
Plant Field served as a spring home to several MLB teams: the Chicago Cubs, Boston Red Sox, Washington Senators, Detroit Tigers, Cincinnati Reds (who trained there for 24 springs), and the Chicago White Sox, the last team to train at Plant Field, in 1954. The stadium was used for plenty of big events over the years, ranging from barnstorming events featuring the likes of Buffalo Bill Cody and Red Grange to college football and political rallies. Pepin Stadium sits on part of the old Plant Field footprint.

FLYING IN

Three airports serve the Tampa Bay market.

The largest is Tampa International Airport, located near both the center of town and Steinbrenner Field, the spring home of the New

York Yankees. (Sit on the left side of a plane approaching from the north and you'll have a view of the ballpark as you land.) Virtually every major and minor airline flies into Tampa International Airport, including Air Canada, Alaska, American, Breeze, British Airways, Delta, Frontier, Havana Air, jetBlue, Southwest, Spirit, Sun Country, United, Virgin Atlantic, and WestJet. It has been extensively expanded and renovated in recent years; where flying into Tampa was once dreadful, it's now a very pleasant trip, though be prepared to walk: the car-rental areas are located relatively far from the main terminal and accessible via tram. *Tampa International Airport, 5503 W. Spruce St., Tampa, Florida 33607; 813/870-8700; tampaairport.com.*

Smaller is St. Petersburg-Clearwater International Airport, located on the west side of the bay. This airport specializes in low-fare carriers across the eastern United States (alas, no Canadian airlines). Allegiant Air is the largest airline flying in from a wide variety of destinations (Albany, Allentown, Harrisburg, Elmira, Fargo, Pittsburgh, Quad Cities, Syracuse), while Sun Country flies in from Minneapolis-St. Paul. It's also small enough so the car-rental agencies (Avis, Enterprise, Budget, National, and Alamo) are truly on site. *St. Petersburg-Clearwater International Airport, 14700 Terminal Blvd., Clearwater; 727/453-7800; fly2pie.com.*

To the south is Sarasota-Bradenton International Airport, located in Sarasota. Many major airlines fly here—Air Canada, Allegiant, American, Delta, JetBlue, United, and Delta—though not necessarily on a daily basis. If you're a Pirates or Orioles fan and planning on spending most of your time in the southern Bay area, this convenient airport is worth a look. *Sarasota-Bradenton International Airport, 6000 Airport Circle, Sarasota; 941/359-2770; srq-airport.com.*

INSIDER'S TIP

If you want to save a few bucks on airfare to spring training, prepare to be flexible. There's so much variance among airline prices these days that you could easily find a much cheaper fare from your city to St. Pete or Sarasota rather than Tampa International; if so, you'll need to make sure that a lower fare is worth the inconvenience of a longer drive.

The same thing goes for Orlando. There's no hard-and-fast

rule about which airport tends to be cheaper. If you have the time, compare fares from both: Orlando is about 75 minutes from Tampa on Interstate Highway 4 (even less if you're staying near Disney World or Kissimmee), and it makes sense to fly into Orlando—even if you're staying in Tampa—when there's a significant difference in airfares. A makeover of I-4 in recent years makes it a smooth drive. Besides, you're on vacation: relax and take in the scenic Florida countryside.

If you fly in, you'll need a rental car to drive between facilities. Beware the fact that the greater Tampa Bay area is now home to electronic tolls that charge vehicles based on license-plate scans. Highway 19 at Drew Street (near the Phillies' complex), for example, now features license-plate scanning, as does the Selmon Expressway heading out of Tampa. You could be nailed by your car-rental company for these tolls as well as administrative fees. If your rental-car company offers to add electronic tolls directly to your bill, say yes: you'll avoid hassle and administrative charges. If you plan on spending any time at all in Florida, considering buying a portable SunPass transponder at any local gas station, drugstore, travel center, or Publix grocery store. If your state already requires a toll reader and you have an E-ZPass account, check the E-ZPass site (*e-zpassiag.com*) to see if your system is compatible.

AL LANG FIELD AND TAMPA BAY BASEBALL HISTORY

The greater Tampa Bay area has been the traditional home of spring training in Florida. There are some remnants of this spring-training history, and you may want to check out some of them during your spring-training visit.

WATERFRONT PARK / AL LANG FIELD

Spring training has been played in St. Petersburg since 1914, first at Sunshine Park (which we discuss later) and then in downtown St. Pete. Al Lang Field and the area to the north have been hosting professional sports in the form of Major League Baseball spring training since 1922, when Waterfront Park opened at the corner of 1st Street Southeast and 1st Avenue Southeast, just to the north of the current Al Lang Stadium location. Waterfront Park hosted several MLB teams over the years—Boston Braves, New York Yankees and the St. Louis Cardinals—before being replaced by a new Al Lang Field in 1947.

Al Lang Field was built south of Waterfront Park and continued hosting Major League Baseball spring training in the form of the St. Louis Cardinals and later the New York Mets. It was named for St. Petersburg Mayor Al Lang, whose efforts in pushing spring training as a tourism promotion led to multiple MLB teams training in the city. The facility was rebuilt in 1977 with lots more shade and concrete, serving as the spring home of the expansion Tampa Bay Devil Rays.

Al Lang Field was given up for dead after spring training 2008, when the Tampa Bay Rays made the move south to Charlotte County.

Waterfront Park was used for spring training beginning in 1916, when the Philadelphia Nationals first trained here from 1916-1921. Other teams calling Waterfront their spring-training home include the Boston Braves (1922-1924), the New York Yankees (1925-1937), and the St. Louis Cardinals (1938-1997), who made the transition from Waterfront Park to Al Lang Field. The Al Lang Field years saw two teams play games there: the aforementioned Cardinals and the New York Mets (1962-1987). The Al Lang moniker dates from the Cardinals years—1947, to be exact—and comes from the original Al Lang, St. Petersburg's local "father of baseball," the mayor of the city who worked tirelessly to bring spring training to town.

When the Cardinals left, the Tampa Bay Devil Rays became the first MLB team to train in its hometown since the 1919 St. Louis Cardinals and Philadelphia Athletics (save the wartime years of the 1940s, when spring training was interrupted).

Today, Al Lang Stadium is used for professional soccer, home to the USL's Tampa Bay Rowdies. Baseball is no longer played there since the playing field was reconfigured for soccer, but you can still take in the Al Lang Field experience by taking in an USL game, which we would recommend. *Al Lang Stadium, 230 1st St. SE., St Petersburg; 727/893-7465; rowdiessoccer.com.*

HUGGINS-STENGEL FIELD

Despite the Yankees' long tradition of training in the Tampa Bay area, there are very few monuments to that history. There is a Monument Park as part of the Steinbrenner Field complex, but most of those honorees don't have direct connections to Tampa or former Yankees training sites.

One monument of sorts is located in a residential neighborhood in St. Petersburg: Huggins-Stengel Field at Crescent Lake Park. At first glance there's not much to Huggins-Stengel Field, just a playing field, dugouts, and a few old buildings. Out past center field there's a bucolic lake—the kind you find scattered throughout Florida—with a modest building sitting down the first-base line.

That lake is Crescent Lake, and it marks the location of what was known for many decades as Crescent Lake Park, the longtime spring home of the New York Yankees, beginning in 1925. There's nothing from the Babe Ruth era remaining, and except for two monuments honoring Miller Huggins and Casey Stengel—for whom the current field is named—there would be no indication this was the place where Ruth, Gehrig, and DiMaggio trained. (The building, however, was used as a clubhouse during the later Yankee days there.)

By 1931, the field was known as Huggins Field, and in 1963, the current name was adopted. The Mets, Orioles, Cardinals, and expansion Tampa Bay Devil Rays all trained at Huggins-Stengel Field in addition to the Yankees.

Huggins-Stengel Field is worth a visit. In springtime, the field is frequently used for college games and high-school scrimmages, so there's a good chance a game will be underway. Take a look around the field and check out the limited amenities; you're basically talking about a field, some chain-link fence, and a small clubhouse. Compare that to the training complexes of today, and you'll have a great appreciation of how much spring training has changed in a relatively short period of time. It's on the National Register of Historic Places, to boot. *Huggins-Stengel Field, 1320 5th Street N., St. Petersburg.*

AL LÓPEZ FIELD

Before there was Steinbrenner Field, there was Al López Field. Located on the current Raymond James Stadium site—just south of the Steinbrenner Field parking lots on Dale Mabry—Al López Field was home to spring training in Tampa before Steinbrenner Field. While the legacy of Al Lang Field lives on because the ballpark still exists at the St. Pete waterfront site, Al López Field has been largely forgotten.

Al López Field opened in 1955 as the spring home of the Chicago White Sox, who trained there through 1959. The Sox were replaced by the Cincinnati Reds, who trained there between 1960 and 1987, departing for Plant City in 1988. (The Plant City ballpark, by the way, still stands and is now used primarily for softball.)

Al López, who managed the White Sox when the team trained in Al López Stadium, ended up outliving the ballpark by a wide margin: the ballpark was torn down in 1988, and López lived to the ripe old age of 97, passing away in 2005. The Tampa Baseball Museum is located in his childhood home; check the previous chapter for details.

PLANT FIELD

Located on what is now the University of Tampa campus, Plant Field served as a spring home to several MLB teams: the Chicago Cubs (1913), Boston Red Sox, Washington Senators, Detroit Tigers, Cincinnati Reds (who trained there for 24 springs), and the Chicago White Sox, the last team to train at Plant Field, in 1954. The stadium was used for plenty of big events over the years, ranging from barnstorming events featuring the likes of Buffalo Bill Cody and Red Grange to college football and political rallies. Pepin Stadium sits on part of the old Plant Field footprint.

In our Tampa/St. Pete overview, we discuss Plant Field, the Henry B. Plant Museum, and ties to spring-training at the old railway hotel. The University of Tampa plays its home games at a ballpark next to Pepin Stadium; a fun visit is to walk through the old Plant Hotel and visualize how a baseball game would have been played in the area at the turn of the century.

The Cubs were the first MLB team to train in Tampa Bay, but not the first in Florida: the Washington Nationals were pioneers of a sort when they set up shop in Jacksonville for spring training in 1888.

SUNSHINE PARK

There's nothing left to St. Petersburg's Sunshine Park, home to spring training in the earliest days of Florida spring training. Located at 22nd Avenue N. & 1st Street N., at what's now considered to be southwest of Coffee Pot Bayou, Sunshine Park (also known as Coffee Pot Park and Coffee Pot Bayou Park) in 1914 hosted the St. Louis Browns, who were enticed to St. Petersburg for spring training by Mayor Al Lang. The all-wood grandstand was put into use by the Browns immediately, as they drew 4,000 fans—paying a whopping quarter per ducat—for a game against the neighboring Chicago Cubs, who arrived at the ballpark by boat from their spring-training home at Plant Field. It was a large ballpark, seating 5,000 in the grandstand, complete with batting cages and sliding pits.

The Browns ended training at Coffee Pot Park after a single year. Later the Philadelphia Phillies would sign a deal to train there between 1915 and 1918. The ballpark also hosted the minor-league St. Petersburg Saints up through 1928. But by then spring training was an activity found in other venues: a ballpark at Waterfront Park opened in 1922 as the spring home of the Boston Braves—and later the New York Yankees and St. Louis Cardinals—and eventually was replaced by the aforementioned Al Lang Field.

BAYCARE BALLPARK / PHILADELPHIA PHILLIES

QUICK FACTS

- **Capacity**: 8,272
- **Year Opened**: 2004
- **Dimensions**: 329L, 401C, 330R
- **Tickets Line**: 215/463-1000
- **Local Airport**: Tampa
- **Dugout Location**: Third-base side
- **Practice Schedule**: The Phillies train at the Carpenter Complex next to BayCare Ballpark. Practices usually begin at 10 a.m.
- **Pregame Schedule**: Gates open 2.5 hours before game time. Phillies batting practice, 10-11:15 a.m.; visitors batting practice, 11:15 a.m.-12:15 p.m.; Phillies infield, 12:15-12:30 p.m.; visitors infield, 12:30-12:45 p.m. Add six hours to each figure for a 7:05 p.m. game.
- **Address**: 601 N. Old Coachman Rd., Clearwater, FL 33765.
- **Directions**: Take Hwy. 19 north of St. Petersburg to Drew Street, where you'll head west until you get to Greenwood Avenue. At Old Coachman Road hang a right and head north; the ballpark is ahead on your right.

NEVER BETTER IN CLEARWATER

Time flies in the world of spring training. Take Clearwater's BayCare Ballpark, now entering its 22nd spring-training season. There are plenty of readers of this book who remember the 2004 opening of this ballpark, and probably more than a few who remember the former spring home of the Phillies, Jack Russell Stadium. It does seem like yesterday.

When BayCare Ballpark opened in 2004, it was certainly one of the nicest ballparks in spring training, and when combined with the adjacent Carpenter Complex, certainly one of the coziest. Today, newer spring-training ballparks have borrowed from BayCare Ballpark and the Phillies' spring-training operation, with most featuring a 360-degree concourse and plenty of unique food offerings. It is the standard by which older spring-training ballparks are evaluated and new ballparks are planned.

But nothing lasts forever, and at some point in the next few years the Phillies will embark on a $300M+ renovation of the ballpark, the accompanying Carpenter training complex, and the retail space south of the ballpark—a building purchased by the Phillies in 2022 —to expand the fan space in the ballpark, add new amenities, and upgrade training tools available to minor leaguers and rehabbing major leaguers. The team announced its intent and has been working with local elected officials on the overall game plan, but has not yet unveiled the specifics or a timeline. The process has been delayed with local county officials spending time on a new Rays ballpark.

Still, there is plenty of enjoyment to be had at a Phillies spring-training game, and the challenge for the team is to enhance the game-day experience without losing any of that magic. Today, BayCare Ballpark is not necessarily the nicest ballpark in the Grape-fruit League, but it certainly is one of the most loved venues: fans come early, leave late, and revel in the spring-training experience. Even if the team is a little lacking on the field, Phillies fans show up to BayCare Ballpark in force.

Once the Phillies unveil their plans, which will likely convert that retail building into a higher-level venue/entryway to the ball-park, expand the concourses, and add more valet parking to the mix, you will likely hear from plenty of old-timers who decry any kind of change at the ballpark. In a way the Phillies are a victim of their success: despite the narrow concourses, the cramped entrance, and the far-off park, a Phillies game is fun. BayCare Ballpark works very well on a functional level; yes, the concourse can get awfully crowded behind home plate. Still, we really can't think of a better time at a spring-training game than to spend the afternoon at BayCare Ballpark.

You know you're in a great ballpark when there are multiple areas providing a great view of the action. Sitting behind home plate in the grandstand, of course, is going to be a great spot. But that's not the only one. When the gates open, fans rush out to Frenchy's Tiki Pavilion in left field to grab one of the bar stools and down a Yuengling or three while soaking in the warmth after a cold and wet Philly winter. Groups can socialize and catch some action in the reserved picnic tables down the third-base line. And families can let the kids run loose while throwing down blankets in the outfield berm. While the official capacity at BayCare Ballpark is 8,272, that assumes every seat is filled and the berm is crammed with fans sitting cheek to cheek.

There is a definite pattern to BayCare Ballpark attendance: the numbers will be on the slower side the first 10 days or so of spring training, but then the crowds begin to pick up to the point where sellouts are common. Those sellouts are fairly inevitable when the Yankees, Pirates, and Red Sox are in town, so plan accordingly. During those sellouts, spring for seats and don't assume you can sprawl out on the berm.

The location of BayCare Ballpark is convenient for fans and the team. The ballpark was built next to the Phillies' existing minor-league training facilities, so things are centralized for the team and for fans wandering the practice fields before games. BayCare Ballpark is right next to Clearwater's main drag (Highway 19) and considerably easier to get to than Jack Russell, even when the Phillies anticipate a sellout. Ample, though somewhat remote, parking in the area also makes things easier for fans.

There are two entrances to the ballpark (one down each line—west and south), but most fans will enter from the west side to a third-base entrance due to parking considerations, and because that's where most of the ticket booths are located. It's currently the signature entrance: besides being closer to parking, the entrance features an attractive fountain plaza and a baseball sculpture. The ballpark itself features the Spanish Mediterranean motif popular in Florida. A concourse rings the entire ballpark, while a second deck features luxury boxes, club seats (with wait service), and group areas. (In the past these west entry gates created a bottleneck.

The ballpark has seen steady upgrades throughout the years. For example: in 2015 a new, bright videoboard almost doubled the size of the old one. For those on the berm or perched on a barstool at Frenchy's, a ribbonboard installed on the ballpark fascia provides scores, information, and more. In 2024, a new sound system and expanded WiFi were installed.

The concourse is where the action is. Behind home plate the concourses are shaded and hospitable, providing easy access to stands selling Philly cheesesteaks and beers of the world. Go down the third-base line and visit the team store before hitting the general Tiki bar area; this is where the Beautiful People hang out, cocktails in hand. So what if the ballgame is secondary? It's spring in Clearwater, and you're in a psychic landscape where Hooters was launched and a beach-bum lifestyle was born. Pass by the twin stacked bullpens (visitors next to the field, home in the back) and spend some time lounging on the berm, soaking in plenty of sun.

Walk back past right field, wave at the poor suckers on Highway 19 who aren't lucky enough to be at a Philadelphia Phillies spring-training game, and enjoy the rest of the action.

INSIDER'S TIP
When shopping for tickets, keep in mind that there are very few bad seats in the park. All are angled toward the pitchers' mound—even those down the first-base line—while a picnic area down the third-base line allows you and a set of friends to reserve your own table for an entire game. Given the popularity of the Phillies in spring training, you may not have much of a selection when it comes time to reserving your seats: you'll want to sit to the left of home plate to take advantage of any shade from the hot Florida sun.

INSIDER'S TIP
At the beginning of spring training the Phillies practice at the next-door Carpenter Complex. They usually begin at 10 a.m.

INSIDER'S TIP
A St. Patrick's Day Phillies game is always a treat, with special merchandise and food specials on tap.

BALLPARK HISTORY

The Philadelphia Phillies have trained in Clearwater since 1947 and were at Jack Russell Stadium from 1955 through 2003. The team opened BayCare Ballpark—originally named Bright House Networks Field, then Bright House Field, and finally Spectrum Field —during spring training 2004.

THE SPRING-TRAINING BALLPARK EXPERIENCE

WHERE TO SIT

With the Phillies dugout on the third-base side, you'll want to sit in sections 113-117 to be closest to the players. You'll be in the sun, but you'll have a view of the home team in action. The berm in BayCare

Ballpark is incredibly popular, especially in left field; you'll want to get there early and stake out a spot to get a good view of the pitchers warming up (and for most spring games, there will be a lot of pitchers warming up). If you do sit in the berm, bring your sunglasses and sunscreen in a plastic container; it's a sun field during an afternoon game. (If you forget the sunscreen, no worries; there are bright-yellow touch-free dispensers located throughout the ballpark, with mounted and portable displays in restrooms, as well as throughout the concourse and berm areas.)

INSIDER'S TIP

As the seating bowl is horseshoe-shaped—that is, the seating down each line curls back toward the playing field—there are very few bad seats in the ballpark, and the Phillies have worked hard to improve what would otherwise be marginal seating areas. For instance, down the third-base line you'll find three levels of terraced seating, the Tiki Terrace, with picnic tables.

If you're looking to sit in the shade, look to the last three to four rows in sections 105-112: they're shaded by the second-deck over-hang on an average day. The Club Level seating (sections 201-203) is also shaded and, as a bonus, padded.

INSIDER'S TIP

The Phillies have slightly altered the seating arrangements in the Tiki Bar area over the years. There is room for 75 or so around Frenchy's, but not every perch will give you a good view of the action. For some, that doesn't matter; others, though, want it all. To assure yourself a good view from the bar, get there early: it's first-come, first-served. (As a bonus, the Tiki Bar serves drinks after the game ends; let the rubes clear out while you have a few post-game adult beverages.) In the past, the terraced seating in front of Frenchy's was first-come, first-served, but it's now sold as reserved seating under the Tiki Terrace moniker.

CONCESSIONS

It wouldn't be a Phillies spring-training game if a cheesesteak sandwich wasn't on the menu. The concession stand directly behind
home plate features Delco's Philly cheesesteaks, served on authentic
Amoroso rolls.

In recent years the Phillies have worked to upgrade concessions,
with menu items like Delco cheesesteaks, crab fries, Boar's Head
sandwiches, and Thurston's strawberry shortcakes appearing every
spring. For Philly expats missing home, the team offers Herr's
potato chips at several concession stands. Also for those missing
Philly: Hatfield hot dogs and brats, Philadelphia Water Ice, Tony
Luke's roasted pork sandwiches, and boardwalk fries.

If you're not an expat, don't worry: there are still plenty of local
favorites on the menu. Our favorites: grouper bites, crab-cake sandwiches, and shrimp avocado tacos with a smoked fish spread. For
the kids, there are plenty of choices, including the old dependables,
like Dippin' Dots and Hershey's ice cream. Also on the menu: Dole
Whip, that lovely pineapple concoction found at Disney World.
Added in 2024: Manco & Manco Pizza.

Otherwise, the four main concession stands scattered throughout
the concourse feature your average ballpark fare. Of special note is
the dedicated McGillicuddy's Beers of the World stand down the
third-base line: it features the widest variety of beers in the ballpark,
including Yuengling. Yuengling represents a marriage of sorts
between Pennsylvania and Florida: Yuengling Beer Company's
roots date back to 1829 when the Yuengling family established a
brewery in Pottsville, Penn., but a 1999 acquisition of a former
Stroh's brewery in Tampa gave Yuengling a toehold in Florida, and
the beer is now marketed as a local beer. Over 120 different brands
of beer are sold at the ballpark in a variety of ways, from single taps
and bottles to Malibu buckets of beer. McGillicuddy's features
brews from local microbreweries Big Storm Brewery, Coppertail
Brewing, and Cigar City Brewery. In a contrast to many other spring
venues, the beer is cheap, as are the cocktails offered at the Clearwater Cocktail Company stand.

And yes, there are cupholders at every seat, so load up on the
food and drink. If you'd rather claim a more relaxed seat, there are
10 picnic tables in center-right field.

INSIDER'S TIP
Do give yourself enough time to acquire food and drink. BayCare Ballpark sits on a small footprint for a ballpark, so there are some crammed spots in the concourse, particularly on the third-base side. You can see the action as you wait in line, but there seems to always be a traffic jam there, between folks visiting concessions and fans passing through.

SHOPPING

Besides the main concession stand on the concourse, the Phillies also offer additional merchandise via a freestanding tent. Green Phanatic dangle hats were a smash in previous years, and in addition to your standard spring-training tees, the Phillies have offered spring-training bobbleheads, Tiki Bar tees and caps, and nail polish in traditional Phillies red and blue. The Phillies Florida operations folks always have something new during spring training.

AUTOGRAPHS

The Phillies enter the field from the left-field tunnel, so your best chance of scoring an autograph is before the beginning of the game as they arrive; head directly to section 120, where the netting ends, and be patient. (Visiting players enter the playing field from a dugout tunnel; they tend to congregate around section 104 down the right-field line.) Depending on the mood of the ushers, you may or may not be kicked out of the area at 12:30 p.m., kids excluded. If you arrive early enough, you can try to attract the attention of a player as they enter or leave the practice fields directly next to the ballpark at the Carpenter Complex; players park between the ballpark and the practice fields as well.

INSIDER'S TIP
If you arrive early enough, spend some time wandering through the Carpenter Complex before entering the ballpark. A sign points the way to each Phillies MiLB affiliate, including the Lehigh Valley IronPigs and the Reading Fightin Phils (the Single-A Clearwater Threshers share the ballpark with the Phillies). The four practice fields are named for

Phillies Hall of Famers: Richie Ashburn, Steve Carlton, Robin
Roberts, and Mike Schmidt.

FOR THE KIDS

A special kids' area in the left-field corner of the ballpark should
keep the young ones busy for hours. A supervised playground area
lets them burn off a lot of steam, while a concession stand devoted
to kid-specific treats will boost them up. You'll still be able to see the
action while watching the kids in the corner of your eye.

PARKING

There are two parking lots to the south and to the west of the ballpark. The lot to the south is small and fills up quickly; the lot to the
west is larger, and if you get there early enough you may snare a
good spot. As you head west on Drew Street, the south lot will be
the one to your right, and you should park there if possible. If that
lot is full, head west and follow the signs; most fans will be directed
to the Joe DiMaggio recreation complex, which isn't far from the
ballpark. If you're coming from the north, check the lot at the
Carpenter Complex, where the minor-leaguers train; we've parked
there and walked the short distance to the ballpark. Parking in all
four spots: $13. In theory, this should be a cashless transaction. Valet
parking is available for $25.

INSIDER'S TIP
There are some alternatives. St. Petersburg College sells $10
parking spots in a lot near the ballpark. At NE Coachman
Park, a little more than a quarter mile from BayCare Ballpark,
the city sells spots for $5. Alas, you won't find any free street
parking in a spot within an easy walk of the ballpark.

INSIDER'S TIP
The Jolley Trolley Phillies Shuttles run from select Clearwater
locations to BayCare Ballpark during select home games. The
Jolley Trolley runs daily between downtown Clearwater,
Dunedin, and Safety Harbor, adding BayCare Ballpark as a
stop in March. The price is right: $2.25 each way, with a

special $1.10 fare each way for seniors and the disabled and a $5 all-day pass. If you're interested in taking the Trolley and avoiding ballpark parking, check out *clearwaterjolleytrolley.com* for more information. There is also a mobile app available, handy for tracking the Trolley's location and estimating waiting times.

INSIDER'S TIP
You may want to consider riding a bike to the ballpark and save on parking. The Ream Wilson Clearwater Trail runs through the city, including directly north of BayCare Ballpark.

INSIDER'S TIP
The Phillies installed a designated ride share pickup area, located at the South Gate of BayCare Ballpark.

SELFIE SPOTS

By far the most popular spot for a selfie is outside the ballpark at the west entrance, where the baseball sculpture in the fountain makes the perfect background for a photo.

IF YOU GO

WHAT TO DO OUTSIDE THE BALLPARK

Clearwater is less than 20 miles outside of the Tampa-St. Petersburg urban core and less than five miles from Dunedin, so you're in the midst of spring-training nirvana. Spring-training cities within easy driving distance of Clearwater include Lakeland (Detroit Tigers), Tampa (New York Yankees), Dunedin (Toronto Blue Jays), and Bradenton (Pittsburgh Pirates). You can expect your spring-training trip to be filled with lots of baseball in the Tampa area.

The thing to do in Clearwater is really nothing: head to one of the many beaches and soak up some sun. We already mentioned Clearwater Beach as a prime activity in our earlier chapter on Tampa attractions. One popular local attraction is Pier 60 Park, located at Causeway and Gulf Boulevard. Pier 60 Park is a white-sand beach that runs north for 1.3 miles and features shops, restaurants, a bait shop, beach concessions, and nightly entertainment. Be warned you won't be the only one heading to Clearwater Beach. After all, March is spring break for a lot of people uninterested in baseball, and they love the sun and the sand enough to flock to Clearwater in search of cheap beer and good food. You can find both at one of the many Frenchy's in the area; they specialize in serving lots of beer and fresh grouper sandwiches. Our favorite is Frenchy's Rockaway Grill (*7 Rockaway St., Clearwater Beach; 727/446-4844; frenchysonline.com*), as you can sit on the deck and enjoy outdoor dining on the waterfront. It's also popular with Phillies front-office personnel, players, and beat reporters. For something more traditional, Bob Heilman's Beachcomber Restaurant (*447 Mandalay Av., Clearwater; 727/442-4144; **heilmansbeachcomber.com***) is old-time Florida at its best, and in the past a traditional haunt of Phillies front-office personnel. The menu features some classics like clams casino, along with a well-selected list of steaks, seafood, and pasta. The Palm Pavilion (*10 Bay Esplanade, Clearwater; 727/446-2642; **palmpavilion.com***) is owned and run by Phillies fan Ken Hamilton, so his outdoor deck is a must-visit for anyone traveling down from Philadelphia. (Nearby: the Palm Pavilion Inn, an old-Florida-style establishment. A night or two there is recommended as well.) And, at more than 90 years old, it's the oldest operating beach pavilion in Florida. Please note: No reservations. Villa Gallace (*109 Gulf Blvd., Indian Rocks Beach; 727/596-0200; **villagallace.com***), a high-brow Italian restaurant, has been a traditional favorite of Phillies players and front-office personnel. Clear Sky Cafe (*490 Mandalay Avenue, Clearwater; 727/442-3684; **clearskycafe.com***) is another seafood hangout also known for its gourmet pizza. We've mentioned Columbia Restaurant in our Tampa/St. Pete overview; there is a Clearwater outpost (*1241 Gulf Blvd., Clearwater; 727/596-8400; **columbiarestaurant.com***). If you want a great view of the entire area, consider Spinners (*5250 Gulf Blvd., St. Pete Beach; 800/448-0901; **bellwetherbeachresort.com***). Located on the 12th floor of the Bellwether Beach Report, Spinners is one of those quaint rotating restaurants you don't see often anymore (or, at least, since Radisson stopped building them). The food is basic but hearty—steaks, seafood, the inevitable grouper—along with a decent drink menu. It takes 90 minutes or so for Spinners to make a complete rotation, so plan on a nice, long, relaxed dinner with some great views of Clearwater.

INSIDER'S TIP
If you're on the nostalgic side, the original Hooters is close to the ballpark. Enjoy. *2800 Gulf To Bay Blvd., Clearwater; originalhooters.com.*

Oh, the beaches. There are a lot of them in the area, with over 26 miles of beaches running up and down the key. Clearwater Beach is the most famous. We're not going to tell you the best beach for your particular desires, but a place we love visiting because of the slower pace is Indian Rocks Beach. If you go, be prepared to make a day of it: Gulf Boulevard, the main drag, is crowded and slow.

A related activity: The Clearwater Marine Aquarium. Until she passed away in November 2021, the Aquarium was home to Winter, the bottlenose dolphin who was famously outfitted with a prosthetic tail after losing her original in a crab trap. But Winter was just one attraction: the whole family can still enjoy seeing various types of sea turtles, river otters, pelicans, stingrays, eel, and more. The aquarium has a noted emphasis on wildlife rescue as well. *Clearwater Marine Aquarium, 249 Windward Passage, Clearwater; 727/441-1790; cmaquarium.org. Adults, $41.95; children (3-12), $32.95; seniors (60+), $39.95.*

INSIDER'S TIP
Highway 19, which runs next to the ballpark to the east, has been upgraded in recent years and is now a major throughway. (It's also now one of those devilish Florida toll roads that work off license plates with no toll booths. Beware.) On the other hand, Old Coachman Road, which runs next to the ballpark to the west, is two lanes, not a toll road, and never very busy. Consult your map or GPS and then head over there for some clear driving.

The Phillies may have moved spring training from Jack Russell Stadium, but one March tradition remains: Lenny's Restaurant *(21220 U.S. Highway 19 N., Clearwater; 727/799-0402; lennys-*

food.com). Phillies players have been coming to Lenny's since it opened in 1980, and the fans soon followed, cramming the restaurant on game days. And when the Phillies moved into BayCare Ballpark, Lenny's was the big winner: the new ballpark is actually closer to Lenny's than Jack Russell is.

Lenny's caters to Phillies fans: in February and March the staff hangs Phillies pennants and other team memorabilia, and a row of seating from Jack Russell Stadium sits outside the restaurant. Lenny's more than doubles its number of customers in March and adds more staff and special dishes designed to appeal to Pennsylvania customers, such as scrapple, as well as a specialized menu that includes the likes of knishes. But the regular menu is great: everyone gets a Danish basket right off the bat, and you'll be hard-pressed to choose between bagels topped with lox and cream cheese, outrageous omelets, or the Redneck Bennie, topped with sausage gravy. The place is crammed with red-clad fans before a home game; arrive early.

WHERE TO STAY

Clearwater is in the western part of the Tampa Bay region, north of St. Pete and west of Tampa. You could stay anywhere within the Tampa Bay area (as we explained in our previous chapter on Tampa Bay) and be within a reasonable drive of the ballpark.

However, Clearwater is a suburb on the rise, with lots of new development and hotels in the area surrounding the ballpark, and it is not difficult to snare an affordable hotel room near the ballpark. Many are within walking distance, although the lack of sidewalks and the busy traffic flow on Hwy. 19 make this a problematic method of arriving at the ballpark.

INSIDER'S TIP
Don't bother trying to figure out where the Phillies players stay during spring training: the team doesn't designate an official team hotel for spring training.

Within a mile of the ballpark are:

- TownePlace Suites by Marriott, 21090 U.S. Highway 19 N., Clearwater; 727/712-3100; *marriott.com*.
- Clarion Inn & Suites, 20967 Hwy. 19 N., Clearwater; 727/799-1181; *clarionhotel.com*.
- Holiday Inn Express, 2580 Gulf to Bay Blvd., Clearwater; 727/797-6300; *ihg.com*.
- Our recommendation: La Quinta Inn Clearwater Central, 21338 Hwy. 19 N., Clearwater; 727/799-1565; *wyndham.com*.

In addition, the hotels on the Campbell Causeway listed in our section opener on Tampa are also convenient to the ballpark: you can take the Causeway to Highway 19 or Old Coachman Road, head north to the next stoplight (Drew Street), and you're right at the ballpark. Be warned Highway 19 has been expanded in recent years and is now a major throughway with tolls, so we'd recommend approaching the ballpark via Old Coachman Road.

FLYING IN

Technically, the closest airport to Clearwater is St. Petersburg-Clearwater International Airport (*fly2pie.com*), located on the west side of the bay. This airport specializes in low-fare carriers. Allegiant Air, for instance, flies directly there from the Allentown, Pittsburgh, and Harrisburg airports, while Sun Country flies from Minneapolis-St. Paul. It's also small enough where the car-rental agencies (Avis, Enterprise, National, Budget, and Alamo) are truly on site.

In case you can't get a flight into St. Pete-Clearwater, you'll want to check out Tampa International Airport—located a very reasonable distance from the ballpark. All the major airlines fly into Tampa.

SPRING TRAINING HISTORY: PHILADELPHIA PHILLIES

The Philadelphia Phillies have held spring training in the following locations: Philadelphia (1901); Washington, N.C. (1902); Richmond, Va. (1903); Savannah, Ga. (1904); Augusta, Ga. (1905); Savannah, Ga. (1906-1908); Southern Pines, N.C. (1909-1910); Birmingham, Ala. (1911); Hot Springs, Ark. (1912); Southern Pines, N.C. (1913); Wilmington, N.C. (1914); St. Petersburg (1915-1918); Charlotte (1919); Birmingham, Ala. (1920); Gainesville (1921); Leesburg, Fla. (1922-1924); Bradenton (1925-1927); Winter Haven (1928-1937); Biloxi, Miss. (1938); New Braunfels, Texas (1939); Miami Beach (1940-1942); Hershey, Penn. (1943); Wilmington, Del. (1944-1945); Miami Beach (1946); and Clearwater (1947-present).

REMEMBERING JACK RUSSELL STADIUM

Even though BayCare Ballpark is a great facility, we can't help but experience a little twinge of sadness when we think about the team's former spring home, Jack Russell Stadium. Opening in 1955, Jack Russell Stadium was a true neighborhood ballpark, a low-slung facility with real box seats and plenty of shade. True, it was small—capacity was just under 7,000, and the clubhouse and office space were cramped—but it was homey, and no matter how bad the Phillies were, the fans flocked down to Clearwater to cheer on their boys.

Today, Jack Russell Stadium as Phillies fans knew it is no more: the grandstand was torn down in 2007 after several attempts were made to find an alternative use. The things that made it charming—the small footprint, the neighborhood location—ultimately worked against it when it came to youth tournaments or other uses. You can't say Clearwater officials didn't do everything they could to save the old place, but at the end of the day it wasn't enough.

Still, the city couldn't completely kill baseball at the site. The playing field was retained and some bleachers were installed. In recent years the field has hosted baseball in the form of college and high-school tourneys. Bring a ball and glove: you can play catch on the same field where Mike Schmidt, Steve Carlton, and Larry Bowa once trained.

TD BALLPARK / TORONTO BLUE JAYS

QUICK FACTS

- **Capacity**: 8,500 (6,200 fixed seats)
- **Year Opened**: 1990; rebuilt in 2020
- **Dimensions**: 328L, 373LC, 400C, 353RC, 328R
- **Tickets Line**: 888/525-5297
- **Local Airport**: Tampa
- **Workout Schedule**: When spring training opens, the team can be found at the Bobby Mattick Training Center at the Cecil B. Englebert Complex (1700 Solon Av., Dunedin). At the beginning of March, the team then shifts major-league practices to TD Ballpark. Traditionally, workouts begin at 9 a.m.
- **Dugout Location**: First-base side.
- **Pregame Schedule**: Gates open 2.5 hours before game time. Blue Jays batting practice and infield, 10-11:20 a.m.; visitors batting practice, 11:20 a.m.-12:20 p.m.; visitors infield, 12:20-12:35 p.m. Add six hours to each figure for a 7:05 p.m. game.
- **Address**: 373 Douglas Av., Dunedin, FL 34698.
- **Directions**: Take Hwy. 19 north from St. Petersburg, then take Sunset Point Road (Route 588) west for two miles, and then head north on Douglas Avenue for a half mile.

ESCAPING THE GREAT WHITE NORTH

TD Ballpark was never regarded as a particularly attractive ballpark: functional at best, the former Dunedin Stadium was loved more for its scenic, throwback location near downtown Dunedin than for its comfort level. It was a small, cramped facility with little shade or amenities, a place to walk away from as soon as the game was over.

A 2020 makeover of the ballpark, as well as extensive renovations to the team's offsite training facility, was a game changer both for the Blue Jays and their many fans. We've always loved attending a spring-training game in Dunedin, but it was more for the total experience than the game: heading to downtown Dunedin for a nice brunch, walking the lovely neighborhood between downtown and the ballpark, and then taking a leisurely stroll back downtown for a post-game beer at one of the many outstanding microbreweries. At a time when spring training is a big business and ballparks have morphed into larger facilities, a game in Dunedin was a throwback, to be sure.

Now, after the renovations, there's a ballpark experience worthy of Dunedin, as the Blue Jays delivered a renovated ballpark that makes the most of a very limited footprint and gives fans an abundance of gathering spots, upgraded concessions, and plenty of new views of the ballpark while keeping—and even enhancing—the intimate atmosphere that made a Dunedin Stadium game an intimate experience. There's still plenty of seating close to the action, but with a new air-conditioned bar and group areas down the left-field line, coupled with a 360-degree concourse that encourages plenty of gatherings with friends and relatives, a TD Ballpark experience now offers more: A cozy family area off the seating bowl to give kids plenty of time to work off some steam before the game begins, an upgraded scoreboard and sound system, refreshed concessions, lots of new colorful Blue Jays graphics, and overhauled restrooms. Yes, there's an improvement for everyone.

The new look at TD Ballpark is classic coastal Florida architecture, with plenty of Blue Jays blue and other bright colors throughout. From the revamped front entrance to an overhauled concourse to the refreshed seating bowl, the TD Ballpark experience is light, sunny, and relaxing. Dunedin is one of the hidden gems in the Tampa-St. Pete area, a refreshing respite from the hustle and bustle along the bay. There's no such thing as a bad spring-training experience, but some experiences are better than others.

The Blue Jays have been training at the TD Ballpark site since the team's 1977 inception, with the previous ballpark configuration dating to 1990. As spring-training facilities throughout Florida have been updated in the last several years, it was clear the experience at TD Ballpark left something to be desired.

Considering the Toronto Blue Jays have now been around for 40-plus seasons, it's remarkable that the team has had only one spring-training site in team history. The Blue Jays began life on March 11, 1977, when the team beat the New York Mets 3-1 in their first game. At that time, the Blue Jays played in 3,417-seat Grant Field, which was one of the oldest ballparks in the Grapefruit League, dating back to 1930.

However, Grant Park didn't keep up with the many new spring-training facilities that were popping up in Florida in the 1980s, and by 1989 the Blue Jays were working on a plan to replace Grant Field with a new ballpark and spring-training facility. As a result, the city of Dunedin invested $2.4 million into a new ballpark at the site of the old stadium, and TD Ballpark became the new spring-training home of the Toronto Blue Jays in 1990.

Most longtime spring-training fans remember the Blue Jays training first at Grant Park and then at Dunedin Stadium. It was known as Knology Park between 2004 and 2008, reverting back to the Dunedin Stadium name, then becoming Florida Auto Exchange Stadium, before reverting yet again to the Dunedin Stadium name in 2018. A new naming-rights deal with TD Bank yields the current TD Ballpark moniker.

The 360-degree concourse totally changed how fans viewed the ballpark and the game on the field. Instead of being restricted to their seats, the new walkway lets fans do exactly what we do at every baseball game: watch some action from our seats, then stroll the ballpark to check out the action from different vantage points. The new layout adds a new air-conditioned bar, Eddie's Bar, open to all if not reserved by a group, as well as an adjoining party deck. The concourse renovation adds a family area with Adirondack chairs, four tops, shaded picnic tables, and its own concessions. The kids can burn off some energy by playing with the corn hole and Connect 4 games, while Mom and Dad can relax with a beer or cocktail.

Two new concession stands were added to the ground-level concourse, each with eight point of sale locations and four beer/soda service locations.

Also added: five suites, including an owner's suite, a players' family suite, and three suites that can be sold separately or combined into one larger event space. These suites, at 325 square feet each, also feature outdoor seating areas. That same upper level features five TV and radio booths, PA/videoboard control space, and a larger press box that will accommodate up to 60 journalists. The field dimensions and outfield wall heights match those found at Rogers Centre.

Getting in and out of TD Ballpark is easier with the addition of six new ticket windows, doubling the number of ticket windows.

INSIDER'S TIP

Some history was made at TD Ballpark during the 2021 MLB season, when the Toronto Blue Jays called it home for the beginning of the regular season while COVID-19 restrictions closed the border with Canada.

The Englebert Baseball Complex, located eight miles away, is where the Blue Jays begin workouts when spring training starts. This is where player development, including extended spring and rehabs, is centered. The entire complex encompasses a large two-story clubhouse building with a long list of workout areas: 4½ fields for MiLB use, 2½ fields for MLB use, one open air agility field for MiLB use, 1 covered agility field (turfed) for MLB use, one inclined agility field for shared MLB/MiLB League use, 13 batting tunnels, covered indoor batting cages, 10½ MiLB gang mounds and 8½ MLB gang mounds.

This clubhouse building features player facilities on the ground floor and team offices on the second, including a covered balcony with a view of the workout areas. These features largely hew to MLB spring-training facilities opening in the past several years, including hydrotherapy rooms, weight rooms, theater-style classroom, food-prep/nutrition areas, plenty of meeting rooms and separate MLB and MiLB clubhouses. In total, the Englebert Complex is now more than doubled in size.

To say the renovations of TD Ballpark were welcome and well-chosen is an understatement. We loved a visit to a Toronto Blue Jays game because of the charms of Dunedin, not the charms of the ballpark. Now, with an extreme makeover, TD Ballpark is now as charming as Dunedin—making a good experience even better. If you miss the feel of old-time Florida spring training, you can certainly find it at TD Ballpark.

THE SPRING-TRAINING BALLPARK EXPERIENCE

CONCESSIONS

The concession offerings are strong on the basics: hot dogs and hamburgers (search out the open grills on the concourse for freshly prepared offerings), chicken tenders, pizza, nachos, and fries. The outfield grill in the family area offers some elevated concessions, including a jumbo dog, chili dog, brat, Italian sausage, and pulled-pork platters, all offered with a variety of sides, including potato salad, cole slaw, baked beans, and macaroni salad. Also available: poutine.

There is an expanded list of beers available, including craft beers from Goose Island, Elysian Brewing, Sweetwater, and Blue Point, as well as microbrews from Bud and Corona. (Be warned they are not cheap: $13 for a craft beer.) Also available alongside beer: wine and hard seltzers.

The specialty bars down each line—the WestJet Flight Deck and Eddie's—have a wider range of cocktail offerings, including frozen drinks, margaritas, well drinks, wine, and a $22 Malibu rum bucket.

INSIDER'S TIP
The Blue Jays do not allow any outside food to be brought inside the ballpark. Only a sealed water bottle, up to 20 ounces, is allowed.

PARKING

The onsite parking spaces are now reserved for season-ticket holders, as part of the former parking lot was devoted to the ballpark expansion. Otherwise, you'll need to park in the surrounding area at $15-$20 per car. You can find cheaper parking within a few blocks of the ballpark, however, as in the parking lot of the local VFW, with some spaces as low as $5. Watch the signs; the area is patrolled, and there are time restrictions in some areas. This lack of available parking is one reason why we park downtown for free and walk the several blocks to the ballpark, either via Douglas Avenue or the Pinellas Trail. The fact that the trail goes directly through a bucolic residential area is a nice bonus; the respite from the hustle and bustle of the greater Tampa Bay area is refreshing.

AUTOGRAPHS

Historically, the best spots for autographs: the open area down the right-field line, where the players go to and from the clubhouse. Players are also known for hanging out outside the playing field during the game once leaving the field of play. Players from both teams come to the edge of the stands to sign autographs before a game as well; visiting players next to the third-base dugout and Blue Jays players next to the first-base dugout and in the bullpen down the right-field line. We're not talking about scrubs here.

If you arrive before the start of games, you'll need to track players down at the Bobby Mattick Training Center at the Cecil B. Englebert Complex (1700 Solon Av.), where the team works out at the beginning of spring training. There are five fields, all open to the public except Field #1. Quite honestly, it's a challenge to attend practices here: there's no public parking at the Englebert Complex, so you'll need to scrounge in the general area for a parking spot.

WHERE TO SIT

The one issue with the ballpark renovations is that they didn't add much in the way of shaded seating. The only seating assured of shade at the beginning of a game is in the last three rows of the grandstands, with more seats on the first-base side becoming shaded during the course of the game. The first several rows in front of the suite level are good spots for shade throughout much of the game. The Blue Jays dugout is on the first-base side, so go for Sections 102-104 or 202-204 for the best views of players. Apply your sunscreen before heading to the ballpark or bring along a tube.

However, there are more spots to grab some shade during a game, including the concourse and the team store. And the upgrade to blue theater-style seating from aluminum bleachers—which could get awfully warm on a sunny day—is welcome, as is the addition of cupholders.

The new spaces on the wraparound concourse provide some new seating options to be considered. In front of the new left-field Eddie's Bar is more theater-style seating. Eddie's Bar is air-conditioned and open to all if not reserved by a group.

If you are like us and spend time wandering the ballpark during a game, consider spending some time in the WestJet Flight Deck, located on the concourse on the right-center-field side. Besides sporting its own bar, the WestJet Flight Deck also features three levels of standing room spots with bar rails, as well as good vantage points of both bullpens. Indeed, the addition of a wraparound concourse gives you plenty of views of both bullpens in a variety of spots.

SELFIE SPOTS

The front entrance has several spots to grab a shot with a Toronto Blue Jays logo in the background.

IF YOU GO

WHAT TO DO OUTSIDE THE BALLPARK

Dunedin is one of the oldest cities in Florida, and for a time was a major seaport in the area. Today, the area is better known for its beaches and its proximity to Tampa/St. Petersburg. If you're craving some rays, you should check out Caladesi Island, which has been called one of the top 10 beaches in the United States. Also worth checking out is Honeymoon Island, which was settled in the 1930s as a honeymoon resort and is now a state park.

TD Ballpark is a mile or so south of downtown Dunedin, which features small shops and restaurants. Chances are you're going to be thirsty before or after the game, and there are a few joints in downtown Dunedin worth a visit; the folks in Dunedin apparently appreciate a snort now and again, because downtown is crawling with bars and brewpubs. No, Dunedin doesn't close down at 7 p.m., as many like to say.

In fact, one of our favorite spring-training experiences is to park in downtown Dunedin, have a nice brunch at one of the many dining establishments, and then walk down the Pinellas Trail south to the ballpark. The walk is less than a mile, and it saves you from the crowds fighting over the few parking spots outside the ballpark. (On weekends you can park downtown without worrying about a time limit in the conveniently located parking lots.) Our personal favorite for brunch on the weekend: the aptly named Café Alfresco, located right on the Pinellas Trail where it intersects Main Street in downtown Dunedin. We're fans of the Crab Cakes Benedict on the weekend, but pastries and espresso drinks are also on the menu. Sit on the covered patio if it's a nice day. *Café Alfresco, 344 Main St., Dunedin; 727/736-4299; cafealfresco.com.*

Also worthy of a morning stop before an afternoon game: Dunedin Coffee Company & Bakery, which serves up a great cup of joe, a mean sweet potato biscuit, and fresh hot cinnamon rolls. *Dunedin Coffee Company & Bakery, 730 Broadway, Suite 3, Dunedin; 727/286-6147; dunedincoffeeandbakery.com.*

If you want to stick closer to the ballpark, Home Plate—which sits between the ballpark and the Pinellas Trail, with a backyard patio on the trail side—offers a lineup of breakfast diner items, some solid lunch offerings, and a few "German" plates like bratwurst goulash and apple strudel. The prices are affordable and the food is solid. No, you can't park there at breakfast and leave your car during the game. *Home Plate, 234 Douglas Av., Dunedin; 727/953-9812.*

Dunedin has turned into a brewpub nirvana, as there are several good ones in the general downtown area. Beer lovers will appreciate Dunedin Brewery, which brews a wide variety of beers on site and billed as Florida's oldest microbrewery. Recommended: the Apricot Peach Ale. There's also a limited food menu and live music on the weekends. Bonus: the brewpub is within walking distance of the ballpark, on the same street—Douglas Avenue. *Dunedin Brewery, 937 Douglas Av., Dunedin; 727/736-0606; dunedinbrewery.com.*

Also worth checking out is 7venth Sun Brewery (*1012 Broadway, Dunedin; 727/733-3013; 7venthsun.com*), a woman-owned and -run brewery with a notable tap menu. Located next to the Pinellas Trail is the Cueni Brewery Co. (*945 Huntley Av., Dunedin; 727/266-4102; cuenibrewing.com*). It's a small space, but there is a great variety of brews on tap; we recommend the Belgian-style ales. Woodwright Brewing (*985 Douglas Av., Dunedin; 727/238-8717; woodwrightbrewing.com*) took over a woodworking shop and transformed it into a gorgeous brewpub space. Highly recommended both for beer and ambiance. Also located on Main Street near the Pinellas Trail: Caledonia Brewing (*587 Main St., Dunedin; 727/351-5105; caledoniabrewing.com*) is located in a converted newspaper building once housing the *Dunedin Times.* The place has been gutted, and now it sports currently trendy longtables designed to create a communal experience. You'll find a wide variety of beers on tap, some brewed onsite and some outside offerings, including mainstream brews like pale ales, reds, and Hefeweizens to exotic offerings like cherry wheats, peppercorn lime Mexican lagers, and lemongrass IPAs. The Dunedin House of Beer (*927 Broadway, Dunedin; 727/216-6318; dunedinhob.com*) has enough big screens and sports programming to fill your March Madness needs, complete with a *very* long beer

list: some 40+ beers and ciders on tap. A little farther afield: Soggy
Bottom Brewing, serving a mean toasted coconut porter. *Soggy
Bottom Brewing, 662 Main St., Dunedin; 727/601-1698;* **soggybot-
tombrewing.com.**
     If beer is not your thing, there are other downtown watering
holes worth checking out. Crown and Bull (the former Kelly's Chic-
a-Boom Room) has been upscaled by local owners. There's less
emphasis on boozy "martoonis" and more emphasis on traditional
cocktails and food prepared with fresh, local ingredients. *Crown and
Bull, 319 Main St., Dunedin; 727-736-5284;* **crownandbull.com.**
     Flanagan's Irish Pub is exactly what you'd expect: a faux Irish
pub featuring Irish beers (Guinness, Harp, and Smithwick's) and
Irish foods like fish and chips, bangers and mash, and corned beef
and cabbage. Expect a big St. Pat's blowout at Flanagan's. *Flanagan's
Irish Pub, 465 Main St., Dunedin; 727/736-4994;* **flanagansirishpub.net.**
     Also downtown: the highly rated Carvor's Fish House, an old-
style Florida hot-fish house featuring (what else?) a killer grouper
sandwich as well as a host of other seafood specialties (fish and
chips, smoked salmon, crab cakes). *Carvor's Fish House, 907 Douglas
Av., Dunedin; 727/754-4240;* **jensenbros-seafood.com.** Or, better yet,
dine waterside at Olde Bay Cafe, located at the Dunedin Marina.
The menu emphasizes grouper (of course!), shrimp, and the fresh
catch of the day. Catch the sunset during a late dinner. *Olde Bay Cafe,
51 Main St. Dunedin; 727/733-2542;* **oldebaycafe.com.**
     We have a host of sports bars in Dunedin as well. For those who
like their food and drinks more traditional in nature, Norton's
Sports Bar is a testosterone haven, featuring 18 televisions
(all showing some manner of sporting event) and seven video
games, including multiple Golden Tee's with big screens. Maybe it's
a guy thing, and maybe it's a little perverse to do thing while on
spring break in Florida, but we love playing video golf on vacation.
Norton's Sports Bar; 1824 Main St., Dunedin; 727/734-2053; **sportsbar-
dunedin.com.** Clear Sky Draught Haus sports an impressive brunch:
just the place to hit before that 1:07 p.m. Sunday matinee. Yes, there
is a Bloody Mary bar on weekends. *Clear Sky Draught Haus, 680
Main St., Dunedin; 727/286-6266;* **clearskydraughthaus.com.**

WHERE TO STAY

Dunedin is in the northwest corner of the Tampa Bay region and adjacent to Clearwater. We cover the hotel scene in the Tampa Bay region in our previous chapter covering Tampa Bay, but if you're a diehard Blue Jays fan and want to stay as close to the ballpark as possible (or on the Gulf Coast, overlooking the water), there are a few hotels worth noting. Don't bother trying to stay at the team hotel: the Blue Jays don't have one.

The Best Western Plus Yacht Harbor Inn (*150 Marina Place, Dunedin; 727/733-4121; bestwestern.com*) is at Dunedin's Marina Plaza and overlooks St. Joseph's Sound. It's an older two-story motel-style establishment, but it's been recently refurbished, and you can't beat the location: besides being on the waterfront it's also the hotel closest to the ballpark—you can walk through downtown Dunedin on your way to a game.

Considerably more upscale: The Fenway Hotel (*453 Edgewater Dr., Dunedin; 844/569-9879; fenwayhotel.com*), a historic old (built in 1924) beach hotel that's been renovated and updated.

Also located less than a mile from the ballpark are the Holiday Inn Express and Suites (*975 Broadway St., Dunedin; 727/450-1200; ihg.com*) and Comfort Suites (*1941 Edgewater Dr., Clearwater; 727/489-5000; comfortinn.com*).

RV PARKS IN THE AREA

It's not really within walking distance, but the Sun Retreats Dunedin RV Resort is located on the Pinellas Trail and close to area beaches. Bring a bike and take the trail to the ballpark. *Sun Retreats Dunedin, 2920 Alt 19. N., Dunedin; 727/784-3719; sunoutdoors.com.*

FLYING IN

The closest airport to Dunedin is St. Petersburg-Clearwater International Airport (*fly2pie.com*), located on the west side of the bay. This airport specializes in low-fare carriers in the United States, but there's currently no airline flying direct from Canada. It's also small enough where the car-rental agencies (Avis, Budget, Enterprise, Hertz, National, and Alamo) are truly on site.

In case you can't get a convenient flight into St. Pete-Clearwater, you'll want to check out Tampa International Airport. All the major airlines fly into Tampa; in addition, Air Canada flies daily from Toronto, and with seasonal nonstop service from Ottawa, Halifax, Montreal and other large Canadian cities, while WestJet flies from Calgary and Hamilton.

SPRING TRAINING HISTORY: TORONTO BLUE JAYS

The Toronto Blue Jays have been training at this site since 1977, first at Grant Field and then at TD Ballpark.

GEORGE M. STEINBRENNER FIELD / NEW YORK YANKEES

QUICK FACTS

- **Capacity**: 10,031
- **Year Opened**: 1996; renovated 2017
- **Dimensions**: 318L, 399LC, 408C, 385RC, 314R
- **Tickets Line**: 800/745-3000
- **Local Airport**: Tampa
- **Dugout Location**: First-base side
- **Pregame Schedule**: Gates open 90 minutes before the game. Yankees batting practice times change daily.
- **Address**: One Steinbrenner Drive, Tampa, FL 33614.
- **Directions**: From I-275: take Exit 41B (Dale Mabry Highway) and proceed north approximately three miles. The ballpark is on your left; Raymond James Stadium will be on your right. Follow the signs for parking. From the airport: take the Spruce Street exit out of the airport. Spruce will turn into Boy Scout Road. You will approach Dale Mabry from the west: stay in the left lanes and turn north (left) onto Dale Mabry. Follow the signs for parking.

YANKEE LEGENDS IN TAMPA

George M. Steinbrenner Field is one of the most popular venues in the Grapefruit League, a status boosted by a 2017 renovation that overhauled major parts of the ballpark. It's basically a miniature Yankee Stadium, as the outfield fences are the same dimensions as those in Yankee Stadium, the decorative elements ringing the grandstand are exactly like those found at the original and new Yankee Stadium, the wind screens down each line spell out YANKEES (just in case you've forgotten where you are), and a miniature Monument Park honoring former Yankee greats is located behind the grandstand.

While Steinbrenner Field was certainly popular in previous years, the 2017 upgrades touched on every fan-facing part of the ballpark. First, a 360-degree concourse added plenty of new seating options for groups and individuals, giving fans the ability to circle the action during a game. It was one of the last large ballparks built for spring training without a concourse level ringing the entire playing field. Fans were expected to stay in their seats and watch the action, not walk around and view the action from different vantage points.

The Steinbrenner Field experience begins in the right-field corner, where a small alternative entrance was expanded into what many fans will experience as the main entrance to the ballpark after parking across Dale Mabry Highway and traversing the pedestrian bridge. Previously, the "front" of Steinbrenner Field was behind the grandstand, the stairs located near the team store and ticket booths. That meant a long walk for the vast number of Yankees fans attending a spring-training game.

Most fans will park across the street at Raymond James Stadium parking and then cross Dale Mabry Highway via bridge to access Steinbrenner Field. In the past, fans were directed from this spot to the back of Steinbrenner Field and a large ticket office, but today this serves as the beginning of the Yankees spring-training experience. The expanded box office, complete with Will Call, is a much more inviting entrance than the old small entryway. Once past the obligatory metal detectors, you have an immediate selfie spot with a NY logo, as well as a view of the bullpen and the playing field.

INSIDER'S TIP

Despite this inviting entrance, think twice about entering here. There are three reasons to bypass this new entrance and head to the "front" of the ballpark. First, there is a moving memorial to 9/11 and the World Trade Center at the front of the ballpark. Second, there's the local equivalent of a Yankee Stadium Monument Park, and it sits outside the ballpark security gates; once you're in the ballpark, you can't leave and reenter. Third, there's a great statue of George M. Steinbrenner. Love him or hate him, he was a seminal figure in baseball history and brought the Yankees back to prominence.

INSIDER'S TIP

Our advice comes with a big asterisk. The Yankees have been renovating Steinbrenner Field's general area behind the grandstand, between the ballpark and the closest practice field. Part of this involves an expansion of player facilities, and we assume there will be some new features aimed toward fans. The work is happening as this book goes to press; we can't wait to see what happens.

What had been mostly open space past the outfield fence is now home to a 360-degree concourse and a series of individual and group seating areas, including reserved seating at a drink rail from each corner to the batter's eye. There are two-story structures in each corner. In right field, the old group seating area has been replaced by a large canopied bar and an abundance of four tops, leading down to rows of food rails and reserved chairs.

Next to the bar: a canopied cabana area that can be sold as a group area or as individual seating areas, complete with all-inclusive ballpark food and drinks. On the other side of the batter's eye, in left field, the seating resumes and runs in front of the high-def scoreboard all the way to the corner. A second level incorporates more canopied drink-rail seating. The spaces on both levels can also be sold as group areas or opened to the public as general admission.

About those concession stands: food and beverage options are now front and center. Previously, concessions were centralized on the outer concourse, requiring fans to totally remove themselves from the action for that beer and brat run. With bars and lounges down each line, it's now easier to grab a beer and not miss any action. While most concession stands are still located in the outer concourse, you now have more options for snaring a beer without missing the action. Many fans will spend time in one of the two new clubs down each line, as they feature large bars and elevated seating. Position yourself in the right spot, and you can see the action from a shaded club area.

The clubs feature different layouts and different themes: one features a photo montage of Yankee sluggers, while the other focuses on great Yankee pitchers. The Bullpen Club sits above the Yankees bullpen in right field, while the Third Base Club sits above the visitors' bullpen in left field. They are packed before the game started, so head there early.

As you walk through the ballpark, pay close attention to the grandstand entry tunnels, as they sport graphics focusing on Yankee history and Yankees spring training. The entryways are arranged by decades. For example, the large graphic focused on the 1940s and 1950s shows players running through spring-training double-play drills under the supervision of Yankee lifer Frankie Crosetti in February 1958. (Inside the tunnel: a smaller display of World Series championships and a nice shot of Mickey Mantle.) On the concourse: banners showing Yankee greats, along with an exhortation for fans to create their own Yankee memories.

The upgrades certainly brought a new life to Steinbrenner Field. Yankees fans—whether in Florida or New York State—love spring training and return for more every March. Even though the renovations touched on every part of Steinbrenner Field, they were understated. There are just enough suites to entice the moneyed (and many of the 12 luxury suites are leased by local firms, not expatriate New Yorkers), and just enough high-end seating in the first few rows of action to please big-buck fans. It is a ballpark built for Yankees fans.

The Yankees feature a practice field next to the monument area outside the park. With its own concession stands, bleachers, and restrooms, the scaled-down practice field is a wonderful place to watch a practice before the actual games start, and a good place to get close to the players.

INSIDER'S TIP
The Yankees also practice at times in Steinbrenner Field, but those practices are not always open to the public. Fans always love the idea of showing up to practices before the game schedule kicks in, but be warned you could show up for a Yankees practice and be locked out of the ballpark.

If you're a Yankees fan, Steinbrenner Field is nirvana, a shrine to Yankeedom. There are plenty of nice New York touches inside and outside the ballpark. Former Yankees greats are immortalized in a walking area outside the front gates: 18 Yankees have had their numbers retired, and these former greats are honored with plaques. Like the Mets, the Yankees commemorate 9/11 with steel from the World Trade Center. When the Yankees win, you can expect to hear Frank Sinatra belting out "New York, New York."

INSIDER'S TIP
The Yankees braintrust and selected guests can be found at spring-training games in Suite 1. It's the one farthest to the left as you're facing the suite level from the playing field.

Steinbrenner Field is centrally located in Tampa, only three miles from the airport and directly across from Raymond James Stadium (home of the NFL's Tampa Bay Buccaneers); chances are good you'll see it from the airplane during your approach if you fly into Tampa.

BALLPARK HISTORY

Steinbrenner Field has been the spring-training home of the New York Yankees since it opened in 1996. At the beginning of the 2008 regular season, it was renamed George M. Steinbrenner Field in honor of Yankees owner and area resident George Steinbrenner; before that it was known as Legends Field.

Before the move to Tampa, the Yankees trained at Fort Lauderdale Stadium between 1962 and 1995. We cover other Yankee-related landmarks in greater Tampa Bay later in this chapter.

Steinbrenner Field is also the regular-season home of the Single-A Tampa Tarpons.

THE SPRING-TRAINING BALLPARK EXPERIENCE

CONCESSIONS

For the most part, fans will head to the rear concourse for food and beverages, a situation that really can't be changed without major alterations to the ballpark. The concessions have been spruced up: there's lots of Yankee blue, and what had more closely resembled a massive food court is now a more refined experience. (The food seems better as well: the jumbo hot dog from Boar's Head is simply outstanding. And plenty of local vendors are still represented by standalone carts.) The usual suspects are on tap: local favorite Yuengling and a host of craft beers like Cigar City's Jai Alai IPA (brewed less than two miles from Steinbrenner Field; we discuss Cigar City later), as well as another notable specialty brew: Pinstripe Pils from Blue Point. If you're there with the family, search out the family bucket of chicken tenders or sliders with fries.

In fact, take the time to peruse all the food options at Steinbrenner Field before committing to a purchase. In 2022, we cruised the concourse before circling back to a surprisingly busy stand featuring plant-based options. There, we purchased a very tasty and very affordable plant-based sausage, topped with sauerkraut and mustard. Now, we don't expect the majority of Steinbrenner Field attendees to go vegan. But the fact that there were enough folks ordering plant-based hot dogs and sausages to keep a a whole stand busy—with the bonus that they offering one of the best vegan sausages we've ever had—says a lot about how concessions are run in Steinbrenner Field to appeal to all baseball fans.

Away from the food stands, the team store has been expanded to a two-story affair, accentuated by a huge traditional top-hat-and-bat logo on the exterior. (One word of warning. If you want to visit the tribute to the George Steinbrenner statue and retired numbers in the Tampa version of Monument Park, do so before entering the ballpark. There is a doorway leading out to the monument area from the team store, but that exit is closed on game day. The monument area is technically outside the ballpark walls, and MLB's spring-training policies prohibit reentry to the game.) If you look at the concessions or the exterior of the new clubs, you'll see metal accented by striping. That's no accident: it's a direct homage to the Yankee pinstripes.

INSIDER'S TIP
The Yankees restrict what can be brought into the ballpark: no outside food or drinks (alcoholic or not).

AUTOGRAPHS

When you enter the training complex from the parking lot, you might see the Yankees on a fenced-in practice field on your left as you circle the ballpark, though in recent years this field has been used less and less for game warmups. Still, it's worth a visit, especially if you want to peruse the monument area before the game. You'll be quite a distance from the players, so don't bother trying to score an autograph from that angle, though you can get closer if you head for ground level and enter the field via a gate behind home plate. The Yankees sometimes warm up on this practice field. In the past, it was hard to snare an autograph, but in recent years the team seems to have put more emphasis on telling players to warm up to fans. Spring training tends to be reunion time for the Yankees as well, and you'll find former greats like Reggie Jackson just hanging out as well. Go ahead; they're happy to talk with average fans, and they're even polite to the professional autograph hunters.

Before spring-training games start you're welcome to attend Yankees practices, which are generally held between 11 a.m. and 2 p.m.

WHERE TO SIT

Before the renovations, there were basically three seating areas in Steinbrenner Field: the lower bowl (controlled by season-ticket holders), the upper bowl (where it was easier to snare a ticket), and the right-field group area. Today, we're hesitant to assign a specific number to the Steinbrenner Field seating areas, as there's so much flexibility in the new areas and more distinct areas to peruse. A conservative estimate of GMS seating areas would be in double figures.

The best seats in the ballpark are bought by season-ticket holders —and there are many in the greater Tampa area—but Steinbrenner Field is so big you can usually find a decent seat. (Warning: a game against a big foe or a popular team training in Tampa Bay, like Boston or Philadelphia, will quickly sell out.) The Yankees' dugout is on the first-base side, so Sections 103-109 and 203-209 will give you the best views of players. Don't assume you can buy a ticket to the far reaches of the ballpark and then head down to grab an autograph: ushers prevent anyone but ticketholders from going down to the field level before a game.

If you desire shade during an afternoon game, sit in the second level behind the Yankees dugout, in Sections 203-210. You can also find shade in the last four rows of the rest of the upper sections (211-220). The 2017 renovation added more shaded seating to the mix.

PARKING

Wear your walking shoes unless you're one of those lucky season-ticket holders with access to a spot directly next to the ballpark. General parking at Raymond James Stadium costs $15 and is a fair distance from the ballpark. You must traverse an overpass over a six-lane highway (Dale Mabry) from the parking lot to the ballpark. From the overpass, you can enter at the new expanded entrance on the second floor or go down the stairs to a main entrance near the souvenir shop.

INSIDER'S TIP
It's a long walk from the parking lot to the ballpark. The Yankees allow those with mobility issues, even without a handicapped car sticker, to be dropped off at the front of the ballpark, where they can take elevators up to the second level.

INSIDER'S TIP
Parking lots open four hours before gametime. They have a somewhat active tailgating culture.

MINOR LEAGUERS

The Yankees minor-league squads do not practice at the Steinbrenner Field complex. You can find them at the Yankees Complex (*3102 N. Himes Av., Tampa*), a longish walk from Steinbrenner Field at the corner of Dale Mabry and Columbus Drive.

SELFIE SPOTS

Monument Park and the Steinbrenner statue are popular spots, but you'll need to grab a selfie there before or after a game: they're outside the ballpark gates, and MLB is strict about no re-admittance to the ballpark once you leave. Inside the ballpark, the most popular is the NY cap logo statue located right inside the right-field entrance. There are lines of folks waiting to take a selfie there before a game. In addition, there are statues of two numbers—#2 (Derek Jeter) and #15 (Thurman Munson)—in the outfield concourse. And, with all the new seating areas, there are plenty of vantage points for social-media pics.

IF YOU GO

WHAT TO DO OUTSIDE THE BALLPARK

Steinbrenner Field is in the middle of Tampa, so the information in our Tampa chapter particularly applies to Yankees fans.

In addition to the general Tampa activities, there are some other noteworthy attractions and restaurants within a short distance of the ballpark that will give you a true flavor of Tampa. Dale Mabry Highway is an interesting stretch of road: between an upscale retail cluster at I-275 and the ballpark is a vast wasteland of strip clubs, gas stations, and fast-food joints. It's not always a place to hang out with the kids, but you can be assured it represents the very essence of Tampa.

Near Steinbrenner Field is La Teresita, a down-home neighborhood Cuban/Spanish joint with some great food: Cuban sandwiches, shredded beef, fried plantains, *frijoles negros, arroz con leche*, and some truly great *ropa vieja*. You can get the food to go (which would make for some interesting tailgating at the Steinbrenner Field parking lot) or sidle up to the counter. It's also a great spot to hit after one of the many Yankees spring-training night games: La Teresita stays open until midnight weekends. *La Teresita, 3246 W. Columbus Dr., Tampa; 813/879-4909;* **lateresitarestaurant.com.**

Close to the ballpark (1.3 miles away): Riveters Tampa, an upscale sports bar with some elevated food options. Open till midnight, the place features 16 big screens for March Madness play and a patio for those lovely Tampa nights. It opens at 11 a.m., which means you'd be better off stopping by after an afternoon game or before a night game. *Riveters Tampa, 2301 N. Dale Mabry Hwy., Tampa; 813/723-5197;* **riveterstampa.com.**

Between Steinbrenner Field and I-275 is the taproom for Cigar City Brewing Company. Though the brewery has outgrown this modest taproom, this is where Cigar City's flagship brews, such as Jai Alai IPA, originated. Today the Spruce Street taproom features a full kitchen and a wide offering of beers, including some selections available only in the brew hall. *Cigar City Brewing Company, 3924 W. Spruce St., Tampa; 813/348-6363;* **cigarcitybrewing.com.** In general, there is an abunance of offerings as you approach I-275 from the ballpark (Sundra, Cooper's Hawk, Union New American).

WHERE TO STAY

Given that most Yankees fans are rather fanatical in nature, many readers of this book will want to stay as close to the ballpark as possible. (One imagines they would sleep in their cars outside the ballpark if they could.) There are hotels within easy walking distance of the ballpark on Dale Mabry, but we don't recommend either of them. (In fact, if the reviews at the likes of Yelp and Trip-Advisor can be believed, you would do well to avoid them.)

To be fair, there are a number of very fine hotels just over a mile from the ballpark, to the south at the Westshore area and to the north, approaching International Plaza. Are they walkable locations? Be warned the ballpark is located in a very car-centric part of Tampa.

Since you likely will have a car at your disposal, you should not feel compelled to stay within walking distance of Steinbrenner Field. That doesn't mean you need to stay miles and miles from the ballpark, however. Steinbrenner Field is less than three miles from the airport, so any of the many airport hotels would work. In addition, there are a slew of hotels within a short drive of Steinbrenner Field, roughly between the ballpark, International Plaza, and the airport to the south, advertising themselves as "airport stadium" hotels—like the Hilton Tampa Airport Westshore (*2225 N. Lois Av., Tampa; 813/877-6688; hilton.com*), Hampton Inn & Suites Tampa Airport Avion Park (*5329 Avion Park Dr., Tampa; 813/287-8500; hilton.com*), Homewood Suites Tampa Airport (*5325 Avion Park Dr., Tampa; 813/282-1950; hilton.com*), and the Hyatt Place Tampa Airport/Westport (*4811 W. Main St., Tampa; 813/282-1037; hyatt.com*). Note that a few of the recommended hotels here are in the Avion Park area, south of the airport: it's a nifty cluster of hotels that provides easy access to your flights and a World of Beer (*5311 Avion Park Drive, Tampa; 813/930-5499; worldofbeer.com*). You won't be able to walk to Steinbrenner Field from these hotels, but their proximity will come in handy if you're staying for multiple games.

Though farther away from the ballpark, the Rocky Point Island

area of Tampa houses many popular hotels. We cover them in the
Tampa intro.

SPRING TRAINING HISTORY: NEW YORK YANKEES

The New York Yankees have held spring training in the following
locations: Baltimore (1901); Savannah, Ga. (1902); Atlanta (1903-
1904); Montgomery, Ala. (1905); Birmingham, Ala. (1906); Atlanta
(1907-1908); Macon, Ga. (1909); Athens, Ga. (1910-1911); Atlanta
(1912); Hamilton, Bermuda (1913); Houston (1914); Savannah, Ga.
(1915); Macon, Ga. (1916-1918); Jacksonville (1919-1920); Shreveport
(1921); New Orleans (1922-1923); St. Petersburg (1924-1942); Asbury
Park, N.J. (1943); Atlantic City (1944-1945); St. Petersburg (1946-
1950); Phoenix (1951); St. Petersburg (1952-1961); Ft. Lauderdale
(1962-1995); and Tampa (1996-present).

PUBLIX FIELD AT JOKER MARCHANT STADIUM / DETROIT TIGERS

QUICK FACTS

- **Capacity**: 9,568
- **Year Opened**: 1966; renovated in 2003 and 2016
- **Dimensions**: 340L, 420C, 340R
- **Ticket Line**: 866/66-TIGER
- **Season Ticket Line**: 863/686-8075
- **Local Airport**: Tampa (preferred) or Orlando
- **Dugout Location**: First-base side
- **Workouts Begin**: Practices begin at 10:30 a.m.
- **Pregame Schedule**: Tigers infield, before 11; Tigers batting practice, 11-11:20 a.m.; visitors batting practice, 11:20 a.m.-12:20 p.m.; visitors infield, 12:20-12:30 p.m. Add five hours for 6:05 p.m. game start.
- **Address**: Publix Field at Joker Marchant Stadium: 2301 Lakeland Hills Blvd., Lakeland, FL 33805. TigerTown address: 2125 N. Lake Av., Lakeland, FL 33805.
- **Directions**: Take Exit 33 off I-4 onto Highway 33 South. TigerTown and the ballpark are approximately 2.5 miles on the left. There is signage pointing out two parking areas next to the ballpark.

THE TRADITIONS OF TIGERTOWN

TigerTown is the last great traditional spring-training complex in Florida, with the relationship between the Detroit Tigers and Lakeland dating back to 1934 (taking a break for the war years, of course), with the team playing first at nearby Henley Field and then Joker Marchant Stadium in 1966. Over those many years TigerTown has evolved into a complete training complex that includes the ballpark, other training fields, dorm, training facilities, and team clubhouses. Only Bradenton's LECOM Park has as much history as does TigerTown, but there's not the same association with one team that Lakeland and TigerTown have with the Detroit Tigers.

Publix Field at Joker Marchant Stadium doesn't look much like it did when opening in 1966. Back then, Joker Marchant Stadium was a very basic facility, with a generic grandstand and the obligatory concessions tucked underneath. The on-field action was the focus; fans were expected to be happy with basic seating and limited concessions. The assumption was that you were in Lakeland to see Al Kaline and Willie Horton work out the winter rust. Heck, the team's former spring home, Henley Field, had more shaded seats than did the original Joker Marchant Stadium.

Not anymore. A 2016-2017 renovation saw a dramatic overhaul to Publix Field at Joker Marchant Stadium, one that expanded the ballpark footprint while adding a slew of fan amenities to the mix. That dreadful brutalist concrete bleacher section down the left-field line is gone, replaced by shaded, modern seating angled toward the infield. The right-field administration building is long gone, replaced by a restaurant and outdoor seating area wrapped around the foul pole, and fans are now able to buy access to an air-conditioned club and 200-capacity picnic area. The bullpens are both located in right field, and a small porch extends into the action in the corner.

The left-field berm area features upgraded concessions in a hospitality pavilion, new Adirondack seating complete with a bar rail, and picnic seating. It's now positioned as a year-round destination. And yes, there is still some grassy berm seating there, just not as much as before. Sitting above the berm: a high-def scoreboard.

In right field: a space the Tigers call the Runway, featuring a long drink rail, new concessions, and additional four-top seating. The Runway is a reference to the site's history as an aerial training center during World War II. When Joker Marchant first opened, the old training runway was still out past right field, as well as Quonset huts used to house pilots and trainers. (The Quonset huts are still there. You can't really see them from the ballpark, but they can be seen from the parking lot.) This is a huge area, providing room to make Publix Field at Joker Marchant Stadium a more accessible ballpark with a 360-degree concourse. In the past, you were pretty much confined to your seat unless you wanted to walk to an autograph area or behind the grandstand and bleachers, but the renovated Publix Field at Joker Marchant Stadium allows you to walk all the way around the ballpark.

The old administration building was replaced by multi-tiered group areas, all featuring Adirondack chairs and tables. The outfield berm was overhauled, with a new scoreboard soaring above a new bar, new picnic seating, and a reserved drink rail (again, complete with Adirondack chairs).

On the player side: a 78,000-square-foot player-development facility houses both the Major and Minor League clubhouses as well as a full weight room, air-conditioned batting cages, and hydrotherapy pools. It's billed as the largest in the Grapefruit

League and replaced the old 1950s-era clubhouse used first by the likes of Al Kaline.

Do not miss an opportunity to attend a spring game at Publix Field at Joker Marchant Stadium, even if you're not a Tigers fan. The handy location between Tampa and Orlando makes it an easily accessible destination for many spring-training fans, and the historic venue is worthy of a visit.

TigerTown is also one of the more historically interesting sites in the Grapefruit League. It was built on the site of a World War II flight school, the Lodwick School. Between 1940 and 1945, more than 8,000 cadets, including British Royal Air Force cadets, attended the Lodwick School of Aeronautics and more than 6,000 graduated. Some of the remnants of that school still exist, including several nearby hangars that have been renovated and used for various purposes. You can see them if you park on the first-base side of Publix Field at Joker Marchant Stadium. Old timers will remember when part of the Lodwick School runway sat beyond the right-field fences.

INSIDER'S TIP

The renovation meant that in 2016 the Lakeland Flying Tigers were displaced to Henley Field (*1125 N. Florida Av.*), the historic former spring home of the Tigers and current home of the Florida Southern College Moccasins baseball team. It served as a temporary spring home for the Tigers the last time Publix Field at Joker Marchant Stadium was renovated, and it's a great experience if you love old ballparks. The grandstand seating has been improved in recent years, but the ballpark exterior is the same Spanish Mediterranean stucco first used when the ballpark opened. We'd recommend taking in a Mocs game during spring training. The Mocs play plenty of night games in March, and you can easily combine a Tigers/Mocs doubleheader. The Mocs play competitive baseball in a Division II Sunshine State Conference (which includes baseball powerhouses like the University of Tampa and Rollins College), and you may see a future pro or two on the field. **Check out the Mocs schedule here.**

INSIDER'S TIP

There are new reminders of Tigers history throughout the training complex. Two surrounding streets are named for Kaline and Horton, while plaques on the first-base side honor Kaline, Joker Marchant, and the 1968 Detroit Tigers. Retired Tigers numbers are displayed on the administrative building.

The best thing about a Tigers spring-training game, however, is the laid-back atmosphere and easy accessibility to players and staff. It still feels like a spring-training game from a bygone era—and in this days of incessant social media and unrelenting marketing messages at the ballpark, that feeling is absolutely priceless.

BALLPARK HISTORY

Joker Marchant Stadium was built in 1966 for $360,000 and named after the city's popular parks and rec director, Marcus Thigpen "Joker" Marchant (*MAR-chant*).

THE SPRING-TRAINING BALLPARK EXPERIENCE

CONCESSIONS

For the most part, you can find the normal ballpark fare at the ballpark: hot dogs, chicken tenders, fish sandwiches, burgers, veggie burgers, peanuts, soda, pizza, beer, ice cream, etc. The pizza, of course, is Little Caesars: the late Mike Ilitch made his money by launching the Little Caesars pizza chain.

But don't limit yourself to a regular dog. A stroll through the concourse yields a wide variety of offerings. At various stands you can also find smoked turkey legs and other barbeque offerings, Tex-Mex, roasted street corn, burritos, salads, mac 'n cheese bowls, tater tots, sandwiches, and strawberry shortcake at an ice-cream stand.

Why strawberry shortcake? The region around Lakeland, especially in nearby Plant City, is known for its early-season strawberry crops, and it's a long-time tradition for the Tigers to sell strawberry shortcake at spring training. Wandering vendors also offer the strawberry delicacies; they're also available at a booth down the third-base line, which serves ice cream as well. And, if it's especially hot, check out the frozen lemonade.

A Michigan Coney Island Dogs stand serves coneys in both Michigan and Flint styles. (Far as we can tell, Michigan coneys are topped with a beanless chili, Flint coneys are topped with loose meat and no sauce. When we last visited the stand, the folks there were patient enough to explain the difference.) The same stand serves Cuban sandwiches and Philly cheesesteaks.

A craft beer/jumbo-pretzel stand is located in the rear concourse, near the first-base side. Beers on tap in the ballpark include Coors Light, Lite, Yuengling Lager, Blue Moon, and Guinness, while many stands offer beer as a secondary beverage. Hard lemonade is on the menu as well, while there are five bars placed throughout the concourse serving cocktails, premium/domestic beers, and wines.

In general, there are far more good food selections at Publix Field at Joker Marchant Stadium than in the past.

INSIDER'S TIP
The Tigers depart from MLB guidelines and prohibit all water bottles, coolers, food, cans, and folding chairs. However, you can bring in food for small children, as well as small strollers.

WHERE TO SIT

The 2017 grandstand renovation added a new canopy to the mix, which increased the number of shaded seats in the ballpark.

One thing that didn't change: season-ticket holders controlling the best seats in the house. The box seats in Sections 100-112 are pretty much controlled by season-ticket holders: Lakeland old-timers who make a point of attending every game and are on a first-name basis with every usher and concessionaire. These seats, however, are not shaded by the new canopy.

The best seats for the rest of us are in Sections 200-210, with the sweet spot between 202 and 210. The new canopy basically covers all the 200-level seating, save the first two rows, and the most shade can be found in Sections 200-206. (The canopy curves, and Section 207 features shaded seating only in the last 10 rows.) The Tigers' dugout is on the first-base side, which means Sections 202-204 will give you the best views of the players entering and leaving the dugout. There are six shaded sections (211-216), increasing the number of covered seats (rows N and up) from 1,246 to 2,098 seats. All chairback seats have cupholders.

The addition of a 360-degree concourse led the Tigers to lower berm prices, and we all love lower ticket prices.

INSIDER'S TIP

The renovations also included the addition of the 34 Club, located atop sections 200-201. It's named for 1934, the year the Tigers arrived in Lakeland. It features an indoor bar and seating, an all-inclusive buffet, and outdoor padded seating for 203 fans. The food offerings are varied—on Sundays, for example, traditional brunch offerings are served—but be warned you might have to share the space with a group or two. We'd recommend it. In addition, four former suites on the third-base side of the press box have been transformed into the On Deck Suite, an all-inclusive space for 36-60 people that includes upscale food and beverages. And if the sun gets to you, take a break at the 1,800-square-foot indoor merchandise store, located at the home-plate entrance.

AUTOGRAPHS

The TigerTown complex encompasses five practice fields in a cloverleaf layout, Publix Field at Joker Marchant Stadium, and Kaline Field, a small diamond located past the Publix Field at Joker Marchant Stadium left-field corner. Before the start of spring training, all practices take place on the five cloverleaf fields and Kaline Field. A roped-off path runs between the practice fields and the clubhouse, and that's the place to snare players once they leave practice, which traditionally begins at 10:30 a.m. Truth is, it's not easy snaring an autograph at Publix Field at Joker Marchant Stadium, as player access tends to be limited. Your best bet is getting to the ballpark as early as possible and working to attract the attention of a player willing to head toward the seats.

Once games start, the minor leaguers take over the cloverleaf fields, with the major-league squad decamping to Kaline Field or Marchant Stadium.

Granada Street runs north of TigerTown. You can park there and watch the workouts from the outfield fence. The practice fields are not always open to the public—in fact, in our experience, the Tigers cut off access more often than most teams, especially on game days —but you can always watch practices from the street. Don't expect anyone to wander out to the home-run fence to sign an autograph, however. From the back of the complex, you can also get some good views of Lake Parker.

If you arrive early enough, you might see players in the parking lot; you can also hang around the parking lot and try to attract their attention as they leave. Players enter and exit near Section 100, the last section in the grandstand down the right-field line, so that's a good place to snare a player as well.

INSIDER'S TIP
A group offering, the Hooters Dugout, is advertised as offering access to players for autographs. Adjacent to Section 100 (down the first-base line), the Hooters Dugout seats between 20 and 40 and includes an all-you-can-eat picnic with ballpark and Hooters food, along with your own server.

PARKING

Parking is $10 on adjacent lots ($8 if you buy in advance online), with an option for $20 premium parking. Get to the ballpark early: most folks head to the main entrance to the ballpark parking lot and traffic gets congested on Lakeland Hills Boulevard. We would not recommend parking in area streets and walking over, though many fans do. Golf carts patrol the parking lot if you have trouble walking a longer distance.

INSIDER'S TIP
As you enter TigerTown, keep to the parking lots to the right. These are the lots on the first-base side. Your car is less likely to be struck by a foul ball in these lots than in the ones on the third-base side.

INSIDER'S TIP
Here's a super-secret back way into the Joker Marchant

Stadium parking areas—especially handy if you're coming from the south. There's an overflow entrance on the south side of the parking lots. To access it, go east (right) on Bella Vista Street (before you hit the TigerTown complex) and hang a left (north) on Gilmore Avenue.

SELFIE SPOTS

The large sign at the entrance of the ballpark, changed out yearly now, is by far the most popular spot for a selfie. There is usually a line of folks waiting to take a shot there.

IF YOU GO

WHAT TO DO OUTSIDE THE BALLPARK

Lakeland is regarded as representing the best of Florida: its economy has benefited from the technology-company growth in both Tampa and Orlando, and it's also benefited from the rise of tourism in both cities. It does live up to the name: there are 38 lakes within the city limits.

This is citrus country, but today's economy is considerably more varied; though many of the 170,000 people in the area either work in the citrus industry or go into Tampa for a job, more work at companies like grocery-store-chain Publix, headquartered in Lakeland. As the area has thrived, so has downtown Lakeland, which has experienced a renaissance of sorts in the last decade. You can find some decent nightlife downtown; worth a visit are Molly McHugh's Irish Pub (*111 S. Kentucky Av.; mchughspubs.com*), which regularly features live music (including music scheduled for a St. Pat's Day street party) and offers standbys like Guinness and Harp on draught; Nineteen 61 (*215 E. Main St.; nineteen61.com*), featuring Latin cuisine; Black & Brew (*205 E. Main St.; blackandbrew.com*), a coffeeshop with sandwiches and salads; Mitchell's Coffee House (*235 N. Kentucky Av.; mitchellscoffee.com*), which features live music on weekends; and Cob & Pen (*1221 Florida Av. S., Lakeland; 863/937-8126; cobandpenlakeland.com*), a unique gastropub with some hidden spaces and great food. Highly recommended: Mojo Federal

Swine & Spirits (*130 S. Tennessee Av. Lakeland; 863/937-4226; mojob-bq.com*), located in the former downtown Post Office and offering traditional Southern barbecue with the usual sides (collard greens, dirty rice, mac and cheese), along with a decent bar and a great happy hour.

As with the rest of Florida, Lakeland has enjoyed a boom in microbreweries. Brew Hub (*3900 S. Frontage Rd., Lakeland; 863/698-7600; brewhub.com*) has a unique business model, combining a contract brewery with a brewery incubator and its own beers. Yes, beer nerds will be geeked out by a visit to the tasting room. Also worth a visit: Swan Brewing (*115 W. Pine St., Lakeland; 863/703-0472; swanbrewing.com*), where the flavors are eclectic—coconut, coffee, prickly pear, tangerine, and more. Be prepared to sit outside; the indoor seating is limited.

Downtown is also home to a historic district, which includes many restored buildings dating back to the early 1900s. It's a typical Florida vintage downtown in terms of architecture, and one gets the sneaking suspicion that the designers of Celebration, Disney's planned community near Disney World, basically stole the layout and feel of Lakeland and recreated it: there's a small lake and a scenic old hotel, The Terrace Hotel, on one end of downtown, and a slew of lakefront buildings with antique stores. Much of the downtown was renovated in recent years, to good effect.

Artsy types will delight in Lakeland. Worth a drive is the campus of Florida Southern College (*111 Lake Hollingsworth Drive; flsouthern.edu*), where nine buildings (dubbed "Child of the Sun") comprise the largest grouping of Frank Lloyd Wright-designed buildings in the world. Built between 1941 and 1948, the initial buildings were constructed by students supervised personally by Wright. You can go to the campus student center and pick up a brochure detailing the history of the buildings before you embark on a self-guided tour.

Also recommended: a drive out to Bok Tower Gardens, which opened in 1929 as a tribute to America by immigrant Edward Bok. Installed at a unusually high site for Florida—295 feet above sea level, one of the highest points of Florida—the site features nearly 50 acres of lush gardens laid out by Frederick Law Olmstead, Jr., a 60-bell carillon billed as a "singing tower," and a 1930s Mediterranean-style mansion. A carillon is a set of bells installed in a tower, played via a keyboard below. It's a unique musical instrument, as the bells do not swing, only the clappers. Carillons are usually found in university and civic buildings, so hearing one in such a setting is an unusual experience, to be sure. *Bok Tower Gardens, 1151 Tower Blvd., Lake Wales; 863/676-1408; **boktowergardens.org.***

One final recommendation: golf. Within a 50-mile radius of Lakeland there are more than 60 golf courses and over 500 holes of private and semiprivate golf courses. Worth noting: Eaglebrooke (*1300 Eaglebrooke Blvd., Lakeland; 863/701-0101; **eaglebrooke.com***) has been awarded four stars by *Golf Digest*, with a design by Ron Garl. One of the best public golf courses in the state is located in nearby Haines City: Southern Dunes Golf Club (*2888 Southern Dunes Blvd., Haines City; 866/TEE-BONE; **southerndunes.com***), a longer (7,227 yards) course with the reputation of being a very difficult play.

Lakeland is also centrally located and makes a good base for spring training, as the city is situated on I-4, the main interstate between Tampa and Orlando. There are four spring-training camps within an easy drive: Pittsburgh Pirates (Bradenton), Toronto Blue Jays (Dunedin), New York Yankees (Tampa), and Philadelphia Phillies (Clearwater).

WHERE TO STAY

Book early. The town fills up on weekends when the Tigers are in town, and a decent hotel room can be scarce. The best time to go is mid-week, in the middle of March, before the end-of-the-month rush associated with spring break in most states.

There is no good hotel within walking distance of Publix Field at Joker Marchant Stadium. There are plenty within a short (under two-mile) drive, mostly along I-4, including:

- Comfort Inn and Suites, Lakeland, 3520 N. Hwy. 98, Lakeland; 863/859-0100; *choicehotels.com.*
- Baymont by Wyndham Lakeland, 4375 Lakeland Park Dr., Lakeland; 863/858-9070; *baymontinns.com.*
- Sleep Inn & Suites, 4321 Lakeland Park Dr., Lakeland; 863/577-1170; *choicehotels.com.*
- Days Inn & Suites, 4502 N. Socrum Loop Rd., Lakeland; 863/797-4606; *wyndhamhotels.com.*

- Holiday Inn Express Hotel & Suites Lakeland North I-4, 4500 Lakeland Park Dr., Lakeland; 888/HOLIDAY; *ihg.com.*
- TownePlace Suites, 3370 U.S. Hwy. 98 N., Lakeland; 863/680-1115; *marriott.com.*

Because you'll be driving to the ballpark anyway, don't feel compelled to stay near Publix Field at Joker Marchant Stadium. Lakeland isn't the sleepy little Florida town it was decades ago, and the resulting growth has led to an abundance of hotels, including chains of all sorts, in the area. (During our last visit to Lakeland, we stayed in a Hilton Garden Inn close to the airport, on the other side of town from the ballpark. It was no big deal to drive to and from the Tigers games, and there were plenty of things to do in the immediate area. But we usually stay in Tampa or Orlando, and the drive is short and sweet.) Most of the newer chain hotels are located off the freeways on the outskirts of town, while the inner part of the city features older places.

If you want a more authentic Florida experience—but one of the priciest in town—check out The Terrace Hotel in downtown Lakeland, just a little over two miles from the ballpark. Opening in 1924 and now a Hilton property, The Terrace features 73 guest rooms, a lovely little veranda, and a spectacular dining room, the Terrace Grill. Make sure you get a room overlooking Lake Mirror. *The Terrace Hotel, 329 E. Main St., Lakeland; 863/688-0800;* **terracehotel.com.**

RV PARKS

The Lakeland RV Resort is located three miles north of Publix Field at Joker Marchant Stadium, conveniently just off Lakeland Hills Boulevard. Part of the Carefree chain of RV resorts, the Lakeland RV Resort has 230 full hook-up sites, a heated pool, and high-speed Internet access. *Lakeland RV Resort, 900 Old Combee Rd., Lakeland; 863/687-6146;* **sunoutdoors.com.**

WHERE TO EAT

Lakeland really isn't considered the fine-dining capital of Florida, but there are a number of good restaurants in the area. You can stick close to the freeway and eat at one of the many chain restaurants, but you can also venture into town for a good meal. Some spots recommended by the locals are:

- Fish City Grill (*1485 Town Center Drive S., Lakeland; 863/683-1243; fishcitygrill.com*). Seafood is the order of the day here, with offerings ranging from oyster nachos to fish tacos and grouper enchiladas.
- Harry's Seafood Bar and Grille (*101 N. Kentucky Av., Lakeland; 863/686-2228; hookedonharrys.com*). This Florida mini-chain combines Southern and Creole cuisine with a variety of seafood.

FLYING IN

Scheduled air service returned to Lakeland International Airport in 2024 in the form of Avelo Airlines (*aveloair.com*) service from various East Coast cities. (Nothing from Detroit, alas.) The closest major airport to Lakeland is in Tampa. It's a bigger airport that is serviced by all the major airlines. The Orlando airport, which is farther away and much bigger, can be daunting, so if fares are equal, you'll definitely want to fly into Tampa.

SPRING TRAINING HISTORY: DETROIT TIGERS

The Detroit Tigers have trained in Lakeland since 1934, save the war years. Other spring-training homes of the Tigers: Detroit (1901); Ypsilanti, Mich. (1902); Shreveport (1903-1904); Augusta, Ga. (1905-1907); Hot Springs, Ark. (1908); San Antonio (1909-1910); Monroe, La. (1911-1912); Gulfport, Miss. (1913-1915); Waxahachie, Texas (1916-1918); Macon, Ga. (1919-1920); San Antonio (1921); Augusta, Ga. (1922-1926); San Antonio (1927-1928); Phoenix (1929); Tampa (1930); Sacramento (1931); Palo Alto, Cal. (1932); San Antonio (1933); Lakeland (1934-1942); Evansville (1943-1945); and Lakeland (1946-present).

ORLANDO / DISNEY WORLD

ORLANDO: FLORIDA'S CROSSROADS

We saw a one-year return of spring training to Orlando in 2024, when the Rays relocated some spring ops to Disney's Wide World of Sports after hurricane damage to Charlotte Sports Park. True, spring training has never been a big deal in Orlando—for many decades, the only franchise training in town was the Washington Senators/Minnesota Twins, and in recent years only the Atlanta Braves trained in Orlando—but Orlando is such an important cog in the Florida tourism industry that coverage in this book is mandatory.

There's no doubt Orlando is an important part of the spring-training experience for many, many fans. With many spring-training fans flying in and out of Orlando and augmenting their trip with a theme-park visit or participation in one of the many college and high-school competitions held during spring-training season—baseball, danceline, soccer, softball, cheerleading—spending time in the area is mandatory for many.

Orlando is still the crossroads of the Grapefruit League, bridging the gap between the many teams training on the northern Gulf Coast and those on the eastern coast. Six teams (Mets, Yankees, Phillies, Blue Jays, Tigers, and Pirates) train within a relatively short car trip, and several college venues are in the area. Though most fans choose to stay close to the spring-training camp of their favorite team, there are many others who decide to set up shop in a central location—like Orlando—and then drive to spring-training and college games across central Florida.

The reason? Orlando relies heavily on the tourist economy and is synonymous with theme parks, so there are plenty of cheap hotel rooms, airfares, and attractions to entertain the family. There's never a lull in the competition for your dollars and attention in Orlando: between large-scale theme parks like Disney World and Universal Studios to more modest offerings like Gatorland, you'll never, ever run out of things to do. You can happily drive down to Publix Field at Joker Marchant Stadium for strawberry shortcake and a ballgame knowing your significant other and your children—those who aren't baseball fans, anyway—will be well-entertained in Orlando.

In addition, Orlando is a national hub for youth sports and activities, and your kids may end up at a baseball, cheerleading, or danceline competition in the area. (Don't be surprised if your flight to MCO is filled with a baseball or softball travel squad.) Generally, the cheapest direct fares from many destinations involve travel to or from Orlando. Or you may want to treat the family to a few days of theme-park action before or after your baseball travels: if piloting

the Millennium Falcon has been a dream for you or your children
(or, let's face it, maybe your parents), then a trip to Galaxy's Edge at
Disney's Hollywood Studios is mandatory.

If you attend spring training to spend 12 hours at the training
complex and soak up every minute of time tracking the exploits of
kids likely to end up at Single-A Rome at the start of the season,
then skip Orlando. For the rest of us, spring training is a renewal on
many levels: a renewal of our baseball passion and a renewal of our
general spirits. After a long, cruel winter we need some time in the
sun, and that doesn't automatically mean solely baseball: it means
baseball and more.

More is in abundance in Orlando—conveniently on the southwest side of town, as all three major Orlando attractions are located
along Interstate 4. (I-4 also leads directly to Tampa to the south,
making it a handy route to Orlando for those attending spring-
training games in Tampa and Lakeland.) The theme-park area is less
than 20 miles away from Orlando International Airport and features
Disney World, Universal Orlando, and Sea World. Also close to
Disney World are the bustling International Boulevard mélange of
hotels and attractions and the Hwy. 192 strip. We'll cover them all
here, making recommendations for hotels and restaurants along
the way.

THE HOUSE OF MOUSE

Is Disney World the happiest place on the planet? Yes. If you can't
have a good time at a Disney World theme park, there's something
wrong with you. The attractions are only getting better and better,
and no company manages queues and waits better than Disney. You
never feel cheated after spending $450 on the family for an entire
day at the Magic Kingdom or Epcot.

Of course, this certainly isn't the most original advice or a secret
to most of you—after all, Disney World is the most popular amusement park complex on the face of the planet—but we're here to tell
you the parks are worth the admission prices. With such a wide
range of lodging, dining, and entertainment options, a stay there
should be high on your shopping list as you cast the perfect spring-
training experience.

First, a general overview. To say that Disney World is a

sprawling complex is an understatement: it encompasses more than 30,000 acres and still hews to the original vision set forth by Walt Disney, who decided on Orlando for a new theme-park location after studying highway maps and touring the area via helicopter. (Indeed: plans for I-4 and Florida's Turnpike created a Florida freeway map that put Orlando squarely in the middle of the state transit system. That's still true today: all roads lead to Orlando.) It features four theme parks, two water parks, more than 30,000 hotel rooms, a major retail and entertainment complex, and a wide range of restaurants and smaller attractions. It is a world onto itself, with its own transit system and police squad.

There are four theme parks under the Disney World umbrella.

- The Magic Kingdom, which is a re-creation and expansion of the original Disneyland in Anaheim, California. It's divided into four "lands"—Frontierland, Fantasyland, Tomorrowland, Adventureland—and includes its own Main Street. Disney stalwarts like Pirates of the Caribbean, Space Mountain, Haunted Mansion, Big Thunder Mountain, and It's a Small World are located here. There's something for everyone: the smaller kids will enjoy the Winnie the Pooh and Peter Pan attractions, while teenagers will appreciate Space Mountain and a new Tron coaster. Fantasyland, in particular, has been upgraded in recent years with a major Seven Dwarfs roller coaster attraction and a high-end restaurant, Be Our Guest, which had been sorely lacking in the Magic Kingdom. The newest attraction: a reimagining of Splash Mountain as Tiana's Bayou Adventure, incorporating characters from *The Princess and the Frog*. The Magic Kingdom is by far the most popular Walt Disney World park.
- Epcot, which combines visions of tomorrow in Future World with a World's Fair-style pavilion of nations in World Showcase. Some of the rides show their age, but in a good way: they're close to the same as when Epcot opened in 1982, which makes great nostalgia for you and a new experience for your kids. The newer and renovated rides, such as Remy's Ratatouille Adventure, Frozen,

Guardians of the Galaxy, and Test Track, are worth the wait; they add an element of speed and freshness to what has traditionally been a laid-back theme park. As a bonus, the annual Epcot International Flower & Garden Festival runs during spring training. If you really need a respite from cold weather, a day in the sun at the immaculately groomed Epcot grounds with a cocktail in hand will soothe your soul. As a bonus: an impressive new fireworks show at the end of the day.

- Disney's Hollywood Studios, which now sports a decided Star Wars emphasis. Joining the existing Star Tours attraction is a themed area, Star Wars: Galaxy's Edge, which features Smuggler's Run, an interactive experience where you pilot the Millennium Falcon, and Star Wars: Rise of the Resistance, an elaborate multimedia experience that runs you through several scenarios until you emerge triumphant. There's more to Galaxy's Edge, including a restaurant, fast food, and the obligatory shops, but you get the idea. There is also a slew of movie-themed attractions (Indiana Jones), thrill rides (Tower of Terror, Rock 'n Roller Coaster), and live shows featuring Disney Channel tie-ins (like Disney Junior Live on Stage), appealing to a wide variety of ages. There's really not a part of Hollywood Studios that's not popular: the attractions at Toy Story Land attract long queues, and even an exhibit showcasing Walt Disney's life attracts crowds.

- Animal Kingdom, which transforms the swamps of Florida into a credible Serengeti Plain. The park is divided into geographic entities (Africa and Asia) as well as themes. For the smaller kids, the Kilimanjaro Safari provides a safe, up-close look at a raft of exotic animals. (If you go on the Kali River Rapids ride, bring along a rain poncho: you will be drenched.) The addition of rides based on the *Avatar* movies attracts hordes of new fans to Animal Kingdom. One of them, Flight of Passage, may be the most impressive attraction in any theme park in the world. Worth the wait.

It takes at least a half day to get the most out of Animal Kingdom or Hollywood Studios, a full day to experience most of Epcot, and in the case of Magic Kingdom, perhaps two days are appropriate.

ESPN WIDE WORLD OF SPORTS

It is one of the busiest sports-tourism venues in the world. When the Atlanta Braves committed to ESPN Wide World of Sports and The Stadium (formerly Champion Stadium) at Disney World in 1998, it put the place on the map. But the Wide World of Sports complex grew over the years to the point where pro baseball was an afterthought, with two arenas, a fieldhouse, and several soccer and football fields attracting youth tournaments and competitions year-round.

As far as youth sports complexes go, it's one of the busiest on the planet. It's also one of the nicest.

Virtually everyone first encounters the complex at a main entrance marked by an enormous globe signifying the Wide World of Sports. Those old enough will remember the original Wide World of Sports show on ABC, where Jim McKay introduced us to athletes experiencing "the thrill of victory...and the agony of defeat." There's little at the actual complex that references the original TV show, alas, but it's nice to see the groundbreaking broadcast memorialized in some form.

After the obligatory selfie at the Wide World of Sports globe and a stroll past an arena, you'll walk up to what's basically the complex's town square, consisting of entrances to The Stadium, the State Farm Field House, ESPN Wide World of Sports Grill, and the Athletic Center, as well as AdventHealth Arena. Close by are tennis courts, a track-and-field complex, soccer and football fields, youth and adult baseball and softball fields, and other athletic fields. The complex is used frequently for a variety of AAU and small-college events, as the State Farm Field House and AdventHealth Arena are used for volleyball, basketball, gymnastics, and more.

NAVIGATING DISNEY WORLD

Some tips for tackling the House of Mouse:

- Plan ahead. Do buy your tickets in advance: Though not mandatory for date-based tickets, you're still best off checking on the Disney website to see if you need a theme-park reservation on busy days, like holiday and over spring break. (Also, if you are using a Sports & Convention park pass, you *do* need to make a reservation.) Buying tickets and making reservations also makes available a Lightning Lane Multi Pass, allowing you to bypass lines on three attractions a day. The Lightning Lane Multi Pass replaces the Genie+, which in turn replaced the old Fast Pass system. By committing to a schedule, you also can schedule meals. The dining options at most of the theme parks can be limited, and if you don't want to eat fast food twice a day, you'll want to make reservations for sit-down restaurants in advance. Call 407/WDW-DINE for reservations and availability or check out the Disney website: you can make sit-down reservations online 60 days in advance of your visit. If you go the quick-service route, preorder your meals on the Disney World app—a download is mandatory for any visitor—to minimize wait times.
- If you have smaller children, check out the character dining options. At Epcot, the revolving Garden Grill Restaurant features Mickey Mouse and friends. At Hollywood Studios, Hollywood & Vine features visits from Disney Junior characters.
- Not everything carries a high price tag at Disney World. If you want the Disney experience without the high admission prices, head over to Disney Springs. The world's largest Disney-merchandise store is here, and kids will love the next-door LEGO Imagination Store. Disney Springs has undergone a huge transformation in recent years and is a great dining destination, including Chicken Guy! from Guy Fieri, Wolfgang Puck Bar and Grill, Jaleo by José Andrés, an overhauled Planet Hollywood, Chef

Art Smith's Homecomin' (with fried chicken to die for), Blaze Pizza, T-REX for a prehistoric meal, a waterfront Boathouse dining venue, and a STK steakhouse with rooftop seating. There is also a slew of retail stores, including UNIQLO, Under Armour, kate spade, and Lilly Pulitzer. If your family is the kind that finds shopping to be relaxing, you'll be able to spend some serious hours at Disney Springs.

- Also free: the late-afternoon feeding at the Animal Kingdom Lodge (located adjacent to the theme park). The resort is spectacular, and the feeding attracts zebras, giraffes, and other exotic animals from throughout the park.

Your first big decision, after you've decided to stay in Orlando, is whether or not to stay at Disney World. Yes, it will be more expensive than staying at the Comfort Inn on International Drive, and rooms in Disney resorts tend to be on the smaller side, but how many times are you going to be at spring training? The extended hours at the theme parks offered only to resort guests is also a persuasive argument for staying onsite.

Disney does make it easier by offering hotel rooms in four price ranges: Deluxe Villa ($450+ nightly), Deluxe ($300+ nightly), Moderate ($240+ nightly), and Value ($140+ nightly). Room rates at Disney World go up in March, but that's because of the prevalence of spring breaks during the month, not because of the hordes of spring-training fans.

There are two Value resorts near ESPN Wide World of Sports: The Art of Animation Resort and the Pop Century Resort. The Art of Animation Resort features plenty of suites (which can be hard to find in the lower-priced Disney accommodations), room layouts inspired by Disney animated classics (Cars Family Suites, Finding Nemo Family Suites, etc.), and a very large pool area. The Pop Century Resort is a sprawling affair that celebrates popular culture of all sorts (not just Disneyana) over the last 75 years or so—a time period squarely aimed at Baby Boomers. A large pool will appeal to the kids, while the Boomer memorabilia in the lobby will appeal to the parents.

Other Value resorts are worth checking out. Though it's closer to

Animal Kingdom than Wide World of Sports, baseball fans and their families will like Disney's All-Star Sports Resort: there's a section with a baseball theme, and the swimming pool is in the shape of a baseball diamond. The All-Star Movies Resort features two swimming pools and a Hollywood theme throughout. The All-Star Music Resort features pools shaped like a guitar and a piano, as well as rooms with different musical genres. Under most circumstances, these resorts are outliers, located far from the four theme parks. But in the world of spring training these resorts truly are All-Stars. More than once during spring training, we've found that the cheapest places to stay in February and March in the general area have been at Disney's Value resorts, so don't assume that just because a resort is on Disney grounds it's more expensive than hotels in the southwest corner of Orlando and Kissimmee.

If staying within walking distance of a theme park is a bigger concern for you, then be sure to check out the Deluxe accommodations close to the Magic Kingdom, Epcot, or Animal Kingdom. For instance, there are three Deluxe resorts on the monorail line servicing the Magic Kingdom, and the iconic Contemporary Resort is a short walk from the Magic Kingdom front gates.

INSIDER'S TIP
Offsite properties operate under the Disney Good Neighbor umbrella and come with some park perks. These are not owned or operated by Disney, but some are located within Disney grounds and have familiar brand names like Hilton, Best Western, Drury, Doubletree, and Waldorf-Astoria. These hotels are usually cheaper than onsite resorts and have some privileges reserved for Disney resorts.

INSIDER'S TIP
A big decision is whether to rent a car for a Disney World visit. The mass-transit system in Orlando basically consists of a lot of cabs, great bus service, ridesharing services, and the Disney transit system. You'll need to arrange your own transport to Disney World via cabs, private buses, and rideshares.

You will need to pay tolls if you do rent a car. While I-4 is not a toll road, there are many toll roads in Orlando, including the Florida

Turnpike and the two main highways leading between the airport and Disney World. It is theoretically possible to make your way to and from Orlando International Airport without paying a toll, but it requires patience and knowledge of the Orlando road system or else a really good GPS mapping app. Check with your rental-car company about how tolls are changed; some will pass along the actual charge plus a small convenience fee, while others will pass along the actual charge plus a large convenience fee.

EATING AT DISNEY WORLD

Staying in Disney World means taking in a meal or three on property. Surprisingly, the food options are mixed. The resorts all have restaurants of some sort—very good food courts in the Value resorts, five-star dining in the Deluxe resorts—but food in the theme parks can be hit or miss.

The best (and some of the most expensive) restaurants in Disney World are located in Epcot's World Showcase. Recommended are Le Cellier Steakhouse in the Canada Pavilion, Via Napoli in the Italian Pavilion, and Rose & Crown Dining Room in the United Kingdom Pavilion (or, if you can't score a sitdown reservation at the Rose & Crown, the quick-service Yorkshire County Fish Shop). Also recommended: Garden Grill, a revolving restaurant where younger kids can meet a slew of Disney characters as they wait for their meals.

The restaurant quality falls off outside Epcot. The best restaurant in Disney's Hollywood Studios (past the expensive Brown Derby) is the Sci-Fi Dine-In Theater, where families sit in cars and watch old science-fiction clips on a big screen a la a drive-in theater. OK food, terrific atmosphere. And in the Magic Kingdom, fast food rules, though the additions of Be Our Guest (the first restaurant in the Magic Kingdom to sell beer and wine) and Jungle Skipper Canteen were worthy additions.

INSIDER'S TIP

As we mentioned, each resort does have some sort of restaurant, whether it be the food court at Disney's All-Star Sports Resort or a Don Shula steakhouse at the Swan and Dolphin. But, surprisingly, the resort food tends to be very good, and we've had plenty of great meals in the lower-end resorts like

Art of Animation and Port Orleans Resort—French Quarter. If you have kids in tow, the Disney pizza is good and can be delivered to your room. You will pay a little more for the privilege of dining at a resort, but it's a much better option than trying to get to an offsite restaurant.

There is something for everyone at Disney World, but there are few sports-related offerings throughout. Our favorite resort, though, is not the All-Star Sports Resort, but rather the All-Star Music Resort, which features family suites, complete with a bedroom for Mom and Dad and two pulldown queen-size beds for the kids. (One caveat: other rooms feature two double beds—no queens—so cramming four people in a room can be a little uncomfortable come bedtime.)

If following March Madness is a priority for you, the only eatery billed as a sports bar within Disney World is Rix Sports Bar & Grill at the Coronado Springs Resort. With 31 TVs broadcasting sports programming and a food/beverage menu featuring craft beers, high-end cocktails, and elevated pub grub, there is no mistaking it for anything other than a sports bar. Other lounges with plenty of sports programming include the bar at Shula's Steak House in the Dolphin Resort and Splitsville in Disney Springs. Once inside the parks, you won't have any access to televised sporting events. One baseball-related eatery of note: Casey's Corner, located on Main Street in the Magic Kingdom. This quick-service diner features ballpark-themed fare: hot dogs, corn dogs, fries, etc. There is baseball memorabilia in the back seating area.

Disney World, 407/WDW-MAGIC (939-6244); disneyworld.com. The standard price for a one-day ticket is $109. Prices per day go down the more days you go to the parks, but they can also go up based on demand.

UNIVERSAL STUDIOS

The Universal Orlando Resort isn't quite as large and sprawling as Disney World, but there are some high-end on-site venues there. The young and hip will want to check out Hard Rock Hotel, while the more staid will want to look at Portofino Bay Hotel or Royal Pacific Resort, which are both Loews properties inside Universal.

The three theme parks at Universal—Universal Studios, Volcano

Bay, and Islands of Adventure—are aimed at a hipper demographic slightly older than the typical Disney age range: whereas Disney has a few thrill rides throughout its four parks, Universal has several with Marvel Comics themes (Spider-Man, The Hulk) at Islands of Adventure, and movie-themed attractions (like Jurassic World VelociCoaster) at Universal Studios. The Wizarding World of Harry Potter at Islands of Adventure and Universal Studios (with the Hogwarts Express running between them) is also immensely popular, so much so that during busy times, you may not be able to even enter the area until some guests have departed. It's still worth a visit for any Harry Potter fan. For younger kids, there's a Dr. Seuss Landing at Islands of Adventure. The Universal CityWalk area is similar to Disney Springs, with restaurants, bars, and shopping.

INSIDER'S TIP

Extremely long ticket lines are par for the course at Universal. Unlike Disney, which offers plenty of ticket agents at each park, just waiting in line to purchase tickets at Universal can chew up the better part of the morning. Buy your tickets online in advance or find an outlet in several hotels and stores throughout Orlando.

Universal Studios, 1000 Universal Studios Plaza, 407/363-8000; **universalorlando.com.** *A one-day pass to Universal Studios purchased in advance costs $119 per park for an adult, $114 for a child (3-9), free for 2 and under. Costs go down for longer stays.*

SEA WORLD AND MORE

Sea World Orlando may not be as glitzy as Universal Orlando or large as Disney World, but it's perhaps a more authentic Florida experience.

Sea World combines tried-and-true attractions with a plethora of dining options, including an underwater grill, and some amusement rides, such as the Kraken (the largest roller coaster in Orlando) and Journey to Atlantis, billed as a combination roller coaster and water coaster. New: Penguin Trek, billed as a family coaster that includes a penguin habitat; and Sesame Street Land, where you and your family can walk down a real-world version of TV's Sesame Street.

The Waterfront at Sea World combines restaurants with shopping and other attractions.

Discovery Cove is a high-end, intensive waterpark experience where you can swim with dolphins, hang out with rays, snorkel in a coral reef, and more. Admission is limited to 1,000 visitors a day, so you won't feel suffocated by swarms of people.

Sea World Orlando, intersection of Interstate 4 and Florida 528/Beachline Expressway, 407/351-3600; seaworld.com. A one-day pass costs $138.99, though they are almost always discounted if purchased in advance online.

ORLANDO HOTELS

One of the nicer things about Orlando is the plethora of hotel options, especially on the western side of town, close to Disney World, Sea World, and Universal Studios. International Drive is a popular destination, and it contains a wide variety of hotel options, ranging from the $60-per-night Econo Lodge to the $400-per-night Ritz-Carlton. There's such a multitude of hotels that a listing here would be futile: you're best off checking out Travelocity, Expedia, or Hotels.com for a fuller listing of available properties. The great thing about Orlando is that spring break doesn't generate enough traffic to significantly drive up hotel prices in the area: you can find a wide number of properties in any price range, and some hotels you assume are expensive—like a Ritz-Carlton or a Gaylord—can be moderately priced thanks to the competition.

For those attending Tigers spring-training games but staying in Orlando or a game farther afield in Tampa, your best bet is a hotel either within the city of Lake Buena Vista or in the southwest quadrant of Orlando. Besides the resorts in Disney World, there are a ton of hotel rooms in the southwest quadrant of Orlando and the western Kissimmee area. Hotel Plaza Boulevard is technically within the grounds of Disney World, but the hotels there are run by outside vendors and include such names as Hilton, Doubletree, Holiday Inn, and Best Western, operating as Disney Good Neighbor Hotels. (You can find more information at *wdwgoodneighborhotels.com*.) You'll rarely spend more than $350 a night on Hotel Plaza Boulevard, with most of the rates are in the $150-$250 range. Families will want to check out the all-suite Doubletree Suites by Hilton

Hotel Orlando (*2305 Hotel Plaza Blvd., Lake Buena Vista; 407/934-1000; hilton.com*)—the only suite hotel on Hotel Plaza Boulevard—while the Hilton Orlando Lake Buena Vista (*1751 Hotel Plaza Blvd., Lake Buena Vista; 407/827-4000; hilton.com*) is within walking distance of Disney Springs. If you're into high-end pools with an awesome lazy river, check out the Hilton Orlando Buena Vista Palace (*900 E. Buena Vista Dr., Lake Buena Vista; 407/827-2727; hilton.com*), also within walking distance of Disney Springs. It's been renovated in recent years.

The prices go down even more once you leave the Disney World grounds. The Orlando and Kissimmee areas around Disney World (especially those on International Drive and Hwy. 192) feature a slew of decent hotels with room rates under $150, with family suites at a hotel like the Clarion Suites running $125 or so a night. You may also want to check out resorts from the likes of Radisson and Hyatt. Virtually every brand-name hotel is represented between Sea World and Disney World.

SPRING-TRAINING HISTORY

One of the sadder things to happen in the spring-training world took place in May and June 2015, when the grandstand at Tinker Field, the former springtime home of the Washington Senators and Minnesota Twins, was torn down.

Baseball has been played at the Tinker Field site since 1914, and the ballpark was named after Joe Tinker—he of "Tinker to Evers to Chance" fame—who came to Orlando after his playing days and made his mark as a developer and land speculator. The original 1,500-seat wooden Tinker Field grandstand was built in 1923 and served as the spring-training home of the Cincinnati Reds from 1923 through 1933, and the Brooklyn Dodgers trained there in 1934 and 1935. In 1936, Clark Griffith moved the Senators' spring training to Tinker Field, and for many years the Twins' AA affiliate played there as well. Almost 1,000 of the seats were moved to Tinker Field from Griffith Stadium when that Washington landmark closed. Even though baseball has been played at Tinker Field since 1914, the final Tinker Field configuration dated back to 1963 and had been updated several times since.

Tinker Field is now gone, torn down to make way for an expansion of Camping World Stadium (the former Citrus Bowl). But it's not forgotten, remembered with a plaza marking the Tinker Field grandstand location. The former spring training and Minor League Baseball ballpark is honored with plaques and a historical timeline. In addition, it features seats from Tinker Field, as well as monuments to Reverend Martin Luther King, Jr. (who attracted a large crowd for a speech) and Hall of Famer Clark Griffith.

In our history chapter we discuss Sanford Stadium and the role it played in baseball integration. The old ballpark where the Boston Braves once trained and Jackie Robinson made his Montreal Royals debut is gone, replaced by a 1951 ballpark that now hosts high-school tourneys every spring and a Florida State Collegiate League team each summer. It's still a lovely place to take in a game. While we don't recommend you make a special trip to see the place because of the toll charges—unless you have fond memories of attending games there in springs past and want to revisit those times, or want to visit the Jackie Robinson sites as we recommend in the history chapter—it's located close to the Sanford airport, a worthy diversion if you're flying into this secondary airport. *Historic Sanford Memorial Stadium, 1201 S. Mellonville Av., Sanford.*

COLLEGE BASEBALL IN THE AREA

If you fly down to Orlando, chances are good some sort of traveling baseball or softball team will be sharing the plane with you. Florida is a mecca for college teams in March, and many of them wind up at college ballparks or former spring-training complexes to cram in as many games as they can during a spring-break trip.

Located northeast of downtown Orlando, right off University Boulevard, the University of Central Florida (UCF) Knights play at John Euliano Stadium (formerly Jay Bergman Field). The athletic facilities at UCF are located in the northwest corner of campus. *John Euliano Stadium, 4000 Central Florida Blvd., Orlando; ucfknights.com.*

FLYING IN

Orlando International Airport is convenient to all parts of the region. While Orlando International is one of those sprawling affairs where trams take you out to remote terminals, it's fairly easy to make your way around—just be prepared for some very significant lines at check-in and security, unless you're vetted by TSA Precheck or the CLEAR program. (When they tell you to be at the airport at least two hours before your flight, they mean it here: it's not unusual to spend 30-45 minutes in the security lines in Orlando.) However, the main concourse of the airport resembles a large mall, so you'll have one last chance to stock up on Disney or Universal trinkets before your flight. Virtually every major and budget airline flies into Orlando International.

Every major car-rental agency is on site as well: Alamo, Avis, Budget, Dollar, Enterprise, Hertz, National, and Thrifty. If you rent with anyone else, you'll need to take a shuttle to an off-site facility. If you're traveling with the family and have a lot of luggage, bite the bullet and pay a little extra to rent from an on-site rental agency. *Orlando International Airport, Airport Blvd., Orlando; 407/825-2001; orlandoairports.net.*

Orlando International is not the only airport in the Orlando area, however. Lakeland Internation features service from a number of East Coast markets via Avelo Airlines (see our Lakeland chapter for details). Orlando Sanford International Airport is a smaller facility located in the northeast corner of Orlando. Allegiant Air uses Orlando Sanford International Airport as an Orlando hub, and it's surprising how many cities are on the Allegiant Air route system with nonstop flights to Sanford (Albany, Allentown, Des Moines, Charlotte, Traverse City, and Elmira, to name just a few). Alamo, Avis, Budget, Dollar, Enterprise, Hertz, and National all rent cars on site as well. Bring your cash, because you'll need to pay tolls to make your way anywhere from Sanford unless you're willing to take the back roads everywhere. If your rental company offers automatic electronic toll payments, take it. *Orlando Sanford International Airport, 1200 Red Cleveland Blvd., Sanford; 407/585-4000; orlandosanfordairport.com.*

SPRING TRAINING IN EASTERN FLORIDA

Eastern Florida is now a hotbed area for spring training, with the Washington Nationals, Houston Astros, New York Mets, St. Louis Cardinals, and Miami Marlins in the area. Spring training at the cities on the Atlantic Ocean side of Florida—West Palm Beach, Palm Beach, Port St. Lucie, and Jupiter—represents more of a traditional experience than you'll find in the hectic tourist towns of Tampa, Orlando, or Fort Myers. We always schedule a trip to the area for a pure taste of spring training; you should as well.

There are five teams training in Eastern Florida, the Treasure Coast, and Palm Beach County. Folks attending games there tend to be mostly hardcore fans, snowbirds, and locals—you don't get many casual fans wandering in as part of a longer Florida vacation. This is spring training at its most basic—and in some ways, its best.

CLOVER PARK / NEW YORK METS

QUICK FACTS

- **Capacity**: 7,000
- **Year Opened**: 1988
- **Dimensions**: 338L, 410C, 338R
- **Ticket Line**: 772/871-2115
- **Ticket Box Office Address**: Ticket Office, New York Mets, 525 NW Peacock Blvd., Port St. Lucie, FL 34986.
- **Local Airport**: Palm Beach
- **Workout Schedule**: Gates open at 9:30 a.m.
- **Home Dugout Location**: Third-base side
- **Pregame Schedule**: Gates open one hour, 40 minutes before game time. Mets batting practice, until 11:15 a.m.; visitors batting practice, 11:15 a.m.-12:15 p.m.; Mets infield, 12:15-12:30 p.m.; visitors infield, 12:30-12:45 p.m. Add five hours for a 6:10 p.m. start.
- **Address**: 525 NW. Peacock Blvd., Port St. Lucie, FL 34986.
- **Directions**: From 1-95, take Exit 121-C (St. Lucie West Blvd.), east to Peacock Blvd, north to ballpark. From U.S. Highway 1: Take Prima Vista Blvd., west to Peacock Blvd., north to the ballpark. The route is well-marked.

A NEW METS SPRING-TRAINING EXPERIENCE

A New York Mets spring-training game tends to be an underrated experience. Port St. Lucie is a little off the beaten path: It's not a major tourism destination like Tampa or Fort Myers, and it's a little dowdy when compared to Palm Beach or even Boca Raton.

We tend to find the snowbirds like it that way, though. Port St. Lucie and surrounding communities like Stuart are very old-school Florida, seemingly immune to the change seen over the last decade in the rest of the state. That's why it's no surprise change comes slowly to the New York Mets spring-training experience as well. Since entering the National League in 1962, the Mets have trained at exactly two venues: St. Petersburg's Al Lang Field and Port St. Lucie's Clover Park.

But change indeed came to Clover Park in the past few years, including an extreme ballpark makeover in 2020. The changes touched virtually every aspect of Clover Park and the adjoining training complex on both the fan and player sides. Clover Park was the beneficiary of a new exterior, expanded concourses, a cheerier color scheme, upgraded player facilities, and enhanced fan spaces. All in all, the Mets and their design team modernized the experience while maintaining the charm of Clover Park's status as representative of small-town Grapefruit League. The $57 million spent by the Mets and St. Lucie County was well-spent.

If you have not been to a Mets spring training game in recent years, you are in for some major changes, beginning upon entry to the ballpark: the concourse has been expanded and a totally new front exterior installed. The new color scheme dumps the solid blue of old and instead employs a lighter palette centered on the team's familiar orange and blue look. Combined with plenty of Mets branding, the new entry plaza is an inviting space with new selfie spots (including a scaled-down Mets dugout and an oversized Adirondack chair) and additional security lines, while retaining and enlarging the 9/11 tribute previously installed outside the ballpark. The parking lot has also been reconfigured with a dedicated turn lane off Peacock Boulevard, making for easier access before a game.

The changes also include new ticket booths and new security points, both of which streamline ballpark entry. Once fans pass security, they'll encounter a new concourse that more than triples the width of the old, narrow rat maze of a concourse. A dead end to the concourse down the first-base line has been blown out, allowing fans to go directly from the grandstand to the right-field party deck and berm without walking through the ballpark seating and blocking the views of other fans.

Interestingly, the new space only included one new fixed concession stand in 2021: everything else was set up as temporary points of sale. In the meantime, the space is an inviting area to hang out away from the seating bowl, with plenty of murals celebrating Mets history. And the branding extends throughout the ballpark, inside and out: for example, a new graphic band on the press-level fascia displays the history of all the Mets logos used over the years: Mr. Met, Mrs. Met, and more. Again, the overall design of the ballpark is made considerably brighter with the addition of plenty of new blue and orange everywhere, ranging from the padded tops of fences in the adjacent workout fields to access points in the concourse.

The interior ballpark upgrades extend down the third-base line. The old Tiki bar behind third base is now gone, replaced by a new group area, a section of four tops, and the Corona Island Bar in left field, featuring a slew of Mexican beers, including Corona, Modelo, and Pacifico. That gives the Mets social spaces down each line where the emphasis is hanging out with friends, not necessarily being glued to the action. That means lots of drink rails, along with some tables.

The deck, by the way, provides a great view of the player-development side of the complex. (Which may be the next target for renovations.)

INSIDER'S TIP
Beginning in 2023 the home and visiting bullpens have been moved off the field of play. The Mets bullpen is located between the Budweiser Terrace and the Mets batting cages, while the visiting bullpen is located behind the left-field wall near the Corona Island Bar and videoboard.

This leads us to the second part of the ballpark renovations, albeit a part that most fans won't see. This includes an expanded home clubhouse (larger than the Citi Field clubhouse), new practice fields, more batting cages, and a better layout for fan access to practices. Fans can see where the new clubhouse is from the third-base side of the concourse, next to the new batting cages. The Mets are one of the teams that separate the major-league clubhouse from the minor-league clubhouse, located next door. Why? We were told the major-league clubhouse should be the goal for minor leaguers; they could see it as part of their reward when rising to the major-league squad.

All the MLB practice fields are next to the ballpark, with the new weight room and expanded clubhouse behind it in the concourse. A synthetic turf workout field now sits next to the grandstand, along with hitting tunnels. The major-league fields are closest to the ballpark deck, with one major-league and one minor-league bunting field adjacent, and minor-league fields beyond. The practice fields were realigned to be closer to fans, with a new central viewing area for major-league workouts. Fans go behind the ballpark to a new sidewalk past right field to enter both the major-league and minor-league fields. Previously, access to player workouts came via a pathway through the woods next to Peacock Boulevard.

Despite the changes, a game at Clover Park is a throwback to the old-time Florida spring-training experience: the palm trees, the alligators, the quaint ballparks located in out-of-the-way neighborhoods. There are no developments within walking distance of the ballpark, just some municipal buildings next door, commercial buildings and warehouses nearby, and an RV resort up the street. No sports bars, no hotels, no entertainment complex, no trendy shops.

While we wouldn't exactly call the location bucolic—commercial development in Florida tends to sprawl, and there's definitely a lot of sprawl near the ballpark—you know you're in Florida when you attend a Mets spring-training game.

INSIDER'S TIP

As you approach the ballpark, take a minute to visit the monument across the street from the main entrance gates and underneath the American flag. The two pillars of steel come from the World Trade Center, salvaged after terrorists struck the New York City landmark on Sept. 11, 2001. They were donated to St. Lucie County by a local chapter of retired New York City firefighters and installed in March 2005. The monument was expanded and moved during the 2020 renovations. It is a sobering reminder that even in this small Florida community, Mets fans are never too far away from New York City.

One thing did not change: a large canopy ensures much of the grandstand seating is in the shade. Only the bleacher seating down the right-field line offers massive exposure to the sun, and the seats between the dugouts are shaded most of the game.

INSIDER'S TIP

The cheapest seats in the house are in the outfield berm. If you're attending a game with a bunch of kids, that's the place to go: the kids can run around while you claim one of the picnic tables in the shade. A few beers from the nearby concession stand won't hurt, either.

Be warned the berm can be a sun field with limited shade, and during an afternoon game you'll spend a lot of time fighting the sun, so bring the sunglasses, caps, and sunscreen.

Because of the large number of New Yorkers in the area, a Mets spring-training game seems like a Citi Field match gone tropical. Interestingly, the New Yorkers didn't tend to live in Port St. Lucie before the Mets moved spring-training operations there in 1988, but the ballpark and the Mets' presence are now cited as prime reasons why New Yorkers have flocked there, increasing the Port St. Lucie population by over 28 percent since 1998.

The complex also houses the Single-A St. Lucie Mets and the Mets' minor-league operations.

INSIDER'S TIP
The Mets buck spring-training norms and begin games at 1:10 p.m., rather than the 1:05 p.m. start favored by most teams.

BALLPARK HISTORY

The New York Mets have trained at Clover Park since it opened in 1988.

The ballpark originally was named for the late Thomas J. White, who founded St. Lucie West and worked to bring the Mets to the area. Naming rights were sold in 2004 to Core Communities, developer of the Tradition development near the ballpark. After the Tradition Field naming-rights deal expired, naming rights were sold to Digital Domain, the visual effects and animation field based in Port St. Lucie. Digital Domain declared bankruptcy in late 2012, walking away from the naming rights deal. The ballpark had a temporary name of Mets Stadium until Core Communities repurchased naming rights before the start of games in 2012, bringing back the Tradition Field moniker. It became First Data Field in spring training 2017, but after Fiserv purchased First Data, the naming rights were transferred in 2020 to another Fiserv company, Clover, which processes credit-card transactions.

THE SPRING-TRAINING BALLPARK EXPERIENCE

CONCESSIONS

While it's not exactly like being in the Big Apple, the concessions at the ballpark will ease the homesickness somewhat. If you're looking for New York takes on traditional ballpark foods, Nathan's hot dogs are served throughout the ballpark, as are hot pretzels, sausages, cheesesteaks, sausages and peppers, foot longs, legendary chicken strips, and deep-fried sweets, like deep-fried Oreos. There's a nice selection of beer—plenty of Modelo and Kirin tallboys, and it's not hard to find Goose Island or some Florida microbrew on tap if a Bud, Bud Light, or Michelob Ultra isn't to your liking. Popular among Mets fans: buckets of ice and six Buds, Michelob Ultras, or Bud Lights selling for $30. With bars in both corners, you're never too far away from a bartender and a beer.

During the renovations, the Mets kept one large fixed concession stand behind third base and added one more in the concourse, while installing temporary points of sale throughout the expanded concourse, including stands focused on cocktails, beer, and pastrami sandwiches. The UltiMet Grill, for instance, is located in the left-field bar area.

The right-field area between the grandstand and the outfield berm has been renovated in recent years, complete with a shaded bar, additional concessions, and four-tops. This is the area designed to explicitly appeal to the millennials who hit the ballpark as a group and spend much of their time socializing. During our most recent visits, the bar was indeed filled with millennials who spent much of their time socializing. That's OK: This is spring training, and if you're a millennial from New York City who has come to Florida for some sun and brews, socializing is certainly a big part of the experience.

INSIDER'S TIP

Clover Park is cashless: only credit/debit cards and mobile-phone tools like Apple Pay and Google Pay are accepted, including at the parking gates. You can exchange cash for a

Clover Park gift card in the Fan Shop and use that card throughout the ballpark.

AUTOGRAPHS

There are no formal places for autographs at the ballpark, so fans gather next to the dugout in hopes of snaring a wayward Met. These efforts usually take place near Section 122, near the Mets bullpen, where players tend to gather.

There's good access to players during workouts before the start of games. The complex features four full diamonds, two half fields, and a small auxiliary workout field. You can enter from Clover Park (on the third-base side) or the minor-league entrance farther north on Northwest Peacock Boulevard. Be warned the Mets don't go out of their way to make you feel at home at workouts: there's no seating and the only place to watch the action is beyond the right-field fence.

There's more access to minor leaguers at the complex. They train on fields #4 through #7, and there's plenty of shaded bleacher seating at fields #5 and #7. Field #7 has the same dimensions as Citi Field and can be seen beyond the Clover Park scoreboard. Be warned that the training complex is closed to the public when the Mets have a home game.

PARKING

Parking is $15 ($25 for RVs) and located adjacent to the ballpark. Have a credit card or a smartphone with Apple Pay or Google Pay enabled: No cash. Arrive early: Entry to the ballpark is now easier thanks to a dedicated turn lane into the parking lot. Golf carts patrol the parking lot if you need a little assistance getting to or from the front gates. Many scout for some free parking on the adjacent streets (across from the ballpark, off Peacock Boulevard, is a popular spot).

WHERE TO SIT

Seating is mainly in two areas: the upper grandstand and the lower grandstand. These are perhaps the most shaded seating areas in spring training; the huge canopy covers all of the upper-grandstand seats (Sections 201-207) and most of the center of the lower-grandstand seats (Sections 101-108). And with all the seats in the ballpark being theater-style chairback seats with cupholders—no bleachers! —a game at Clover Park is a comfortable experience.

The Mets dugout is on the third-base side, so if you want a good view of the players, buy tickets in Sections 104, 106, 108, or 110.

As mentioned, the right-field bar area is a popular destination during a game. Also popular: the drink rails and four tops down the left-field line, beyond the Tiki bar. These areas are especially popular before games begin, so if you have a crappy seat and want a better view of the action, head down there when you arrive at the ballpark to claim your spot. But with the addition of plenty of drink rails and spots designated to stand and watch the action, we saw plenty of folks abandon their fixed seating for a SRO spot overlooking the game.

FOR THE KIDS

The right-field berm is a perfect place for the kids to cut loose, if there's not a rowdy crowd at hand.

MINOR-LEAGUE COMPLEX

The minor-league complex is located directly north of Clover Park, while the main practice field is located directly west of the ballpark. The minor-league complex features a separate entrance and parking area; access it via Peacock Boulevard. You can see it from the left-field party deck.

SELFIE SPOTS

There are four recommended spots, and three are outside the ballpark gates, so plan ahead. The first is the 9/11 tribute, which we discussed above. The second is a scaled-down Mets dugout complete with logo; you can pretend you are Steve Cohen and directing the new course of the team. The most popular spot, and one that generates a line, is an oversized blue Adirondack chair with a Mets logo.

The fourth spot isn't really a spot, but a series of spots. Inside the concourse is a series of graphics adorning the concourse walls, with some honoring Mets greats and others combining looks at great moments in Mets history. Pick a spot and click away.

IF YOU GO

WHAT TO DO OUTSIDE THE BALLPARK

Port St. Lucie has evolved into one of Florida's great—and vastly underrated—vacation spots, providing access to old Florida while also offering a slew of options when it comes to one of the state's main pastimes: golf. What makes Port St. Lucie different is the sanction of the PGA. The PGA runs a club and learning center in Port St. Lucie and has established a museum there as well, all under the auspices of the PGA Village.

The PGA Golf Club (*1916 Perfect Dr., Port St. Lucie; 800/609-9067; pgavillage.com*) features three championship courses. The Ryder Course, designed by Tom Fazio, features rolling hills and a lot of water hazards; the Wanamaker Course, also designed by Fazio, has a classic Florida feel; and the Dye Course, designed by Pete Dye, has a links-style layout. Many of the hotels have an agreement with the golf club for room/links specials. If your game is not quite up to a championship-course level, some time at the PGA Learning Center —which features a driving range and several practice holes for work on the short game—is in order.

The PGA doesn't have a monopoly on golf in Port St. Lucie, though. Most of the courses are attached to housing/retirement communities and not open to the public, alas; there's only one municipal 18-hole course run by the city, and only a few public courses, such as the notable Fairwinds Course in nearby Fort Pierce (*4400 Fairwinds Dr., Fort Pierce; 772/462-1955; fairwindsgolf.com*).

In general, St. Lucie County is a bucolic area, and you might want to spend some time enjoying the scenery before or after a game. One favorite spot is the Port St. Lucie Botanical Gardens (*2410 SE. Westmoreland Blvd., Port St. Lucie; 772/337-1959; pslbg.org*), which features an impressive selection of both local and exotic fauna.

AFTER THE GAME

There are the usual chain and fast-food restaurants in the area, including several on Peacock Boulevard approaching the ballpark, so you won't go hungry.

If you're interested in beer and a burger after the game, Duffy's is a local chain of sports bars offering good food, a decent variety of beer, and an abundance of big-screen TVs showing sporting events of all sorts. (If you happen to be at spring training during March Madness, Duffy's is the perfect hangout; chances are good you'll find your favorite team's game on one of the many TVs.) We'd recommend you head south to the nearby Duffy's in Stuart, located in the heart of the historic downtown area. Florida is in a transitional state these days: the ways of old-time Florida—the ways we associate with the traditional spring-training vibe—are rapidly disappearing under the weight of a gazillion strip malls and retirement complexes. Stuart is a throwback to old-school Florida, with a vibrant downtown on the waterfront. The downtown Duffy's features a patio (with flat-screen TVs; no escaping sports here), a traditional sports-bar décor, and a friendly staff. Take some time to walk around downtown Stuart: there are plenty of watering holes, but the real attraction is the chance to soak up some real Florida atmosphere. The same goes for nearby Fort Pierce and Jensen Beach: if you're planning a multiday trip, some time spent poking around the old downtowns in the area is time well-spent. *Duffy's, 1 SW. Osceola Blvd., Stuart; 772/221-4899; duffysmvp.com. To get there from Port St. Lucie, head south on Hwy. 1 (also referred to as Federal Highway) to downtown Stuart. The route can be a little challenging, but it is well-marked; as you head south on Hwy. 1, keep in mind the exit to downtown Stuart is on the left.*

If you have antsy kids, Bowlero *(1600 NW. Courtyard Circle, Port St. Lucie; 772/408-5800; bowlero.com)* features 48 lanes of bowling, a video arcade, batting cages, laser tag, and an indoor 9-hole miniature golf course. Perfect for rowdy kids and tired parents.

Hop Life Brewing *(679 NW. Enterprise Dr., Suite 101, Port St. Lucie; 772) 249-5055; hoplife.com)* is a typical new breed of brewery, operating out of an industrial park, offering food from a food truck and featuring plenty of outdoor seating. Recommended: the raspberry beer if on tap.

MLB and MiLB Mets players are known to hang out at the Bravo Supermarket cafeteria (*2820 W. Port St. Lucie Blvd., Port St. Lucie; bravosupermarkets.com*), especially the Latin American players homesick for some *tequeños* or *rabo*. Bravo is a chain of supermarkets found across Florida, but the Port St. Lucie location has been known for attracting Mets players for years. Don't go and gawk; go and order some great homecooking.

WHERE TO STAY

There are several hotels within a mile of the ballpark, which is perfectly walkable. The Mets' spring hotel in 2024 was the Spring-Hill Suites by Marriott (*2000 NW. Courtyard Circle, Port St. Lucie; 772/871-2929; marriott.com*).

South of the ballpark on Peacock Boulevard are several chain hotels also within walking distance, including Holiday Inn Express Suites West (*601 NW Courtyard Circle, Port Saint Lucie; 855/799-6861; ihg.com*), Hampton Inn and Suites (*155 SW. Peacock Blvd., Port St. Lucie; 772/878-5900; hilton.com*), and Springhill Suites (*2000 NW. Courtyard Circle, Port St. Lucie; 772/871-2929; marriott.com*). All three feature suites as well as regular hotel rooms. You will also see plenty of golf condos advertised on the likes of VRBO and AirBnB.

INSIDER'S TIP

Unless you're an utter cheapskate and want to avoid the very reasonable parking fee at Clover Park, there's no good reason to stay next to the ballpark (unless the idea of combining golf with your stay appeals to you). During our last spring visit to the area we had a wonderful stay at the Hilton Garden Inn at PGA Village/Port St. Lucie (*8540 Commerce Centre Dr.; Port St. Lucie, 772-871-6850; hilton.com*).

RV PARKS

RV fans should note the presence of the high-end St. Lucie West Motorcoach Resort just down Peacock Boulevard from the ballpark (*Outdoor Resorts of America, 800 NW Peacock Blvd., Port St. Lucie; 772/336-1135; motorcoachresortstluciewest.com*). It's billed as a motorcoach-only resort (limited to Class A RVs), and a quick glimpse inside the gates showed some lovely landscaping and clean facilities. It features its own 9-hole par-3 course, lighted tennis courts, and high-end amenities like cable TV and WiFi, but it requires a four-night minimum and is quite spendy: $175/night. Farther away is the Port St. Lucie RV Resort (*3703 SE. Jennings Rd., Port St. Lucie; 772/337-3340; portstluciervresort.com*), but the 55+ facility carries a daily price of $65,

FLYING IN

The closest airport to Port St. Lucie, some 40 miles away, is Palm Beach International Airport. Most major airlines fly into PBI, including Air Canada, Allegiant, American, Avelo, Breeze, Delta, Frontier, Sun Country, JetBlue, Southwest, United, and Spirit, though some feature only seasonal service. Delta, Frontier, JetBlue, Southwest, and United fly from New York City-area airports to Palm Beach International. *1000 James L. Turnage Blvd., West Palm Beach; pbia.org.*

An alternative is Orlando Melbourne International Airport, located less than 60 miles north of Port St. Lucie. It's a small airport, and the only major airlines flying in are Allegiant, Delta, Sun Country, and American Airlines, but not always daily. *1 Air Terminal Pkwy, Melbourne; mlbair.com.*

If you're planning on visiting several spring-training sites, you may want to fly into Orlando and then drive down to Port St. Lucie. Most of the 125 miles between Orlando and Port St. Lucie are on I-95 and the Beachline Expressway or, alternately, the Florida Turnpike.

SPRING TRAINING HISTORY: NEW YORK METS

The New York Mets have had only two spring-training venues in team history: St. Petersburg's Al Lang Field (1962-1987) and Port St. Lucie (1988-present).

PALM BEACH COUNTY

With four teams training at two complexes some 20 minutes apart, Palm Beach County has emerged as a very appealing spring-training hub. You can count on the two complexes hosting games daily, and if you time your trip well, you can cram a lot of baseball into your vacation. Add in Clover Park, the Mets' spring home—

some 45 minutes to the north—and you have enough baseball to satisfy the biggest fan.

If you've never been there but want to take in some high-level baseball and high-level living, Palm Beach County is a great spring-training destination. True, it's not the cheapest place to visit when it comes to hotel rooms or airfares, but Palm Beach County will be worth the time and expense for most visitors. In this chapter, we'll present a short overview of spring training in Palm Beach County. In the following chapters, we'll cover the specific areas near CACTI Park of the Palm Beaches and Roger Dean Chevrolet Stadium.

Though Palm Beach County encompasses some 1,941 square miles, most of it is rural and not of much interest to tourists. You'll spend your time close to the ocean in the northwest corner of the county, in a 25-mile corridor running between Jupiter to the north and West Palm Beach/Palm Beach to the south, all east of Florida's Turnpike. This all makes commuting times manageable, and it also exposes you to both the modern Florida experience as well as historic Florida. It's no surprise this baseball corridor parallels the original Florida East Coast Railway line running through the state all the way to Key West. Which is entirely appropriate, as Henry Flagler—who launched and expanded the Florida East Coast Railway—was also the man who brought winter and spring baseball to Florida.

HENRY FLAGLER: A FLORIDA BASEBALL PIONEER

Henry Flagler was certainly a man of vision. As a founder of Standard Oil with John D. Rockefeller and Samuel Andrews, Flagler made his fortune while helping establish one of America's first great industrial firms. Flagler was a colorful figure, a teetotaler who nevertheless profited greatly from an investment in a whiskey distillery. His experience in negotiating railroad contracts for the young Standard Oil—an experience that saw Flagler and Rockefeller outmaneuver the powerful Jay Gould on oil-shipping contracts—positioned him well to put together a modern railway network that united the Florida east coast.

Armed with extensive financial assets, Flagler turned his attention to Florida, both as a tourist destination and as a financial investment. After being hospitalized in 1882-1883, Flagler spent much of his recuperation time reviewing Florida land opportunities. In 1883, Flagler and Rockefeller toured Jacksonville and St. Augustine, scouting out financial opportunities—visits that led Flagler to invest in his first Florida hotel, St. Augustine's Ponce de Leon Hotel. It took several years, several rounds of railway investments, and plenty of personal transformations, but by 1912 Flagler had created a train line running between Jacksonville and Key West.

Along the way, he built grand hotels to serve those railway travelers. By 1890 he had contracted with Brooklyn and Chicago teams to train at his St. Augustine hotel: an early effort to capitalize on spring-training tourism. Two other noteworthy Flagler hotels were in Palm Beach: The Breakers and the Royal Poinciana. Flagler saw baseball as a tourist attraction—not uncommon in the day, as we've seen in previous chapters—and imported Negro League players like John Donaldson, Smoky Joe Williams, and several members of the Cuban Giants to play baseball and work in his hotels.

Spring training would be part of the West Palm Beach experience for decades, whether it was Connie Mack's Athletics training at Wright Field or the Atlanta Braves training at Municipal Stadium. Both those ballparks are gone, but The Breakers still stands, part of historic downtown Palm Beach. (Alas, The Breakers that Flagler built was lost to fire in 1925. The current Breakers was built by his widow.)

We'll cover attractions near each of the ballparks in the following chapters, as well as hotel options. No matter where you stay, there are some Palm Beach and West Palm Beach experiences to consider in your planning.

Downtown West Palm Beach has the trendy Clematis Street district, offering a variety of restaurants and bars to serve every taste. We'd recommend Grease Burger Beer and Whiskey Bar (*213 Clematis St., West Palm Beach; 561/651-1075; **greasewpb.com**) for a burger and a brew. It's the best of both worlds: a gastropub featuring flavorful burgers while also sporting 20 high-def displays to catch all the March Madness action. Similarly noteworthy: If a straight-up sports bar is more to your liking, there's a local outpost of the Duffy's chain (*225 Clematis St., West Palm Beach; 561/249-1682; **duffysmvp.com**). Though not a sports bar, Lynora's (*207 Clematis St., West Palm Beach; 561/899-3117; **lynoras.com**) serves a mean pie and plenty of high-end Italian pasta dishes. Batch (*223 Clematis St., West*

Palm Beach; 561/708-0000; **batchsouthernkitchen.com**) presents a high-end Southern cuisine: pimento cheese, jackfruit sliders, fried chicken, cathead biscuits, deviled eggs, and more. This is really a starting list; there are dozens of great spots in the Clematis Street district, and you can't go wrong by just parking nearby and strolling around until something catches your eye.

Across the channel from downtown West Palm Beach is Palm Beach. The Breakers is on the east seaward side and worth a visit, if just for a cocktail at the Seafood Bar. If the aforementioned Henry Flagler history interests you, his Whitehall Palm Beach estate is now the Flagler Museum (*One Whitehall Way, Palm Beach; 561/655-2833;* **flaglermuseum.us**). The Flagler Museum is a link to a much different time in American history: a Gilded Age where expense was no consideration, and the most opulent designs became reality. Yes, you could drive to Mar-A-Lago on South Ocean Boulevard—the north-south main drag in the resort area—and take a picture of the historic estate.

Shopping is also a prime activity in Palm Beach, where the Worth Avenue area features the likes of Neiman Marcus, Saks, and plenty of specialty shops and restaurants.

ROGER DEAN CHEVROLET STADIUM / MIAMI MARLINS / ST. LOUIS CARDINALS

QUICK FACTS

- **Capacity**: 6,834
- **Year Opened**: 1998
- **Dimensions**: 330L, 355LC, 400C, 350RC, 325R
- **Ticket Line**: 561/775-1818
- **Local Airport**: Palm Beach
- **Workout Schedule**: Gates open at 9:30 a.m.
- **Dugout Locations**: Cardinals on first-base side, Marlins on third-base side
- **Gates Open**: 1½ hours before game time
- **Pregame Schedule, Cardinals**: Batting practice, until 11:15 p.m.; visitors batting practice, 11:15 a.m.-12:15 p.m.; visitors infield, 12:15-12:30 p.m.
- **Pregame Schedule, Marlins**: Batting practice, 10:10-11:10 a.m.; visitors batting practice, 11:10 a.m.-12:10 p.m.; Marlins infield, 12:10-12:20 p.m.; visitors infield, 12:20-12:30 p.m.
- **Address**: 4751 Main Street, Jupiter.
- **Directions**: From I-95, exit at Donald Ross Road (exit 53) and travel east to Parkside Drive. Make a left and follow Parkside Drive to the Roger Dean parking lots, located on the right.

DOUBLE DUTY IN JUPITER

Roger Dean Chevrolet Stadium is one of the oldest ballparks in the Grapefruit League, opening in 1998. In many ways, it's showing its age, especially when compared to the new spring-training palaces opening in recent years. The concourses are cramped and far from the action, there's no 360-degree walkway, and the popular berm space was removed. Still, a visit to Roger Dean Chevrolet Stadium is one of the more pleasant experiences in the Grapefruit League: The St. Louis Cardinals and the Miami Marlins present a laid-back environment during the spring-training season.

Providing such a laid-back experience is a paradox, to be sure, as Roger Dean Chevrolet Stadium is one of the busiest ballparks in professional baseball. Besides hosting the Marlins and Cardinals in spring training, the ballpark also hosts two Single-A MiLB teams and a slew of other community events. The emphasis, understandably, isn't on luxury: it's on running a smooth operation that can be sustained year-round. (Yes, year-round: in off-months you'll see events like beer festivals on the schedule.) Some might call it a little bland, but there have been efforts in recent years to upgrade the facility, and there are plans out there for a more elaborate makeover

that includes new clubhouses and the removal of the existing clubhouses to make room for a 360-degree concourse. These changes are
now planned for 2025 after spring training ends, set to open in 2026.

Yes, this is yet another delay in the renovation of Roger Dean
Chevrolet Stadium, work that began in 2023—planned to the point
that the Florida State League teams relocated to CACTI Park of the
Palm Beaches for part of the summer. Despite this false start,
construction is not expected to impact spring training in 2025.

But the work is needed to allow the ballpark to compete with
other spring-training facilities—a status important for both the
Cardinals and Marlins, both in the pursuit of free agents and in the
development of youngsters. At Roger Dean Chevrolet Stadium,
there's no concourse ringing the inside of the ballpark: the limited
concourse and concession area are located behind the grandstand.
There's really no theme associated with the ballpark, as it's not done
up in Spanish style like many other Florida stadiums, for instance.
Instead, Roger Dean Chevrolet Stadium is ringed with native oaks
and palmetto trees in a very understated manner. Baseball is serious
business at Roger Dean Chevrolet Stadium.

Originally Roger Dean Chevrolet Stadium was also the spring-
training home of the Montreal Expos, with the Florida Marlins
training up the road in Viera's Space Coast Stadium. However,
when Jeffrey Loria sold the Expos and bought the Marlins, he
retained the Florida rights and property that had belonged to the
Expos, and he decided to move the Marlins' spring training to
Jupiter while still paying on a spring-training lease in Viera. The
word was that Loria wanted the team to train closer to his home in
Palm Beach, but team officials insist that the swap was made in
order to market the Marlins to Palm Beach County.

Though the ballpark itself is cramped, the entire complex is
spacious. It includes 12 major-league practice fields (six for each
team), two half-sized infields, and three clubhouses (one for the
Marlins, one for the Cardinals, one for the visiting team). If you go,
be prepared for some walking, as practice fields used by both teams
are not particularly close to the main parking ramp and adjacent
parking area serving the ballpark.

As noted, there are plans for an extensive renovation of Roger
Dean Chevrolet Stadium costing some $108 million, slated for a 2026
debut: demolition of existing clubhouses to make room for addi-

tional outfield seating, replacement clubhouses, free WiFi, relocated bullpens, new scoreboard; new group spaces, and other improvements. Funding will come from tourism taxes and the teams, with work set to begin after this spring.

Roger Dean Chevrolet Stadium was designed as part of the larger residential/retail Abacoa development in eastern Florida. It was named for West Palm Beach car dealer Roger Dean, whose family bought the naming rights; the Roger Dean name still lives on at a local dealership, even though Dean himself passed away in 1999. A naming-rights renewal in 2018 saw the name changed from Roger Dean Stadium to Roger Dean Chevrolet Stadium.

Be warned that Roger Dean Chevrolet Stadium can be one of the more expensive venues in the Grapefruit League. The price to any spring-training game at Roger Dean Chevrolet Stadium is the same no matter what team is playing, and that means you're paying as much to see the Marlins as you are the Cardinals. No offense to Marlins fans, but the Cardinals are by far the better spring-training draw, and it seems a little out of whack for tickets to be the same for both teams.

INSIDER'S TIP

Tickets to Marlins games are easier to acquire than tickets to Cardinals games. Cards enthusiasts tend to be fanatical about their team from the beginning of spring training through the end of the season.

Some say a game at Roger Dean Chevrolet Stadium is one of the greatest experiences in spring training. It is a throwback to the days when the emphasis was on the game and not on the amenities. Of course, many say that's a false choice—in a place like JetBlue Park or Hammond Stadium, baseball still comes first and foremost, despite what's going on at the party deck—but a game at Roger Dean Chevrolet Stadium is a more low-key event, to be sure.

BALLPARK HISTORY

The St. Louis Cardinals have trained at Roger Dean Chevrolet Stadium since it opened in 1998. The Montreal Expos trained there from 1998 through 2002, and in 2003 the then-Florida Marlins began training there.

THE SPRING-TRAINING BALLPARK EXPERIENCE

CONCESSIONS

In general, the food at Roger Dean Chevrolet Stadium is above average for spring-training vittles. The signature concession offering is the Dean Dog, a 1/3-pound all-beef hot dog served on a special bun with grilled onions and peppers. It can be found at the grilles at each end of the concourse.

The first-base MVP Grille features some food items you'd expect to see at Busch Stadium, including toasted ravioli with marinara sauce. Now, we wonder why someone would toast ravioli (and yes, we've had it at Busch Stadium), but if you like your ravioli toasted, you can also find it at Roger Dean Chevrolet Stadium.

The better food choices: a basic Chicago-style dog (with celery salt, tomatoes, relish, etc.) dubbed the Chicago Cubs Hater Dog, ribs, or the mahi tacos.

If you want a beer outside the standard Bud offerings, it's worth your time to search out better beers like Yuengling or other Florida microbrews.

INSIDER'S TIP
Behind the grandstand is a great place to escape the sun, but there's no view of the field. If you want some shade and short lines for beer and mixed drinks, head for the Guanabana's hut down the left-field line, which features four tops and beverage service.

PARKING

If you spend a lot of time at spring training, you get used to paying for parking. And, indeed, you'll be directed to park in a lot next to the ballpark or in an adjacent parking ramp, paying $10 for the privilege.

Most of you will enter the ballpark area on Parkside Drive,

heading north from Donald Ross Road right off the freeway. As you head north on Parkside Drive you'll drive past Florida Atlantic University until you reach University Boulevard. Go through the four-way stop, and the first right will take you to the north side of the $13 parking ramp. The ballpark is on the east side of the ramp, so park as far to the east side as you can.

This is a large ramp, designed to fill the needs of Roger Dean Chevrolet Stadium.

You can also park for free in the next-door Abacoa Town Center, placing you close to some interesting post-game drinking and dining. If you enter the area from Parkside Drive, hang a right on University Boulevard and go past the ballpark complex until you hit Edna Hibel Way. Hang a right; past the first building on the left you'll find another free parking ramp putting you within a block of Town Center Drive, which we'll discuss later in this chapter. And there's another free parking lot off Main Street on Chancellor Drive, putting you only four blocks from the ballpark. Parking in the Town Center is free, but there are time limits if you park on the street. Three hours will probably be enough time to catch a game but watch the clock anyway: the area is patrolled.

INSIDER'S TIP
If you're heading to the Roger Dean Chevrolet Stadium complex to witness Cardinals practice, park on the street and not in the larger parking ramp: you'll be close to the workout fields, which you enter on University Boulevard. If you're showing up for Marlins practice, park in the small parking lot off Parkside Drive and walk through the entrance close to the ballpark.

AUTOGRAPHS

Both teams will stop to sign autographs as they come on and off the field: the Cards down the right-field line and the Marlins down the left, at the end of the new extended netting. Both teams are known for being accessible during spring training.

In addition, players from both teams are known for being accessible during workouts, but the teams take different approaches to access. The Cardinals limit fan access to Fields 1 and 6; the Marlins allow access to every field on their side of the complex. There are separate entrances for the workout areas. Marlins fans enter from the parking lot next to the ballpark, while Cardinals fans enter on a path past the small team parking lot on University Boulevard. If the path was numbered, it would be approximately 1050 University Boulevard.

Be prepared for some sun on the uncovered bleachers.

WHERE TO SIT

Most of the seats in Roger Dean Chevrolet Stadium are chairback seats with cupholders; you'll be physically comfortable in Sections 101-124 (in the lower grandstand) and Sections 201-213 (in the upper grandstand). Sections 301-304 are auxiliary bench bleachers; not the most comfortable seating in the ballpark.

If sitting near the Cardinals dugout is important, shoot for sitting in Sections 105-110. If sitting near the Marlins dugout is important, Sections 116-120 are best.

Many fans were disappointed when the right-field berm was scrapped in favor of a new party deck and an all-you-care-to-eat area. Those tickets were popular with walkups, as they were sold only on the day of the game. But any fans who were irritated with the loss of the berm were replaced by fans absolutely thrilled with good seating and good food. These Bullpen Club seats aren't the greatest, but they do offer much in the way of amenities, such as all-inclusive food and beverage service. (Sans alcohol, of course: you're on your own for the beer tab.)

Roger Dean Chevrolet Stadium is one of the few ballparks where an SRO ticket is worth something. There's a wide walkway between the two seating sections of the grandstand, and the back section is raised. This allows for the sale of SRO tickets in a marked area in the walkway; the seating is raised so high there's very little chance of having your view blocked by an SRO tick-etholder should you buy a ticket in the first row of the back section of the grandstand. In addition, there is a large SRO area down the third-base line, between the end of the grandstand and the bleachers.

If shade is an issue for you, sit in the back of the grandstand. Recent improvements added shading on each side of the second-level press box/suite area. We'd recommend sitting in the last two rows in sections 204-209.

INSIDER'S TIP

Check out the Tiki-themed concession stand down the left-field line, next to the bullpen. Technically, it's a chickee (a hut with a raised floor and a thatch roof, used by Florida Seminoles for centuries), but since we have Tiki huts at many other spring-training ballparks, we'll stick with that verbiage. Concessions from the nearby Guanabanas restaurant were sold there, including delicacies like empanadas. It's billed by the Roger Dean Chevrolet Stadium folks as a social space: besides being a concessions center, the area features tables topped by purple, pink, and yellow Guanabanas logo.

SELFIE SPOTS

The entrance to the ballpark is a fine spot for a selfie.

IF YOU GO

WHAT TO DO OUTSIDE THE BALLPARK

There's a definite Jupiter lifestyle: lots of golf and fishing interrupted by good meals and cheap drinks. True, Palm Beach County is one of the more upscale areas of Florida—rivaling Naples and Sarasota in incomes and amenities—but you'd never know it from the clientele at local hangouts, where millionaires rub elbows with beach bums, all resplendent in their casual clothing.

Between Jupiter and the rest of Palm Beach County, you'll be able to go out every night to a good restaurant without going to the same place twice.

Many folks, mostly Cardinals fans, stick to the general Jupiter area during spring training. Jupiter is home to a planned Florida community, Abacoa, with all the good and bad that it entails. When the ballpark first opened, it was in the middle of nowhere. Since then, the surrounding development has expanded to the point where there are things to do should you decide to stay near the ballpark. You can find plenty of restaurants and movie theaters nearby, since downtown Abacoa is located directly next to the ballpark.

Most of the attractions are located on Town Center Drive and Main Street, which feature a range of bars and restaurants. A place to run into Cardinals and Marlins players enjoying a post-game meal is Copacabana Cuban Cuisine (*1209 Main St., Suite A-101, Jupiter; 561/360-3378; copacabanacubancuisine.com*), specializing in Cuban specialities like *ropa vieja, lechon asada, masita de puerco fritas,* oxtails, and the traditional Cuban sandwich. Yes, there's a full bar, and yes, there's a lengthy Happy Hour.

The Civil Society Brewing Company (*1200 Town Center Dr., Suite 101, Jupiter; 561/855-6680; civilsocietybrewing.com*) has emerged as our favorite postgame pit stop: the beers are top notch, and the specialty of the house is a line of hoppy IPAs. Expect a huge crowd after the game, as the place is usually slammed with baseball fans. Highly recommended. DAS Beer Garden (*1203 Town Center Dr., Suite 116, Jupiter; 561/776-8669; dasbeergarden.com*) is a small place specializing in German food and local beers. It's a good spot if you don't want to go hungry to the ballpark on weekends—try the hash with elk sausage. (Alas, on weekdays DAS isn't open before after-noon games.) The Stadium Grill (*1203 Town Center Dr., Jupiter; 561/630-9669; stadiumgrilljupiter.com*), across the street from the ballpark, was renovated in 2017 and is a great spot before or after the game. It is what it is: a good neighborhood spot suitable for a drink and some bar food. As a bonus, the Stadium Grill is also a short walk from the Edna Hibel Way parking ramp discussed in the previous section.

A hidden gem in the Abacoa area: Leftovers Café (*451 University Blvd., Jupiter; 561/627-6030; littlemoirsjupiter.com*), where the emphasis is on fresh seafood. No, no leftovers here: just offerings like blue crab egg rolls, grilled swordfish, and a slew of daily specials at affordable prices. Highly recommended.

When in Jupiter, you should check out the seacoast. The Jupiter Inlet Lighthouse (*Lighthouse Park, 500 Capt. Armour's Way, Beach Rd and Hwy. 1, Jupiter; 561/747-8380; jupiterlighthouse.org*) is the oldest structure in Palm Beach County, first lit on July 10, 1860. Designed by George Gordon Meade, a lieutenant at the Bureau of Topo-graphical Engineers and later the general who defeated Robert E. Lee at Gettysburg, the lighthouse is still a working facility. It's open

Wednesday-Saturday, 10 a.m.-2 p.m., with a $12 admission charge for adults, $10 for seniors, and $6 for children.

There are other spring-training venues within an easy driving distance. You could head 35 miles up the coast to Port St. Lucie (where the New York Mets train), or drive the very short distance to West Palm Beach, where the Washington Nationals and Houston Astros train.

DINING OUTSIDE THE BALLPARK AREA

Between Jupiter and Palm Beach there are restaurant options for all tastes and price tags. As you might expect, the emphasis in most restaurants is seafood, although steakhouses are also popular in the area. And even though the well-heeled hang around the Palm Beach area in the spring, there are enough casual-dining establishments for the average spring-training fan.

Duffy's Sports Grill is a local chain of sports bars known for its burgers and chicken wings, with two locations in Jupiter. *Jupiter West, 6791 W. Indiantown Rd., Jupiter; 561/741-8900. Jupiter East, 185 E. Indiantown Rd., Jupiter; 561/743-4405; duffysmvp.com.* Another sports bar (i.e., lots of televisions) worth checking out, but one with a more upscale menu: The Woods Jupiter (*129 Soundings Av., Harbourside Place, Jupiter; 561/320-9627; woodsjupiter.com*). Being this is Palm Beach County, the Woods Jupiter has both the trappings of a sports bar (the bar experience is emphasized, and there's an extensive wine list) and an upscale menu. Yes, it's owned by Tiger Woods.

Those looking for a more upscale experience will have plenty of opportunities to drop a lot of cash on a high-end meal. Once you have scouted out the best of Jupiter, you have the rest of Palm Beach County to explore. Captain Charlie's Reef Grill in Juno Beach (*12846 US 1, Juno Beach; 561/624-9924; captaincharliesreefgrillfl.com*) is worth seeking out; its wine list has been profiled by *Wine Spectator*, and the menu is renowned for featuring seafood caught earlier in the day.

We cover more Palm Beach/West Palm Beach/Jupiter hotspots in the area overview chapter.

WHERE TO STAY

A Courtyard by Marriott (*4800 Main St., Jupiter; 561/776-2700; marriott.com*) is across the street from Roger Dean Chevrolet Stadium. Room rates during spring break run between $380 and $434, if you can get a room.

Otherwise, only one other hotel is within a mile of the ballpark: Homewood Suites (*4700 Donald Ross Rd., Palm Beach Gardens; 561/622-7799; hilton.com*). There are plenty of hotels within a close driving distance of five miles or so; most are of the chain variety. The Cardinals' team hotels in 2024 were the Embassy Suites (*4350 PGA Blvd., Palm Beach, 561/622-1000; hilton.com*) and Wyndham Grand Jupiter at Harbourside Place (*122 Soundings Av., Jupiter; 561/273-6600; wyndhamhotels.com*). No team hotel for the Marlins.

You can also look to Palm Beach and West Palm Beach for a hotel room as well. (The next chapter lists a few more.) Those cities are at the most 20 miles from the ballpark and feature a huge selection of hotels at a wide variety of prices, ranging from the likes of The Breakers (*One South County Rd., Palm Beach, 888/BREAKERS; thebreakers.com*) or the Brazilian Court (*301 Australian Av., Palm Beach, 561/655-7740, thebraziliancourt.com*) at the high end to the more affordable chains, such as Hampton Inn or Residence Inn.

RV PARKS IN THE AREA

There are no RV parks close to the ballpark; the closest is several miles away. In general, this is not RV territory.

FLYING IN

The closest airport is Palm Beach International Airport, which is about 25 miles away from the Jupiter area. Most major airlines fly into PBI, including American, Air Canada, Allegiant, Delta, Frontier, JetBlue, Southwest, Spirit, Sun Country, and United, but sometimes on a seasonal basis. *Palm Beach International Airport, 1000 James L. Turnage Blvd., West Palm Beach; pbia.org.*

You may also want to consider flying into Fort Lauderdale Airport or Miami International Airport and then driving to Jupiter if the fares are significantly cheaper. Miami International Airport is only 84 miles away from Roger Dean Chevrolet Stadium—and Fort Lauderdale Airport is even closer—so if you can save a few bucks for the price of a short drive, you should do so.

SPRING TRAINING HISTORY: ST. LOUIS CARDINALS

The St. Louis Cardinals have held spring training in the following locations: St. Louis (1901-1902); Dallas (1903); Houston (1904); Marlin Springs, Texas (1905); Houston (1906-1908); Little Rock (1909-1910); West Baden, Ind. (1911); Jackson, Miss. (1912); Columbus, Ga. (1913); St. Augustine, Fla. (1914); Hot Wells, Texas (1915-1917); San Antonio (1918); St. Louis (1919); Brownsville, Texas (1920); Orange, Texas (1921-1922); Bradenton (1923-1924); Stockton, Cal. (1925); San Antonio (1926); Avon Park, Fla. (1927-1929); Bradenton (1930-1936); Daytona Beach (1937); St. Petersburg (1938-1942); Cairo, Ill. (1943-1945); St. Petersburg (1946-1997); and Jupiter (1998-present).

SPRING TRAINING HISTORY: MIAMI MARLINS

In 1993, the Florida Marlins first held spring training in Cocoa, at the former spring home of the Houston Astros. (The former Cocoa Expo Sports Center—now the Coastal Florida Sports Park—still stands and is used for youth baseball.) The site was shifted to Viera's Space Coast Stadium in 1994, and then the Marlins moved to Roger Dean in 2003 when Jeffrey Loria completed his sale of the Montreal Expos and purchase of the Florida Marlins. Roger Dean Stadium was built as a joint project between the Expos and the Cardinals; that interest was retained by Loria when he shed the Expos.

CACTI PARK OF THE PALM BEACHES / HOUSTON ASTROS / WASHINGTON NATIONALS

QUICK FACTS

- **Capacity**: 7,858 (6,500 fixed seats, 1,358 berm seating)
- **Year Opened**: 2017
- **Dimensions**: 335L, 408LC, 405C, 408RC, 335R
- **Ticket Lines**: 561/404-8209, 844/676-2017 (Nationals), 877/935-5668 (Astros)
- **Local Airport**: Palm Beach. You can also check out Fort Lauderdale or Miami fares.
- **Home Dugout Locations**: Houston on third-base side, Washington on first-base side.
- **Address**: 5444 Haverhill Rd., West Palm Beach, FL 33407.
- **Directions**: The ballpark is located between Haverhill Road and Military Trail, south of 45th Street, between Florida's Turnpike and I-95. From the Turnpike, take Exit 107 onto State Highway 710 East; from there take a right onto Haverhill Road. From I-95 South, take Exit 74 onto 45th Street; from there head west to Haverhill Road and the ballpark. From Miami: Take either the Turnpike or I-95 North. From the Turnpike: Head north until you hit Exit 99, State Highway 704, then turn a left on Haverhill Road. From I-95 North, take Exit 74 onto 45th Street; from there head west to Haverhill Road and the ballpark.

NEW BEGINNINGS IN WEST PALM BEACH

After some initial growing pains, spring-training games at CACTI Park of the Palm Beaches have evolved into well-run, entertaining events for fans of both the Washington Nationals and Houston Astros.

If you spent any time in Arizona for spring training, you'll recognize the basic design of CACTI Park of the Palm Beaches: It bears more than a passing similarity to Camelback Ranch–Glendale or Salt River Fields at Talking Stick. The goal in all three complexes is to offer an immersive spring-training experience, one that takes you through training fields and workout facilities before setting foot in the ballpark. This is a definite design trend in recent years at spring-training facilities, one executed to great success in West Palm Beach.

Which is good news for baseball fans in general as well as baseball fans in Palm Beach County. The area was home to spring training for decades, whether it was the Philadelphia/Kansas City Athletics training at Wright Field (later Connie Mack Field) or the Atlanta Braves and Montreal Expos training out of West Palm Beach Municipal Stadium. Indeed, spring training in the area dates to the turn of the century (see the previous Palm Beach County overview chapter on how Henry Flagler promoted spring training in the region).

There is only one other two-team facility in the Grapefruit League: Roger Dean Stadium, spring home of the St. Louis Cardinals and Miami Marlins. Since the opening of that complex in 1998, there have been tremendous advances made in spring-training design, and CACTI Park of the Palm Beaches reflects those advances. Each team had considerable input into their setups, and they made some distinctly different choices about how things are arranged. The Nationals' clubhouse is built into the first-base side of the ballpark and connected to the concourse, with players heading in through the bullpen. The Astros occupy all space past the left-field concourse in a more traditional spring-training design, with common areas in the middle.

Going to a spring-training game at CACTI Park of the Palm Beaches is worth an early entrance, as you should take your time and walk through your favorite team's training complex before entering the ballpark. The Astros' training fields are to the north, and the Nats' training fields are to the south, with parking lots on each side. You may not have a choice where you park but arriving early to the complex means you can circle around should your desired parking lot be closed. You'll see the ballpark and complexes from a distance.

No matter where you park, the walkways will guide you to a front plaza, one of the ballpark's signature items. Because of the high water table—this is Florida, after all—it wasn't possible to go down very far, so the decision was made to go up, in a very subtle manner, which leads to a concourse level some 14 feet above the parking-lot and playing-field levels. As you move through the training fields and to the ballpark's front entrance, you're gently moving up in elevation and traversing bridges before reaching a promontory that looks upon the plaza and a lake.

Speaking of the plaza: It certainly is a place for fans to gather and meet both before and after the game. It's some 34,000 square feet on all levels, offering an inviting entrance to the ballpark on the third-base side. And, in this age of the selfie, there are two other signature items off the plaza that proved to be immensely popular: 20-foot-tall logos in front of each team's entry area.

Once inside, you'll see a seating bowl, a 360-degree concourse 20 feet wide with both team's clubhouses/offices (Houston on third-base side, Washington on first-base side). It's not a huge ballpark, with 6,500 fixed seats and room for 1,358 more on the outfield berm. There is no cross aisle in the seating bowl, so all seating descends from the concourse (where the handicapped seating is located). The second level features premium seating: there are six suites (three on each side of press box) as well as covered party decks down each line. The suites are not traditional suites: the windows open to the playing field, giving them more of a Florida feel. In addition, the outside seating is at the same level as the inside—there are no fixed seats, but fans can arrange their own seats and take advantage of the outdoor drink rail.

Many fans will judge this ballpark by its shade. With the third-base line running due north, the sun will be at the back to fans behind home plate. By the end of the third inning, or so, most of the seats will be in the shade thanks to a large canopy installed over the grandstand. (Still, this is Florida: put on some sunscreen before entering the ballpark or seek out the sunscreen stand. More on that later.) The design is light and airy.

Speaking of the canopy: the cantilevers are not as dense as those found in other ballparks. The ballpark features minimally structured stucco, accented with wood panels. The whole site is part of Palm Beach County's Art in Public Places, and the plan was for local artists to create rectangular planes creates shading, graphics, team history, highlights, and more on the fan's journey from parking to entrance. Take a close look as you walk inside and outside the ballpark: the details are subtle, but still striking.

INSIDER'S TIP
The ballpark opened in 2017 as The Ballpark of the Palm Beaches. In 2018, it was FITTEAM Ballpark of the Palm Beaches under a naming-rights deal that since ended. The CACTI Park of the Palm Beaches was unveiled in 2024 after a naming-rights deal with Travis Scott's hard-seltzer company.

There are development limitations: there's a 13-acre lake on the site, and there's an easement on 27 more acres. In the end, 120 acres was available for the training complex. Some of that easement will be seen in the canal to the south of the site and crossing that canal will be part of the experience. A park was completed by spring training in 2018, adding to the area's bucolic nature.

CACTI Park of the Palm Beaches is a worthy addition to the Grapefruit League and a distinct improvement over the former Nationals and Astros spring homes.

THE SPRING-TRAINING BALLPARK EXPERIENCE

CONCESSIONS

You'll find the standard ballpark goodies: hamburgers, hot dogs, soda, beer (both macro and craft), barbecue, Philly cheesesteaks, freshly prepared funnel cakes, and ice cream at various points of sale booths throughout the ballpark. When CACTI Park of the Palm Beaches opened, there were issues with long lines at the concession stands, but once the kinks were worked out, lines were shorter. You can bring in a sealed bottle of water and refill it at drinking fountains, with filtered cold water available.

The District Taproom features a wide variety of beers. As well, we found offerings from Houston's Karbach Brewing Company. You will find a wider selection of craft beers at the dedicated bar down the third-base line.

AUTOGRAPHS

Astros fans will want to arrive early and head to the third-base side, as the team will enter the ballpark from the left-field corner and make their way to their dugout. (Alas, there's no open walkway as there was at Osceola County Stadium. But plenty of players still stopped to sign autographs, in our experience.) The Nationals enter the field from the bullpen. Again, plenty stopped to sign autographs on their way to the field during pregame ceremonies. Note that the netting was extended for spring training 2020, so scout out locations as soon as you arrive.

Another strategy: head early to the ballpark (10:30 a.m.) and catch the home team's batting practice in the training fields, as players move between there and the clubhouse.

PARKING

Parking at the complex is $15—credit card only, no cash—and there is plenty available. Two main unpaved lots are located north and south of the ballpark, and there are golf-cart shuttles in use. The unpaved lot is accessible from both Haverhill Road and Military Trail, and the handicapped parking sections are in a paved area west of the main ballpark entrance, off Haverhill Road. If you park on the south side, you'll enter the ballpark complex via the Nationals workout facilities. One of the advantages of the West Palm Beach location: there's plenty of four- or six-lane access to the ballpark. Don't worry if you are directed to a spot far from the ballpark gates: golf carts run fans between the ballpark and their parking spots. Alas, no more valet parking.

WHERE TO SIT

With third base running due north, the sun will be at the back of fans behind home plate at the start of a game. By the time a game is a third over most of the seats will be in the shade thanks to a large canopy installed over the grandstand.

We try to head directly for the patio furniture installed in the right-field concourse. This is open seating, and there's nothing better than watching a ballgame in the shade (thank you, scoreboard!) on a comfortable lounge chair. Also open seating: the Picnic Patio down the left-field line, where $34 gets you all-inclusive food and drink.

If you can, we'd recommend moving up to the second-level deck. Large areas can be reserved for groups, but if there is no group reserving the space, it's worth checking out. The party deck seats 100 and features microbrews from the local brewery. The craft-beer selections are plentiful and there are plenty of tables for hanging out with friends and catching the game. You can also see the Palm Beach skyline from the second level.

A unique seating area for spring training: On the first-base Nationals side is a field box with open seating. It's being billed as on-field loge box, complete with food and drink rail and waitstaff service. It seats 68.

INSIDER'S TIP
If you find yourself in the sun for most of a game, head to the
MD Anderson Cancer Center tent, located next to the team
store. In the past sunscreen was offered there.

FOR THE KIDS

A games area with the likes of ping pong and corn hole is in the left-
field corner.

SELFIE SPOTS

The 20-foot-tall logos in front of the grand plaza were hits with fans,
who lined up to take shots. They proved to be mandatory stops
before fans entered the ballpark.

IF YOU GO

WHAT TO DO OUTSIDE THE BALLPARK

Given that the Astros and Nationals spend a lot of spring training
taking on the Cardinals, Marlins, and Mets in nearby Jupiter and
Port St. Lucie, you can easily hunker down for a week in the greater
Palm Beach area and see your favorite team five or six times. You
will still need to find things to occupy your time between games.
While there's not a lot to do in the industrial and residential areas
surrounding the ballpark, there's plenty of things to do in the area.
We cover them in the Palm Beach County overview chapter.

WHERE TO STAY

There are no hotels within a mile of CACTI Park of the Palm
Beaches, but there are several within two miles, including several
right off I-95 in the city's Metrocentre area. These are perfect for
families:

- Holiday Inn Express & Suites West Palm Beach

Metrocentre, 2485 Metrocentre Blvd., West Palm Beach;
561/472-7020; *ihg.com.*
- Residence Inn West Palm Beach, 2461 Metrocentre Blvd.,
  West Palm Beach; 561/687-4747; *marriott.com.*
- Homewood Suites West Palm Beach, 2455 Metrocentre
  Blvd., West Palm Beach; 561/682-9188; *hilton.com.*
- Springhill Suites West Palm Beach, 2437 Metrocentre
  Blvd., West Palm Beach; 561/689-6814; *marriott.com.*

Astros fans will want to check out Hilton Garden Inn West Palm
Beach (*1675 Palm Beach Lakes Blvd., West Palm Beach; 561-683-0069;
hilton.com*), located five miles from CACTI Park of the Palm
Beaches. The hotel, partially owned by Astros owner Jim Crane,
sports a decor decked out in hints of blue and orange, the Astros
colors, as well as baseball themed artwork. This was the Astros'
team hotel in 2024, of course, and is usually unavailable during
spring training.

There is an abundance of hotel rooms in the greater West Palm
Beach area, including many closer to the ocean. Staying downtown
(cheaper) or in Palm Beach (expensive) are also options. Or you
could stay in the Jupiter area (see our Roger Dean Stadium chapter
for details) and then drive down for games. You'll miss rush hour if
you're heading to the ballpark for an afternoon game.

RV PARKS

There are no RV parks within a mile of the ballpark, but there are
several within a short drive, including Vacation Inn Resort of the
Palm Beaches (*6500 N. Military Tr., West Palm Beach; 561/848-6170;
vacationinnrvpark.com*), billed as an upscale facility geared more
toward ownership and long-term rentals; and Palm Beach RV Park
(*1444 Old Okeechobee Blvd., West Palm Beach, 561-659-2817; palm-
beachrvparks.com*), another upscale facility with only monthly
rentals. In general, RV resorts and parks in West Palm Beach are
geared toward longer-term, season rentals, not daily or weekly
arrangements.

FLYING IN

The closest airport is Palm Beach International Airport, which has been upgraded in recent years and now provides a pleasant travel experience. Most major airlines fly into PBI, including Allegiant, American, Air Canada, Delta, Frontier, JetBlue, Southwest, Spirit, Sun Country, and United, but sometimes on a seasonal basis. American Airlines and JetBlue run nonstops between Reagan National and Palm Beach International, while Southwest flies direct between BWI and PBI. Alas, there are no nonstops between Dulles and Palm Beach International. United runs nonstops direct from Houston on a seasonal basis. *Palm Beach International Airport, 1000 James L. Turnage Blvd., West Palm Beach; pbia.org.*

You may also want to consider flying into Fort Lauderdale Airport or Miami International Airport and then driving to Jupiter if the fares are significantly cheaper. Miami International Airport is only 77 miles away from CACTI Park of the Palm Beaches—and Fort Lauderdale Airport is even closer—so if you can save a few bucks for the price of a short drive, you should do so.

SPRING TRAINING HISTORY: HOUSTON ASTROS

The Houston Colt .45s began their history with training camp in Apache Junction, Ariz., in 1962-1963. In 1964, spring training was shifted to Florida and Cocoa, where the Astros trained until 1984. (The former Cocoa Expo Sports Center—now the Coastal Florida Sports Park—still stands and is used for youth baseball.) In 1985, the Astros moved to their spring-training home in Kissimmee, wrapping up that history in 2016. Osceola County Stadium is still in use, but it was converted to a soccer facility in 2020.

SPRING TRAINING HISTORY: WASHINGTON NATIONALS

The Washington Nationals/Montreal Expos have held spring training in the following locations: West Palm Beach (1968-1972); Daytona Beach (1973-1980); West Palm Beach (1981-1997; 2017-present); Jupiter (1998-2002); Viera (2003-2016). The team's former home in Viera, Space Coast Stadium, still stands and is used for amateur sports.

Made in the USA
Monee, IL
30 August 2024

64166240R00144